The History of United States Cultural Diplomacy

New Approaches to International History
Series Editor: Thomas Zeiler, Professor of American Diplomatic History, University of Colorado Boulder, USA

Series Editorial Board:
Anthony Adamthwaite, University of California at Berkeley (USA)
Kathleen Burk, University College London (UK)
Louis Clerc, University of Turku (Finland)
Petra Goedde, Temple University (USA)
Francine McKenzie, University of Western Ontario (Canada)
Lien-Hang Nguyen, University of Kentucky (USA)
Jason Parker, Texas A&M University (USA)
Glenda Sluga, University of Sydney (Australia)

New Approaches to International History covers international history during the modern period and across the globe. The series incorporates new developments in the field, such as the cultural turn and transnationalism, as well as the classical high politics of state-centric policymaking and diplomatic relations. Written with upper level undergraduate and postgraduate students in mind, texts in the series provide an accessible overview of international diplomatic and transnational issues, events, and actors.

Published:
Decolonization and the Cold War, edited by Leslie James and Elisabeth Leake (2015)
Cold War Summits, Chris Tudda (2015)
The United Nations in International History, Amy Sayward (2017)
Latin American Nationalism, James F. Siekmeier (2017)
The History of United States Cultural Diplomacy, Michael L. Krenn (2017)

Forthcoming:
International Cooperation in the Early 20th Century, Daniel Gorman
The International LGBT Rights Movement, Laura Belmonte
Reconstructing the Postwar World, Francine McKenzie
International Development, Corinna Unger
Women and Gender in International History, Karen Garner
The Environment and International History, Scott Kaufman
The United States and Latin America in the Contemporary World, Stephen G. Rabe
The History of Oil Diplomacy, Christopher R. W. Dietrich
The Nineteenth Century World, Maartje Abbenhuis
Global War, Global Catastrophe, Maartje Abbenhuis and Ismee Tames

The History of United States Cultural Diplomacy

1770 to the Present Day

MICHAEL L. KRENN

Bloomsbury Academic
An imprint of Bloomsbury Publishing Plc

BLOOMSBURY
LONDON · OXFORD · NEW YORK · NEW DELHI · SYDNEY

Bloomsbury Academic

An imprint of Bloomsbury Publishing Plc

50 Bedford Square	1385 Broadway
London	New York
WC1B 3DP	NY 10018
UK	USA

www.bloomsbury.com

BLOOMSBURY and the Diana logo are trademarks of Bloomsbury Publishing Plc

First published 2017

British Library Cataloguing-in-Publication Data
A catalogue record for this book is available from the British Library.

ISBN:	HB:	978-1-4725-0860-7
	PB:	978-1-4725-1001-3
	ePDF:	978-1-4725-0922-2
	eBook:	978-1-4725-0878-2

Library of Congress Cataloging-in-Publication Data
A catalog record for this book is available from the Library of Congress.

Cover image © Howard Sochurek/The LIFE Picture Collection/Getty Images

Typeset by Integra Software Services Pvt. Ltd.

To find out more about our authors and books visit www.bloomsbury.com.
Here you will find extracts, author interviews, details of forthcoming
events and the option to sign up for our newsletters.

For Lisa, who makes life better every single day

CONTENTS

SERIES EDITOR PREFACE

New Approaches to International History takes the entire world as its stage for exploring the history of diplomacy, broadly conceived theoretically and thematically, and writ large across the span of the globe, during the modern period. This series goes beyond the single goal of explaining encounters in the world. Our aspiration is that these books provide both an introduction for researchers new to a topic, and supplemental and essential reading in classrooms. Thus, *New Approaches* serves a dual purpose that is unique from other large-scale treatments of international history; it applies to scholarly agendas and pedagogy. In addition, it does so against the backdrop of a century of enormous change, conflict, and progress that informed global history but also continues to reflect on our own times.

The series offers the old and new diplomatic history to address a range of topics that shaped the twentieth century. Engaging in international history (including but not especially focusing on global or world history), these books will appeal to a range of scholars and teachers situated in the humanities and social sciences, including those in history, international relations, cultural studies, politics, and economics. We have in mind scholars, both novice and veteran, who require an entrée into a topic, trend, or technique that can benefit their own research or education into a new field of study by crossing boundaries in a variety of ways.

By its broad and inclusive coverage, *New Approaches to International History* is also unique because it makes accessible to students current research, methodology, and themes. Incorporating cutting-edge scholarship that reflects trends in international history, as well as addressing the classical high politics of state-centric policymaking and diplomatic relations, these books are designed to bring alive the myriad of approaches for digestion by advanced undergraduates and graduate students. In preparation for the *New Approaches* series, Bloomsbury surveyed courses and faculty around the world to gauge interest and reveal core themes of relevance for their classroom use. The polling yielded a host of topics, from war and peace to the environment; from empire to economic integration; and from migration to nuclear arms. The effort proved that there is a much-needed place for studies that connect scholars and students alike to international history, and books that are especially relevant to the teaching missions of faculty around the world.

We hope readers find this series to be appealing, challenging, and thought-provoking. Whether the history is viewed through older or newer lenses, *New Approaches to International History* allows students to peer into the modern period's complex relations among nations, people, and events to draw their own conclusions about the tumultuous, interconnected past.

Thomas Zeiler, University of Colorado Boulder, USA

ACKNOWLEDGMENTS

There are many, many people I need to thank – not so much for their particular assistance with this volume, but for their sustained help, encouragement, and professional courtesies over the past fifteen or more years. When I started the work on my 2005 book about U.S. art exhibits sent abroad during the Cold War, I was a complete and absolute novice in terms of understanding culture or cultural diplomacy. Much like the stereotypical unsophisticated visitor to the local art museum I just "knew what I liked!" Had it not been for the extraordinary generosity of my peers and the patient assistance of numerous archivists, the art book would never have come about and, of course, this present monograph would not be in your hands.

Of special note is Jessica Gienow-Hecht, who was kind enough to allow me to participate in what turned out to be some of the most exciting and thought-provoking conferences I have ever attended – the Culture and International History (CIH) gatherings in Wittenburg, Frankfurt, and Berlin. Discussing the field of cultural diplomacy with scholars from around the world helped to shape my own developing ideas and forced me to get up to speed on the literature and theories. Over the years she read more drafts of some of my work than any scholar should have to endure, always with her sharp and critical eye focused on making the piece better. Ken Osgood has been a valued colleague for many years. His work on public diplomacy and his perceptive comments on my work have pushed me to be a better historian. I met Laura Belmonte at the CIH conference in Frankfurt, where I was instantly struck by her deep and precise thinking about U.S. propaganda and cultural diplomacy – as well as her infectious sense of humor that, as anyone who sits through a three-day conference knows, is an absolute necessity. I appreciated her comments on an early draft of Chapter One, which proved to be the toughest to write. Conferences also brought me into contact with Giles Scott-Smith and Nicholas Cull, two scholars who quickly made clear not only their willingness to help with my own research but also that my resulting work had best meet their own high standards – or face the wrath of their incisive wits! Walter L. Hixson was one of the first scholars to cite my initial foray into the world of cultural diplomacy when he noted my work on the "Unfinished Business" exhibit at the 1958 world's fair in his important study, *Parting the Curtain: Propaganda, Culture, and the Cold War, 1945–1961*. I have appreciated his assistance and admired his scholarship for many years. David Snyder, who was instrumental in my participation at a conference on U.S. public and cultural diplomacy during the 1970s, also proved to be a demanding, and effective, coeditor for the published collection that emerged from that gathering.

There are many other scholars I could name – and I am quite sure they will let me know that I did not – but I also want to give my thanks to the archivists and librarians at the National Archives, Library of Congress, Archives of American Art, Smithsonian Institution Archives, and the archives of the Phillips Collection, Museum of Modern Art, and the National Gallery of Art. All of them helped me many years ago when I first stepped into the rather daunting world of cultural diplomacy and patiently guided me through the process.

And there are two individuals, in particular, that I would like to thank. The first is Martin Manning. I remember during the early research into the art book when my graduate assistant ran into my office and breathlessly exclaimed, "There is a guy named Martin Manning you have to talk to." At that time, Martin was working with the United States Information Agency and he headed up the agency's Historical Collection – which soon came to be known by every scholar who worked in those records as the "Manning Collection." Martin not only scrupulously assembled a first-rate collection of books, articles, and primary sources, but his willingness to share these with researchers became legendary as well. He did not simply show you the records and tell you to have fun – he was, in a very real sense, a collaborator with every researcher who entered his library. He is also a first-rate scholar in his own right, and my continuing friendship with him was one of the best things to come out of the art book.

The other person who needs to be mentioned is Margaret Cogswell. During the course of my initial research into the art book, someone suggested that I needed to speak with her. And so I did – many, many times. Margaret was a pioneer in so many ways. Not only was she one of the early and forceful proponents of American cultural diplomacy, but she was also one of the first women to work in the official bureaucracy of the American programs, going beyond the planning of U.S. cultural exhibits to traveling the world, both as a curator and an active participant. Interviewing her was always an experience – her excitement and passion for the work she did never abated and it was absolutely contagious. When she passed away in February 2016, she left behind many friends and a legacy of dedication to the power of art.

A very special thank-you goes to Tom Zeiler. It was a few years back when I first approached Tom about participating in the series he was editing and suggested that I might be able to produce a comprehensive study of U.S. cultural diplomacy. His initial enthusiasm gave me a sense of the possibilities for such a study. These were rapidly overrun by the terrifying realization that I had gotten myself into a sprawling project for which I had but the slightest

outline. As I slogged through Chapter One I was overcome by the feeling –
perhaps typical of many academics – that the work was doomed to failure.
When I sent the first draft to Tom I cringed at imagining his response that
would likely begin, "Well, there are a couple of good things here, but...."
Instead, what I got is what every author needs from an editor – valued
words of encouragement and support, coupled with clear and meaningful
suggestions for revision. I hope that this book merits the wonderful support
I have received from Tom, from a small army of colleagues and archivists,
and individuals such as Peg Cogswell.

And, finally, allow me a well-earned note of appreciation for my wife,
Lisa. We met and married later in life and so she never had the pleasure (or
agony) of watching me write a book. As she watched our study reduced to
what could only appear to be disorganized piles of books, articles, and notes
(and witnessed the slow, but steady, encroachment on her side of the study
desk), she must have wondered exactly what she had gotten herself into.
But she also came to understand the enormous commitment of time such a
project calls for and each time she pulled the study door closed and told me
that she would make sure that neither kids nor cats would interrupt me, I
felt that familiar twinge of guilt at the selfishness our profession sometimes
demands. That she still professes her love is a lasting testament to her kind
heart and immense patience in dealing with me.

Introduction

Thirty years ago it would have been relatively unusual to see the words "culture" and "diplomacy" used in the same sentence.[1] But the flood of publications in the recent past reveals a great interest in the study of U.S. cultural diplomacy. Numerous books and articles have been published examining nearly every facet of the nation's efforts to utilize culture as a tool for international relations. Some have focused their attention on individual cultural genres, such as art, music, dance, theater, literature, and sports. Others have taken a somewhat broader approach by breaking down the cultural efforts into topics such as "high" culture or "popular" culture. Some scholars have focused their attention on the bureaucratic structures that support those efforts, such as the Department of State or the United States Information Agency (USIA). The scholarship has also looked into the role of nongovernmental actors. More recently, as the studies have multiplied, researchers have attempted to create an overarching theoretical framework that attempts to bring the diverse strands of the literature together under one roof, including a growing body of work that examines cultural relations as one aspect of internationalization and globalization.

This study is not an attempt at a somewhat overgrown historiographical essay, although it relies very heavily on the important work done by other scholars in the past couple of decades. Instead, by combining the work of some wonderful researchers with my own substantial work in the field of U.S. cultural diplomacy, I aim to tell the story of America's long history of attempting to use culture as an instrument for achieving foreign policy goals. Of equal importance will be my goal of using the domestic battles concerning cultural diplomacy to illustrate the immense difficulties the American nation has faced in trying to define exactly what it is and what it stands for, that is, to define American identity at home and abroad.

For those readers looking for *the* study that finally answers the question of exactly what cultural diplomacy is, the ideological concepts of this book might prove frustrating. Cultural diplomacy, due to the very fact that it deals with the equally slippery term "culture," has proven difficult to define with absolute precision. Does it encompass high culture, low culture, middlebrow culture, and popular culture? Do sports and science count as culture? What about ideas? Is it simply propaganda in sheep's clothing? Is culture part of public diplomacy, the same as public diplomacy, or something entirely different? After deliberating on these questions I came to believe that in trying to intellectually patrol the border crossings between what is and what is not cultural diplomacy I was missing out on important opportunities to investigate a richer, more fascinating, and, ultimately, more illuminating picture of this relatively new field of study for American diplomatic historians.

Just as U.S. ambassador Cynthia P. Schneider entitled her 2006 article "Cultural Diplomacy: Hard to Define, But You'd Know It If You Saw It,"[2] what I "see" as cultural diplomacy starts from very basic definitions. For me, the one provided by William A. Rugh, but shared by many other scholars, addresses examinations of so-called soft power, which Rugh defines as deriving "from American culture if that culture is admired and respected abroad. 'Culture' in this sense means literature, art, performing arts and music, including both 'high culture' and popular culture – and education."[3] Such a definition is deceptively narrow. Already, Rugh expands the concept of culture from its "high" manifestations (fine art, theater, literature) to include the "low" examples of culture (television, Hollywood movies, comic books). As I will argue in this volume, however, an analysis of cultural diplomacy that focuses entirely on the cultural *products* utilized by U.S. diplomats is unnecessarily exclusive of the cultural ideas and philosophies that, in fact, led to the appearance of those products. Concepts such as freedom of expression, equality, social justice, and democracy were equally important – and certainly just as controversial – weapons in the cultural diplomacy arsenal. The first operating assumption of this study, then, is that only by combining the product with the idea can we gain a fuller picture, both of what cultural diplomacy is and what it aims to accomplish.

A second assumption arises directly from the first. By considering such a broad spectrum of what constitutes the cultural component of cultural diplomacy – high art, popular culture, ideas – this study starts from the position that America's cultural diplomacy did not begin from (or, in some ways, end up at) the notion that this form of interaction with the world could and should emanate entirely from the official foreign policy bureaucracy of the U.S. government. Thus, if we now see cultural diplomacy as something that is carried out by both official *and* unofficial agents, we also expand the chronological framework. By beginning my study with Thomas Jefferson's efforts to dispel French notions of American degeneracy in the late 1700s I have quite consciously included a long history of "non-official" acts of cultural diplomacy before stepping into what has more or less been defined as the beginnings of "official" U.S. cultural diplomacy in the late 1930s.

It might be seen as an act of contrition. A few years back I participated in a round-table review of Thomas Zeiler's book *Ambassadors in Pinstripes: The Spalding World Baseball Tour and the Birth of the American Empire*. Although my analysis was generally quite favorable, I could not resist a somewhat snarky comment about "whether efforts such as the baseball tour can fairly be called cultural diplomacy at all.... Perhaps, but if not, then one of the main criticisms of studies of cultural diplomacy rears its ugly head: that the scholar simply reads too much into episodes that were merely entertaining diversions rather than important barometers of America's rise to power."[4] This, with no apparent appreciation of irony, from someone who devoted an entire book to U.S. art exhibits sent overseas during the Cold War! But it is also a recognition of my increasingly strongly held view that we should not be defining the chronology of America's cultural diplomacy solely through the ability to be able to name this or that agency or government official that "started" it all. Simply because the U.S. government was a little slow (by about a century and a half) to recognize the power of culture and establish new offices, new job titles, and even entirely new bureaucracies to put it to work for American diplomacy should not stop us from investigating other avenues by which the nation's culture intersected with its foreign policy. After all, it might fairly be argued that Jefferson's actions in the late 1700s began a line of thought in which U.S. officials, consciously or unconsciously, imagined some sort of link between American culture at home and its possible uses abroad.

Finally, and perhaps most controversially, this study will argue that trying to assess the significance of American cultural diplomacy from the perspective of its direct and specific "impact" on the foreign audience is neither entirely obtainable nor, at least as regards this book, of overwhelming importance. There has been a consistent debate among scholars in (and outside of) the field concerning cultural diplomacy's impact, but the basic premise of this study is that it is a ticklish problem. Most of the information available from the Department of State and USIA records, as well as the collections of non-state actors and institutions that participated in the programs, contains fragmentary evidence – some news clippings, personal assessments, and anecdotal stories. (The USIA was established in 1953 as the "official" government agency responsible for most of the nation's information and cultural activities overseas.) Not surprisingly, much of this evidence is laudatory. Official U.S. cultural representatives naturally wanted the programs to appear successful; private sources also wanted the efforts to be seen as having a positive impact so that government support would continue. In addition, the entire issue of impact is muddied by a lack of consensus on exactly what "impact" means. Foreign newspaper editorials, polls taken of the attendees, and "guest books" placed by U.S. officials at many of the cultural shows can all give us some indication of how popular (or unpopular) these presentations were or how many people attended. Popularity and viewership, however, do not necessarily translate clearly or effectively into such things as treaties signed or rejected, trade pacts made or unmade, allegiance to and/or antipathy toward this or that nation or policy. Finally, the entire debate around defining the concrete impact of an art show, or a concert, or a film often moves us away from a deeper understanding of what the United States *wanted* these cultural programs to accomplish; what they *hoped* the foreign audience would grasp. This, at least to me, is just as important in terms of understanding what U.S. foreign policy is as any other policy declaration by American statesmen. After all, the announcement of the Monroe Doctrine elicited almost nothing in the way of a direct impact when it first appeared. Yet, most scholars would agree that the doctrine was significant in terms of what it told us about U.S. desires and dreams in the international realm. That a government-sponsored jazz performance did not immediately force the destruction of the Berlin Wall should not, therefore, detract from its importance in understanding the means and desired ends of American diplomacy. Of even greater importance for this book is the idea that the study of America's cultural diplomacy reveals not simply how the United States wished to be seen and understood by the overseas audience. It illuminates nothing less than the sometimes-torturous path the country has taken in trying to create a national identity at home.

This study adopts a fairly straightforward chronological approach to the topic. Chapter One examines the early origins of American cultural diplomacy from the late eighteenth century through the nineteenth century. These were largely "unofficial" efforts that sometimes resorted to what were, admittedly, somewhat strange tools in order to present a picture of America to the world. Beginning with Thomas Jefferson's use of a stuffed animal to increase national prestige, America's cultural ambassadors during the 1800s included missionaries, escaped slaves, boxers, baseball players, and the nation's most famous writer of the late nineteenth century. There was, however, a nearly imperceptible glimmer of the future as the U.S. government (having little concept of cultural diplomacy) timidly entered the fray in the 1860s by publishing the inaugural volume of the *Foreign Relations of the United States* series as an early attempt at public and cultural diplomacy during the Civil War – and then quickly withdrew from the field. In this chapter, as with those that follow, both the physical manifestations of American culture and the ideas that often helped to produce them will be featured as aspects of the nation's nascent cultural diplomacy. In Chapter Two, the more definite outlines of America's cultural diplomacy take shape. From the early 1900s through World War II the three most significant presidents of that period – Theodore Roosevelt, Woodrow Wilson, and Franklin Delano Roosevelt – all took stabs at establishing more formal and official frameworks for carrying their country's culture to the world. Each of the men understood the power of culture, but they also clearly perceived that utilizing culture as a means of diplomacy risked accusations of government interference in cultural matters in which it had no business or, even worse, of charges that the United States was engaging in the insidious act of propaganda – something associated with Imperial and Nazi Germany and the communist Soviet Union, not democratic America. They therefore moved slowly and cautiously, often attempting to blur the lines between "official" and "unofficial" purveyors of cultural diplomacy, or arguing – as Wilson and FDR would do – that wartime dangers necessitated the use of all the weapons in the American armory.

The first years after World War II, as the Cold War became a term familiar to more and more Americans, are the focus of Chapter Three. Surveying the successes, and quite cognizant of the failures, of TR, Wilson, and FDR, U.S. diplomats in the late 1940s and early 1950s plunged into the world of cultural diplomacy with high hopes but little practical experience or understanding of the domestic ramifications. In their attempts to dispel Soviet propaganda that consistently portrayed the United States as a materialistic, grasping, militaristic nation, entirely barren of culture, American officials began to assemble their weaponry, such as painting, music, theater, and literature, establish an official bureaucracy to organize the programs, and send the art and artists out to the waiting world in order to tell the "truth" about America, its ideals, and its people. Spectacular successes in reaching millions in the foreign audience were matched by equally spectacular fireworks at home when the American public and suspicious congressmen savaged the efforts as needlessly expensive, worthless in terms of achieving concrete goals, evidence of government overreach, and, most damaging, un-American. In addition, U.S. officials discovered, neither for the first nor the last time, that some issues – particularly America's ugly race problem – proved difficult to really tell the truth about.

What many American cultural diplomats, and a number of scholars, have called the "golden age" of U.S. cultural diplomacy is covered in Chapter Four. Beginning with Dwight D. Eisenhower's establishment of the USIA in 1953 and an American "cultural offensive" to try and match the Soviets' efforts, the remainder of the 1950s witnessed some of the largest – yet still controversial – examples of America's cultural diplomacy during the Cold War period. Culminating in America's participation in the first post–World War II world's fair in Brussels in 1958 and the U.S. cultural "invasion" of the Soviet Union with the American National Exhibition in Moscow in 1959, the Eisenhower years saw the fullest expression of official U.S. cultural diplomacy in the nation's history. As more Americans, inside and outside of government, came to believe that culture was an effective weapon against the communist menace, even the incessant sniping from a handful of angry congressmen and pundits could not stem the growth of the cultural diplomacy bureaucracy.

Almost as quickly as cultural diplomacy rose to prominence, it slowly dissolved from the 1960s through the 1990s. This steady decline is the focus of Chapter Five. John F. Kennedy's "Camelot" seemed to suggest that culture would play an even more important role in American foreign policy, but Kennedy's untimely death, a terrible, costly, and unpopular involvement in Vietnam, and a civil rights problem that stubbornly refused to simply go away led to changes in America's approach to cultural diplomacy. As the Watts riots and Martin Luther King's assassination piled upon the growing death toll in Vietnam, and then Vietnam bled over into domestic violence and Watergate, the entire structure, meaning, and goals of U.S. cultural diplomacy came under greater scrutiny. As the Cold War became but a memory, and conservative congressmen gained ascendancy, the questions of both the need for cultural diplomacy and whether the cultural efforts truly reflected what was "American" came back into vogue. By 1999 and the end of the USIA, it appeared the critics had won the battle. The cultural diplomats quietly packed up their art exhibits, closed their libraries, silenced the music, and folded their tents.

And, then, along came 9/11 and everything changed. That change is the topic of the Conclusion. With the shattering attacks on New York and Washington, DC, more and more Americans asked where the hatred and misunderstanding of their nation came from. It was not entirely surprising that, again faced with an external threat, the U.S. government responded by reestablishing programs of cultural diplomacy. Once again, American culture would help the world understand the truth about the nation, dispel anti-American propaganda, and pave the way for mutual understanding and respect. As the nature of the threat had changed so, too, did the forms and aims of the newest manifestation of American cultural diplomacy. Defining the new enemy as emanating from nations suffused with the Islamic religion and Muslim culture, U.S. officials decided to direct their cultural assault at one particular demographic – the young, who were deemed both more malleable and more susceptible to popular culture. Hip-hop groups replaced symphonies, videos were the new art exhibits, and American sports stars reached out to young men and women. Of course, these new initiatives were met with the same concerns, controversies, and criticisms as in the past; in addition, with no USIA to fall back on the issue of whether the government agencies or private institutions were the proper homes for the new cultural offensive gained more traction.

In sum, therefore, my focus will be on the different forms and methods that have been employed since the late eighteenth century to the present day (with a heavier focus on the twentieth century), as U.S. cultural diplomacy grew from its more than humble beginnings in the shape of a decaying, stuffed moose to sending orchestras, theater troupes, art exhibits, hip-hop groups, and much more around the world. In doing so, I wish to illuminate not only the changes that have taken place but also the continuities that persisted throughout the trials and tribulations that accompanied the nation's efforts to use culture as an instrument of American foreign policy. In doing so, a main theme emerges: for over 200 years the United States has used culture in an attempt to explain itself to the world, to increase its prestige and the respect from other nations, to fend off attacks from enemies and/or serve as a weapon against those enemies, and to encourage other nations and peoples to support American goals and interests around the globe. A consistent element has been the desire to tell the world the "truth" about America, to highlight its positive aspects and downplay the negatives.

Telling the truth about America, as we shall see, has never been as easy, straightforward, or consistent as one might first imagine. The United States has, from its beginnings, been a fairly polyglot nation containing a variety of racial and ethnic groups and political, religious, social, economic, and even cultural beliefs. In fact, the history of the nation actually reveals sometimes radically different definitions about exactly what *is* "America." Over the years, those differences have not faded away in the fabled melting pot. Therefore, the truth broadcast to the rest of the world has often been confusing and contradictory to the foreign audience. After all, if the American people cannot agree on the essential truths about their country, it is even less likely that the people of the world will be able to clearly see them.

In addition, America's cultural diplomats have struggled to come to terms with some truths. Race is foremost among these issues; the history of U.S. cultural diplomacy is also a story of the tortured tales relayed to the world about equality, civil rights, and progress, as well as the sometimes cynical, sometimes wildly successful, often embarrassing attempts to use "notable African Americans" as cultural ambassadors. The international audience has also witnessed the oftentimes vicious clashes that have occurred when the "truths" that are trumpeted abroad run afoul of what others in the American public and Congress consider to be basic and unassailable American ideals. Ugly incidents of censorship and "black lists," arguments about what is and what is not "art," and bitter contests over the government's proper role in the nation's cultural affairs were often aired to a world audience that could only wonder what, exactly, those Americans were trying to say.

These, and other, problems also illuminate another consistent factor: the question of who, or what, should really be handling the ticklish issue of culture and diplomacy. To study the history of America's cultural diplomacy is akin to watching a group of children play the old game of "hot potato." The responsibility for carrying out cultural activities abroad started in private hands, slowly evolved toward more government control, then just as often ended with the government throwing it back to the private sector. Even within the government, the issue of what office should take the reins of cultural diplomacy has been a living example of the "Potomac two-step." The Department of State went through spasmodic episodes of directing the nation's cultural diplomacy. When it got tired of dealing with the always-controversial program, it was more than happy to ship it off to a completely new office, the USIA. The USIA soon grew weary of some parts of the effort and threw them to the Smithsonian Institution. And in the last decade or so of the USIA's slow slide to extinction, the cultural activities of both State and USIA morphed into another new agency, the United States International Communications Agency in 1978, which then changed back to the USIA in 1982, which was then gobbled up by the Department of State in 1999 with its functions now included in the new office of Under Secretary of State for Public Affairs and Public Diplomacy. Culture was the redheaded stepchild of U.S. diplomacy.

And, finally, my hope is that this study captures something of the passion of those who fought long and hard to see cultural diplomacy become a part of the nation's foreign relations. It is the story of people such as Margaret Cogswell, someone who transformed from a name in the documents I was researching, to a valuable source of information, to a friend who will truly be missed. In 1964, she was part of a program entitled *Communication through Art* that sent American art experts into Pakistan, Turkey, and Iran to both display their own work and connect with their peers. She experienced a "midnight ride by moonlight from Agra and the Taj Mahal to New Delhi at relatively breakneck speed along a road that had no signs, but was encumbered with bullock carts, peacocks, and speeding trucks. It was up to the driver to avoid them – he did." Despite these hair-raising adventures and other problems, she felt that the program demonstrated that "communication *can* occur, through art, between countries." In words that ring as true today as they did over five decades ago, Cogswell concluded, "In a tumultuous world, art is one of the lifelines which we throw out to each other – lifelines of shared experience and understanding. To try and do this – and to discover better ways of doing it better – is what *Communication through Art* was for."[5] If she were with us today, it is not hard for me to imagine that she would still be screaming down moonlit roads, barely avoiding peacocks, and throwing out cultural lifelines to today's tumult-ridden world.

It is these issues, and many others, that are raised by America's cultural diplomacy that help to explain my continuing fascination with the topic. For what all of the debates, and arguments, and misunderstandings, and passions reveal is not simply the truth that the United States wished to tell the world. They illustrate, in often stark relief, the various truths about a nation that, nearly 250 years after its founding, still struggles to define what it is, who its people are, and what it stands for.

CHAPTER ONE

Identity Crisis and the Beginnings of U.S. Cultural Diplomacy

The United States in the late eighteenth century was a new nation facing a host of challenges. Its economy was in shambles as the result of years of destructive warfare. The British market was virtually closed to the United States, and trade with other nations ebbed and flowed with each new conflict between the European powers. Although victorious in its revolution against Great Britain, America's military position could hardly have been more perilous. The British still held Canada and refused to relinquish fortifications in northwestern lands claimed by the United States. Both the Spanish and French, allies during the American Revolution, had become – with the defeat of the British – competitors for territory and markets. Even the devastated tribes of Native Americans could, at times, provide a menacing threat.

Along with these quite palpable challenges, however, the United States also faced something of an identity crisis. While technically a "united" nation, in truth America was beset by internal tensions and regional animosities. At the Constitutional Convention it became clear that small states were suspicious of large states; northern and southern states jousted over where the nation's capital would be located; and the issue of slavery nearly derailed the entire gathering. Beyond this evidence on the domestic front that America was a nation in search of itself, there were equally troubling ruminations coming from abroad suggesting that the United States was intellectually bereft and culturally backward; that its people were crass, boorish, and uncivilized. The word that most disturbed people such as Thomas Jefferson was "degenerate," the term being bandied about, particularly by French natural scientists, to describe both the American nation and people.

Matters might never have reached such levels of international significance had it not been for Georges-Louis Leclerc, Comte de Buffon. Born in 1707, Buffon became by the mid-1700s the preeminent natural historian in all of Europe. He spent most of the four decades before his death in 1788 working on his monumental study, *Histoire Naturelle*. In thirty-six hefty volumes Buffon laid out his new interpretations of the natural world including explanations for the wide variety of plants and animals that existed in different areas of the world. Through the intellectual twists and turns in page after page, and volume after volume, Buffon basically concluded that environment (particularly climate) was primarily responsible for shaping the flora and fauna of a particular geographical setting. He went further, claiming that these various environments led to either the improvement or "degeneration" of the life forms within each sphere. Most notably, he set his sights on the North American continent where, he argued, degeneracy was in full bloom. As biologist Lee Alan Dugatkin explains, Buffon theorized that "as a result of living in a cold and wet climate, all species found in America were weak and feeble. What's more, any species imported into America for economic reasons would soon succumb to its new environment and produce lines of puny, feeble offspring." Nor did Buffon stop with the animal and plant life; the Native Americans, exposed to these degenerating forces, had become "stupid, lazy savages."[1]

American readers could easily connect the dots: if the environment and climate of North America produced substandard plants and animals and even transformed human inhabitants into degenerates, then the American colonists must also eventually reap the same stultifying results. Indeed, other Europeans had already jumped to that very conclusion. Prussian clergyman Cornelius de Pauw declared that "the Europeans who pass into America degenerate, as do the animals.... This degradation of humanity must be imputed to the vitiated qualities of the air stagnated in their immense forests, and corrupted by noxious vapours from standing waters and uncultivated grounds."[2] In short, "Buffon's theory was an attack on the manhood of the American patriots and was particularly galling to those republicans who saw themselves as the Anglo-Saxon masters of a future empire extending across the continent to the Pacific Ocean."[3]

Although a number of American commentators attempted to rebut Buffon's theory of degeneracy, Thomas Jefferson took it one step farther and thereupon produced and employed what might rightly be viewed as the first artifacts of American cultural diplomacy. As the American minister to France from 1785 to 1789, Jefferson was well placed to appreciate the impact Buffon's writings had on the European audience. But Jefferson, himself an avid amateur scientist, realized that the impact of the Frenchman's theory went beyond the purely academic world: "He understood that the very survival of the United States of America rested in part on how its relations – especially trade relations – developed with European countries, and the extent to which people from other lands would immigrate to the United

States." If Buffon's theory was right, "why should any country develop trade relations with America, a degenerate land?…This was precisely the sort of propaganda that Jefferson feared was the natural outcome of Buffon's ideas – if they remained unchallenged. Degeneracy, which started out as a natural history argument, was being used as a tool against America."[4]

As both scientist and diplomat, Jefferson could not let Buffon's theory remain unchallenged. Even before arriving in France to take up his official duties he took up his pen to answer the theory of degeneracy. In 1780, Jefferson received a request from a French diplomat in America for more information about the former's native state of Virginia. The result was the first and only book written and published by Jefferson during his lifetime – *Notes on the State of Virginia* – which he completed in 1781 and tinkered with for the next few years. Much of the manuscript was made up of direct answers to the questions posed by the French diplomat dealing with the soil, waterways, geology, forests, agriculture, and animal and plant life in Virginia. Jefferson also took the opportunity to expound on his political views and dealt in some depth with the critical issue of slavery. He also directly addressed Buffon and his theory. By the time Jefferson began his work on *Notes*, Buffon had been publishing volumes of his *Histoire Naturelle* for over three decades, and his international reputation could not have been higher. This did not deter Jefferson from directly assaulting the very bases of the elder scientist's theory. He attacked Buffon's misuse (or outright ignorance) of relevant evidence. Reminding his readers that the fossils of massive creatures had been unearthed on the North American continent, Jefferson argued that while "the naturalists of Europe" continued to insist that these were merely the remains of elephants and hippos it was clear to anyone with eyes that "the tusks and skeletons are much larger than those of the elephant, and the grinders many times greater than those of the hippopotamus, and essentially different in form." Moving on to the claims that the existing mammals in America were puny in comparison to their European relatives, Jefferson was blunt: "It does not appear that Messieurs de Buffon and D'Aubenton have measured, weighed, or seen those [quadrupeds] of America."[5]

Very quickly, however, Jefferson turned his discussion into a nationalistic assault on the idea of American degeneracy (and, naturally, European superiority). In response to Buffon's argument that the inferiority of the native inhabitants of America was clearly demonstrated by their lack of developing great thinkers and inventors, Jefferson fired back, "Yet I may safely ask, how many good poets, how many able mathematicians, how many great inventors in arts or sciences, had Europe, north of the Alps, then [prior to the Romans] produced? And it was sixteen centuries after this before a Newton could be formed." Jefferson admitted that there were "varieties in the race of man," but he doubted "whether the bulk and faculties of animals depend on the side of the Atlantic on which their food happens to grow, or which furnishes the elements of which they are compounded? Whether nature has enlisted herself as a Cis or Trans-Atlantic partisan?" And, as Buffon's arguments had been extended to the European colonists of the New World, Jefferson issued his own challenge: France had nearly twenty million people, and England nearly ten million. America had but three million white inhabitants and yet, "We produce a Washington, a Franklin, a Rittenhouse. France then should have half a dozen in each of these lines, and Great Britain half that number, equally eminent."[6]

That Jefferson intended his *Notes* as a direct attempt to counter Buffon's insinuations of American "degeneracy" is clear from the fact that the book was first published (in a limited edition) in France in 1785. It would not be published in English until 1787. When the written word did not have the desired effect of forcing Buffon and his associates to renounce their theory of America's inferiority, Jefferson decided to move on to more tangible rebuttals. Having already suggested that the European scientists had never seen, let alone seriously studied, the animal life of North America, Jefferson decided to remedy this deficiency. His first effort in this regard was only marginally successful. Shortly after arriving in France to take up his diplomatic duties Jefferson sent to Buffon the skin of a large American panther. The Frenchman was only marginally impressed with the pelt, but he did invite Jefferson to dine with him. Jefferson jumped at the chance for face-to-face debate with the aging scientist. The result of their meeting was a modest retreat on Buffon's part concerning the panther skin and a bold challenge to the upstart American. Following Jefferson's boasts that American deer and, in particular, the American moose would put similar European species to shame, Buffon declared that "if I could produce a single specimen with horns one foot long, he would give up the question."[7]

Seizing this opening, Jefferson immediately corresponded with friends and associates back in America requesting that the remains of a moose be shipped to France. Just the skin of the animal would not do; Jefferson wanted a full-sized, stuffed specimen to present to Buffon. Somewhat surprisingly, given the rather primitive state of Atlantic shipping in those days, Jefferson was delighted to hear that on September 28, 1787, his moose (along with a variety of antlers from elk and deer) had arrived, more or less intact. In his letter to Buffon introducing the massive animal, the American apologized that "the skin of the moose was drest [sic] with the hair on, but a great deal of it has come off, and the rest of it is ready to drop off." Despite its rather shabby appearance, the moose became the first object to be successfully utilized as part of America's cultural diplomacy. Buffon, upon seeing for himself the size of the animal, apparently promised Jefferson that he would make amends in the next volume of his *Histoire Naturelle*. Unfortunately, this never took place as Buffon passed away just a few months after receiving Jefferson's moose.[8] His theory of degeneracy would remain part of the conversation in natural history circles well into the nineteenth century, but Jefferson's moose marked the opening volley in the war to influence foreign opinion concerning America and its people.

Following in Jefferson's footsteps, nineteenth-century Americans who went abroad and helped shape foreign attitudes about the United States were a motley crew indeed, ranging from ex-slaves, to missionaries, to figures from the relatively new worlds of professional sports and mass entertainment, to a variety of tourists, including the best-known American writer of the late 1800s. Unlike Jefferson, who was a government-appointed representative of the United States, these men and women did not operate with any official government sponsorship or, in many cases, any distinct notions that they were serving as unofficial cultural ambassadors. Yet, all of them took to the international field as Americans, and whether the talk was about slavery, or baseball, or God, each of them addressed those issues from a uniquely American perspective. All considered themselves patriotic; all of them believed, to one extent or another, that along with their books and speeches, their bibles and boxing gloves, they carried with them the greatness of their nation. And all were determined to have an impact on the foreign audience. If, in fact, it is safe to say that the "image" of America that these individuals created overseas was often confusing and sometimes contradictory, we should not be so very surprised or concerned. Their America, after all, was neither monolithic nor had a homogeneous population. More than 600,000 Americans would die in the mid-nineteenth century fighting over what the American nation really was. Little wonder, then, that the "messages" about America relayed to the foreign audience during the nineteenth century were not always clear or consistent; they reflected the inchoate rumblings of a nation still searching for its identity.

Some of the first Americans who followed in Jefferson's lead by taking their message abroad were motivated not by science but by faith. Missionaries from a variety of faiths and representing different components of American society traveled overseas for much of the nineteenth century, taking along their bibles, their beliefs, and an unflagging certainty that their god, and their nation, should be shining examples to the world. They were joined by a dizzying array of moral reformers representing groups such as the Woman's Christian Temperance Union and the YMCA/YWCA that, while not always associated with a particular church or denomination, used the word of God to promote "good" habits or battle against sinful behavior (drinking, smoking, etc.). In seeking their ultimate goal they certainly did not suffer from a lack of hubris. As historian Ussama Makdisi observes, "They wanted to introduce true American Christianity to all of humanity, and in the process, to effect the 'Conversion of the World'."[9]

For many years, these moral warriors were described as merely additional foot soldiers in the march of American empire. In the standard story of American diplomacy, they were harbingers of imperialism or, more precisely, an insidious form of cultural imperialism. And there is certainly some truth to this assessment: "There is no need to deny what is obvious: as much as the term 'cultural imperialism' paints an admittedly broad stroke, the term has resonated for the simple reason that Western, including American, missionaries did overwhelmingly justify the subordination, if not always ethnic cleansing or extermination, of native peoples during a genocidal nineteenth century." Their impact on America's imperial expansion is also clear. In his study of America's moral reformers working overseas, Ian Tyrrell describes their efforts in the late 1800s as having "enlarged what could be termed the external 'footprint' of the United States in the 1880s and 1890s, creating conditions wherein a more vigorous economic and political expansion could be seriously considered."[10]

Relegating such missionaries and reformers to the role of bit players in America's territorial and economic expansion of the 1800s and characterizing their work as merely part of a larger picture of cultural imperialism tends to obscure their more important work as early examples of America's cultural diplomacy. To be sure, they did not carry out their activities at the behest of the U.S. government, nor did they receive anything resembling state support or guidance. In fact, for some missionary groups America's imperialism posed a real and troubling obstacle to the achievement of their goals. Therefore, before characterizing these nineteenth-century missionaries and reformers as simply marines with bibles a closer look at their work and aims is necessary.

That the individuals and churches intent on spreading God's word could be just as chauvinistic, culturally insensitive, and even at times just as imperialistic as their fellow Americans is undoubtedly true. (We have but to remember the ringing jingoism of Reverend Josiah Strong in the 1880s and 1890s to understand that for some, Christianity and colonialism were not necessarily contrasting ideologies.[11]) Nevertheless, for many of the reformers and missionaries who braved the hardships of overseas travel in the 1800s their goals were often expressed in less brutal, loftier terms. As Tyrrell explains, "Moral reform groups and missionaries often thought of their work as analogous to empire – but a kind of Christian moral empire that rose above 'nation,' and one nobler in aspiration than the grubby motives of gold and glory." When they landed on foreign shores, Makdisi argues, "They came not as crude military crusaders but as the redeemed 'artillery of heaven'."[12]

To a large extent, the first barrages from this artillery landed most heavily in the Middle East, particularly the "Holy Land" of Palestine. American missionaries were, in fact, merely the shock troops for a sustained invasion of the region by American tourists throughout much of the nineteenth century. Most of them were "Protestant Christians, who saw themselves as having a particularly meaningful connection on the strength of their religious beliefs." And many of them fully believed that this land was quite literally *their* land due to the "popular self-perception that Americans were not only the literal inheritors of God's favor but also better versed in the Bible ... than Europeans."[13] For the missionaries, however, the Middle East was not merely a pilgrimage; they had work to do. Many of them came directly from the classrooms of the Andover Theological Seminary and were supported in their travel by the American Board of Commissioners of Foreign Missions founded in 1810 in Massachusetts. They carried with them, therefore, powerful religious beliefs tinged with not a little streak of Puritanism. Their purpose was clear – to bring the true American Christianity to every corner of the world, most especially the Middle East: "In this American quest to reclaim the world for Christ, no place figured more profoundly than the Holy Land." There was a good deal of reclamation work to do – the region, although bathed in biblical references, had degenerated into an area inhabited by "idolatrous Christian sects and forsaken Jews. Most blatantly, however, there was the ascendancy of Islam." The first missionaries sent forth by the American Board set sail in late 1819 and many more would follow, all vowing to "renovate a world" by bringing the true word of god to the heathens. In some ways, they were the first purveyors of what would later be called "soft power:" "They wanted to conquer spiritually where others had prevailed through force."[14]

This "soft" approach, however, served to reveal a particularly troubling strain of nationalism when American "truth" ran into foreign "others." Christian duty was often heavily leavened with hubris, national arrogance, and loathing of the very people who were to be saved. As Mark Twain remarked later in the nineteenth century, one of the most famous American travelers to the Holy Land religiously clutched his handkerchief and his pistol: "Always, when he was not on the point of crying over a holy place, he was on the point of killing an Arab."[15] Somewhat ironically, it also helped to illuminate in a stark and devastating fashion the issues that arose when "others" within the United States tried to participate in explaining the truth about America to the world. Nowhere was this more apparent than with African American cultural diplomats who struggled to represent a nation that condemned them to slavery or second-class citizenship because of their race.

African American missionaries who went abroad representing both their nation and their race faced an especially ticklish problem. In his study of the African Methodist Episcopal (AME) Church and its missionary efforts in the late nineteenth and early twentieth centuries, Lawrence Little claims that the group "espoused a rhetoric of liberty and equality that promoted American democratic ideals and included African Americans within the civil polity of the nation." With its missionaries on the front lines, the Church fought for a "global application of American liberty by globalizing issues of oppression and identifying with oppressed people around the world." For the AME Church, the battles for liberty at home and abroad were intimately connected: the bigotry and racial violence faced in America were simply an "offshoot of the political, social, and economic domination that European and American imperialists were attempting to impose upon the rest of the globe."[16] The Church's work, therefore, seemed clear enough: oppose racism in the United States and imperialism overseas.

For some African Americans, this was the chosen path. In Elliott Skinner's massive study of the efforts by black Americans to influence their nation's foreign policy toward Africa, he details numerous individuals and groups working "to get the white man off the back of African peoples the world over." They operated through official channels (including the handful of African Americans working for the Department of State) and unofficial lines of persuasion to express their discontent over the European partition of Africa in the late 1800s and the continuing damage done to that continent by imperialism.[17] For others, including many members of the AME Church, it was more complicated. First and foremost, they recognized the difficulty inherent in their goal to spread "American liberty" around the world when liberty in America for their own people was an uncertain proposition at best. In other words, it was difficult to stand as apostles for freedom when the freedom enjoyed by African Americans was severely circumscribed by unofficial racism and official segregation. In addition, it was extremely risky for African American missionaries to criticize imperialism. This could easily offend the European colonial masters in Africa and render the missionaries persona non grata. Particularly in the late nineteenth century they could also easily incur the wrath of an American government (and a sizeable portion of the American public) that seemed intent on constructing an empire for the United States. In dealing with these problems, the AME missionaries demonstrated the ways in which serving as unofficial American cultural diplomats sometimes came with a price.

According to historian Lawrence Little, some leaders of the AME Church found a way to reconcile their professions about spreading "American-style liberty" around the world with American imperialism. Many of these leaders considered themselves "members of a black religious bourgeoisie," and thus had a "vested interest in the American ideals, institutions, and culture they had helped to produce." Thus, while they continued to view their missionaries as agents for liberty and equality, they came to share with their white counterparts a certain cultural arrogance about the people they were trying to save. As with the white missionaries working their way through the Middle East, black missionaries saw themselves as "chosen by God. It was their duty, they believed, to spread the gospel to the unredeemed peoples of the world, especially those of color." But they would spread more than the word of God. They also believed that the "Christian values" that were intrinsic to America – particularly "hard work" and "thrift" – were equally needed by those "unredeemed peoples." In short, their mission was not simply to create good Christians, but good workers, good consumers, and good citizens. Imperialism, whether of the European or American variety, therefore became a force for positive change by helping to uplift the benighted denizens of Africa and elsewhere. And imperialism had an added benefit for the struggle for civil rights at home: "organizing and incorporating colonial people into the AME Church contained a religious-political message that demonstrated that people of color were capable of self-government and undermined basic premises of black inferiority."[18] They continued to preach the value of American liberty, but it was a liberty that now required a certain amount of colonial tutelage in order to fully reap its benefits.

Other African Americans who traveled abroad during the early nineteenth century confronted the contradictions of "American liberty" more directly and critically. Focusing their attention on Great Britain they also carried a distinct message by pointing a damning finger at the most obvious chink in America's rhetoric about freedom and equality – slavery. The United States worked manfully to avoid a direct confrontation with the issue for years with compromises flying fast and furious: the three-fifths compromise at the Constitutional Convention, the Compromise of 1820, the Compromise of 1850, and the Kansas-Nebraska Act were all political dressings applied to the gashes dividing North and South over the issue of slavery and its expansion. A small, but vocal, group of abolitionists worked in America to end slavery, but most of their fellow citizens feared them as dangerous radicals who would lead to a split in the Union or, even worse, the nightmare of millions of free blacks within the nation. In an effort to apply more direct pressure on the American people and national government some abolitionists traveled abroad hoping to receive both monetary and political assistance from the one nation that seemed to be taking the lead in abolishing slavery – Great Britain.

In August 1845, Frederick Douglass left America for a nearly two-year trip to Ireland and Great Britain. Douglass was certainly the most famous free black in America due to the publication earlier in 1845 of his *Narrative of the Life of Frederick Douglass, an American Slave*, which chronicled his years as a slave, his breathtaking escape from his master, and his life as a free black in Massachusetts. In fact, the appearance of his book and his precipitous flight abroad were linked, for Douglass and many of his supporters came to fear that his former master – now knowing his ex-slave's whereabouts – would come north to claim his property. But other factors also drew Douglass and a number of other free African Americans to Great Britain in the first half of the nineteenth century. As he recalled in his 1881 autobiography, "A rude, uncultivated fugitive slave, I was driven to that country to which American young gentlemen go to increase their stock of knowledge – to seek pleasure, and to have their rough democratic manners softened by contact with English aristocratic refinement."[19] Most important was that nation's "'moral prestige,' a consequence of its decision in 1833 to abolish slavery in the West Indies." Although Britain's stance on slavery and the slave trade was not entirely altruistic, it was the first major nation to take a stand against the "peculiar institution." African Americans who traveled there in the early 1800s often commented on the "supposed absence of racial prejudice... and its liberating effect on African American travelers."[20]

Douglass and other American abolitionists also came to Britain with the idea of joining forces with anti slavery forces in that nation and using that foreign opinion to pressure the U.S. government to take a more active stance against slavery. During his visit to Ireland and Britain, Douglass gave numerous lectures in town halls, churches, and other public venues describing the brutality of slavery, its pernicious impact on American society, and calling on his audiences to help in ending this inhumane practice. As Douglass so eloquently put it in an 1846 address, "I may be asked, why I am so anxious to bring this subject before the British public – why I do not confine my efforts to the United States?" His answer was clear: "Slavery is the common enemy of mankind, and all mankind should be made acquainted with its abominable character…. [T]he slave is a man, and, as such, is entitled to your sympathy as a brother."[21] The challenge was not so simple as it might initially appear. While Great Britain wore the mantle of anti slavery by enacting emancipation in some of its colonies and taking action against the international slave trade, this did not translate into the "racial paradise" that some travelers from the United States expected to encounter. As scholars Alan J. Rice and Martin Crawford pointedly note, "Douglass's lectures formed only part of a range of representations of race and slavery in America transported across the Atlantic in the same period." His fiery oratory had to contend with "ethnological" exhibits of "primitive Africans," a variety of American and British black-face performers (whites who blackened their faces and portrayed black Americans utilizing every cringe-worthy stereotype they could muster), and racist caricatures and articles in leading British newspapers and journals. Douglass persevered, however, and his efforts "helped to internationalize the African American struggle for full human rights" and "demonstrated how the struggle resonated far beyond the community itself in a relationship with other continents forged within what Paul Gilroy has more recently termed a 'black Atlantic' discourse." By the time Douglass departed in 1847, he had "played a major part in turning the tide of opinion from hostility, apathy, or ignorance toward support for abolition."[22]

In some ways, it might be argued that Douglass's forays into foreign lands to try and explain slavery and America's race problem provided an impetus for what could be considered the first – and extremely tentative – official action by the U.S. government in the realm of cultural diplomacy. The appearance in 1861 of the inaugural volume of the *Foreign Relations of the United States* certainly marked an important milestone in the history of public diplomacy in which the American government took direct steps to inform the larger public about the goals and inner workings of the nation's foreign affairs. As Aaron W. Marrs notes in a recent history of the *FRUS* series, the first volume came about in response to congressional demands for documentation concerning newly elected President Abraham Lincoln's foreign policy. Over 400 pages of official letters and memos were sent to Congress and as Marrs argues the intent was clearly to "sell" the Civil War to the American people: "modern readers can assess the early *FRUS* volumes as a sign of what the Lincoln administration wanted the American public to know about its foreign relations efforts during the first months of the conflict." Yet, it was evident that the foreign audience was equally important: "U.S. posts abroad also transmitted copies of *FRUS* to foreign governments, and American representatives reported that the public release of documents had a positive impact." One might argue that *FRUS* is not cultural diplomacy at all, but merely propaganda in another form. There is some merit in this point of view, for the volumes that were published during the Civil War did not contain a complete record of America's diplomacy. Some matters were excluded entirely, while some of the other correspondence printed in *FRUS* was heavily edited.[23]

Nevertheless, a strong argument can be made that the *FRUS* series began, perhaps unknowingly, what would come to be regarded as official cultural diplomacy. Three issues, in particular, support that conclusion. First and foremost is the publication of a special issue of *FRUS* in 1866. This was a volume devoted entirely to expressions of condolences from home and abroad following the assassination of President Lincoln in 1865. As Marrs concludes, "The 'Lincoln Volume' afforded the opportunity, however tragic the occasion, to combine public affairs and public diplomacy. The volume not only gave voice to a global expansion of solidarity and support, but also demonstrated the resiliency of the American system of government." The messages from grieving Americans – including some Southerners – suggested to the foreign audience that the United States was once again truly united. Those from overseas, which included formal expressions of sorrow from foreign governments and spontaneous outpourings of support from individuals and private organizations, were used to portray international respect for both Lincoln and his now reunified and powerful nation. In addition, the Civil War *FRUS* volumes directly confronted the domestic issue of slavery. The inaugural volume contained explicit messages from Secretary of State William Seward arguing that slavery was the basis of the Civil War. He even advised the U.S. representative in Russia, where Czar Alexander II had recently emancipated the serfs, to make it clear that even before the outbreak of the Civil War "it was expected that under the operation of moral, social, and political influences then existing the practice of slavery would soon cease." Finally, the very fact that the United States, alone among the world's governments, even attempted the printing of a "thorough, accurate, and reliable" account of the nation's foreign affairs sent a very strong message about the strength of a democracy and the value of openness.[24] It would not be until the twentieth century, however, that the American government seemed to completely grasp the value and power of culture as a tool for official international communication.

In the years following the Civil War, therefore, private individuals and groups continued to shoulder most of the responsibility for bringing U.S. culture to the world. Prior to the Civil War most of these efforts revolved around the expression of ideas – scientific, spiritual, moral, and political – to spread the word about the nation's cultural foundations and achievements.

Decades of a rarely spoken, but deeply ingrained, sense of cultural inferiority meant that only a few direct manifestations (literature, art, music) of American culture made their way abroad. By the time the war ended, however, some in the United States thought it appropriate to actually show their cultural products to the world. A perfect example of this effort was the American participation in the Fine Arts Department of the 1867 Exposition Universelle held in Paris. Since there was as yet no official government agency to assist in representing the United States at foreign exhibitions and fairs, the art show for the 1867 exhibit was selected, organized, and funded by private American organizations and individuals. When appeals by these individuals and organizations to the U.S. government for assistance were met with suspicion and apathy from Congress, the National Academy of Design (founded in 1825 by various American artists and supporters of the arts) eventually appointed its own committee to oversee the work and ultimately relied on a selection committee made up of artists, art dealers and critics, and private citizens. The committee relied on appeals to collectors, individual artists, and museums to secure the works ultimately shown in Paris.[25]

While the American show in 1867 was entirely in private hands, it nevertheless served as an important step in America's cultural diplomacy. As Carol Troyen explains in her marvelous study of the U.S. exhibit in Paris, the show was "designed to present to an international audience the achievements of American culture and to demonstrate that American art was the equal of its machinery and inventions." The organizers made a pointedly nationalistic argument in urging congressional support by claiming that government funding was necessary to "secure a proper representation of the art of the country in Paris." The nearly 120 pieces of American art (paintings, sketches, and sculpture) were evidence that a "new, patriotic self-assurance had for the moment displaced the nation's deep-seated cultural insecurity and, full of naïve enthusiasm, America in 1867 sent its best contemporary art to be measured against Europe's greatest modern masters." To that end, landscape paintings dominated the American collection and were chosen to send a particular message: they "immortalized the optimistic spirit of antebellum America, and proclaimed the country to be expansive, unspoiled, and indomitable." From our present-day standpoint, it was certainly a very impressive gathering of works by artists such as Winslow Homer, Frederic Church, and Albert Bierstadt. However, the American art barely made a dent in the seemingly impervious armor of European cultural superiority. The only work that seemed to garner much interest was a magnificent painting of Niagara Falls by Church that managed to win a silver medal. To a large extent, the French and British critics turned up their collective critical noses and dismissively characterized most of the American art in Paris as mere imitations (and poor ones, at that) of the far better works by European artists. And as a prelude to the controversies that erupted over American art exhibits sent abroad during the Cold War, there was plenty of finger pointing in the wake of the disappointing showing by American art, including accusations that the French purposely relegated the works by the upstart Americans to less than prestigious settings in the exhibit hall. However, "It was the selection of works that was most frequently blamed for the failure of the American display." The most pointed criticism charged that "the entries from the United States were neither native nor descriptive enough, and insufficiently documented the characteristic aspects of certain typical American scenes."[26] In short, they failed to properly exhibit the true American culture – another argument that would appear again and again as U.S. cultural diplomacy picked up steam in the mid-twentieth century.

There was, however, another American exhibit at the Paris fair that exceeded the popularity of the fine arts on display – and also served as an indication that another form of U.S. culture was beginning to find its way abroad. A large selection of photographs featuring the American landscape succeeded where the American landscape paintings apparently failed. The photos received praise in the European press and even won a gold and a bronze medal. The reason for the different reception seemed clear. American painting still seemed wedded to its European heritage – hence its inability to portray the "real" America. The photographs, however, allowed the foreign audience to clearly and precisely understand that "America is still to us a new world, and anything which gives us a true representation as a photograph, is sure to be looked upon with wondering eyes."[27]

The photographs shown in Paris in 1867 were significant for their role in illustrating that the American culture sent abroad after the Civil War differed from the examples of the early- and mid-nineteenth century. In place of scientific discourse, appeals to the spirit, forthright confrontations with race, or even the fine arts, the latter decades of the 1800s were dominated by popular culture in the form of sports, tourism, and mass entertainment. Although profit was often a motivating factor behind these efforts, each of them – in one way or another – also carried forward powerful messages about the American nation from which they came. In their own fashion, they served as cultural markers denoting America's rise to world power in the late nineteenth century.

Throughout the nineteenth century the United States and Great Britain competed for economic, military, and political power. On occasion, as with the War of 1812, the competition devolved into a bloody struggle. This battle for prestige and power, however, was also carried out on smaller battlefields. The sport of boxing was in the midst of its glory years in Great Britain and more than one Englishman believed that their people's success in the boxing ring was a sign of "national virility."[28] Thus, when the British heavyweight champion Tom Cribb toed the line against the American ex-slave Tom Molineaux on September 28, 1811, a crowd of over 20,000 people gathered outside of London to watch another battle for national honor against the upstart Americans. Molineaux earned the grudging respect of the British public a few years earlier when he put up a valiant stand against Cribb, but by 1811 – with "national virility" being more and more vigorously challenged by their former colony – the crowd was out for blood. And they got what they wanted: Cribb manhandled his challenger before knocking him cold in the eleventh round.[29]

While the fight meant more to the British – Molineaux, as a black former slave, elicited little support from his American countrymen – it was evidence of a new interest in competitive sports that was heightened by what historian Elliott Gorn refers to as the "nationalistic overtones" that burst forth when the combatants in a sporting event came from different nations. This was shown very distinctly in 1860 when the Irish-born American fighter John C. Heenan traveled to England to battle Tom Sayers for the heavyweight championship of the world. Partisans on both sides of the Atlantic cheered on their "national" champions, and for those seeking an outlet to patriotic aggression the fight certainly did not disappoint. Lasting over two hours the fight turned when Heenan broke his arm. The American refused to surrender, however, and "Sayers slowly beat Heenan's handsome face into an ugly mask," leaving Heenan nearly blind. As was often the case in these brutal, bare-knuckle bouts, the end came not because of the action in the ring, but the violence outside of it. When policemen tried to stop the bout, the crowd rushed into the ring and a riot ensued, forcing the fight organizers to declare a draw.[30]

During the first six decades of the nineteenth century, American boxers traveled to Great Britain to try and wrest the heavyweight championship from British hands, simultaneously serving as proxies in the international competition between the United States and England. In the latter years of the 1800s, however, the balance of power – both in the ring and in the world – began to slowly shift in favor of the Americans. At the same time that boxing lost favor among much of the British public, it enjoyed a tremendous rise in popularity in the United States (despite the fact that prizefighting was illegal in every state). As some historians have suggested, this new public excitement for the sport was due in part to fears that American men were losing their "masculine" heritage. Other Americans, such as Theodore Roosevelt, viewed boxing and other competitive sports as good training for the most pressing task at hand – building a U.S. empire.[31]

The rising popularity of sports in America brought forth a new personality on the national stage – the sports celebrity. And in late nineteenth-century America none was more famous than John L. Sullivan, the heavyweight champion of the world. Born to Irish immigrants in 1858 Sullivan literally fought his way out of poverty by taking up prizefighting. By 1882 and his defeat of fellow Irish-American Paddy Ryan, Sullivan was acclaimed as the new champion. He spent much of the next few years performing in plays, boxing exhibition matches, engaging in prodigious amounts of drinking and carousing, and, occasionally, defending his title. In 1887, with money running low, Sullivan and his advisers decided to invade foreign soil. In October of that year he set sail for Great Britain. During the next few months, he toured the "old country" of Ireland and England. Although most of the British upper class derisively dismissed the Boston Strong Boy as a thug masquerading as a gentleman, the British and Irish masses mobbed Sullivan everywhere he went. Even the Prince of Wales made time to meet the American champion. Boxing, once the sport that promoted Great Britain's "national virility," had a new star and some observers found a parallel between the handing of the heavyweight belt to Sullivan and the growing American international presence that threatened Britain's preeminent position in the world.[32]

Sullivan's trip to England and Ireland, while it generated tremendous interest among the public in those nations, was basically a one-off event. Although Sullivan did travel abroad in later years most of these excursions were long after his championship days were behind him. His only other tour abroad during his reign as heavyweight champ was a disastrous trip to Australia in 1891 when he toured with an acting company and starred in a play. The nearly unanimous view of the Australian audiences was that Sullivan should stick to boxing.[33] Another American sports figure, however, had grander plans and designs.

In the late nineteenth century, as the United States began constructing its overseas empire, entrepreneur Albert Spalding was building an empire of his own around the increasing American fascination with sports, particularly baseball. His company produced sporting goods to feed the new demand for bats, balls, and gloves, and by the 1880s he was already raking in the profits. Spalding was a man with vision and by 1888 – also like the United States – he was ready to push into foreign markets. His plan? Send two baseball teams on a "world tour" to promote the United States, the sport, and – of course – the line of sporting goods available through Spalding's company.[34]

As Robert Elias notes in his comprehensive study of baseball and U.S. foreign policy, a number of scholars agree that sports – particularly baseball – were used to promote American interests abroad: "Troops, corporations, and churches were not the only U.S. emissaries overseas. American missionary zeal was also passionately expressed through baseball." That the "American way of life" was superior to all others was widely accepted and "Americans believed they had the one true sport – baseball." The baseball tours were, according to Elias, "often described as 'invasions of foreign territory'." Spalding was not the first American to recognize the potential of such "invasions," but he did not give up on the idea when tours to Great Britain in 1874 and Cuba in 1879 and 1886 failed to achieve much popularity or impact. He simply decided that his own effort needed to be bigger and flashier.[35]

For his "World Baseball Tour," Spalding wanted star power and he got it when he convinced Cap Anson, the new manager of the Chicago White Stockings, to bring his team along on the trip around the globe. Anson's best playing years were behind him, but he was the most recognized name in baseball and the White Stockings were winners of numerous titles. To play against Anson's team, Spalding recruited what he called the "All-American Team," led by another baseball hero, John Montgomery Ward. The two teams embarked on a grueling tour that began in the fall of 1888 and ended in the spring of 1889. During those months, the tour barreled through New Zealand and Australia, Ceylon, Egypt, Italy, and France, and finished up with a swing through England and Ireland. Crowd size and reaction varied, from bored befuddlement to genuine interest, and in England the Prince of Wales (who seems to have become his nation's official greeter of foreign sports figures) attended a game.[36]

There is little doubt that Spalding saw the tour as a business venture: "implant the game abroad, he reasoned, and equipment would have to be bought from someone like him." Historian Thomas Zeiler, however, argues that there was more than mere moneymaking behind the baseball mogul's grand endeavor. Even Spalding realized the tour would likely lose money in the short term, but he and his fellow sports entrepreneurs were "not completely removed from the nationalistic and globalizing impulses that pointed to expansion and Great Power status" for the emerging United States. He therefore "linked baseball to a U.S. presence overseas, viewing the world as a market ripe for the infusion of American ideas, products, and energy. Through globalization during the Gilded Age, he and other Americans penetrated the globe." Even President Grover Cleveland found time to meet with Anson and the Chicago team in the White House prior to their departure for the first stop in Australia and proudly declared that they were the "best representatives of the national game to the Australian people."[37]

Sport was but one manifestation of the growing popularity of a relatively new phenomenon in the United States – mass entertainment. Prior to the late 1800s, Americans seeking amusement often had to rely on small venues – theaters, saloons, and impromptu sporting events. Technological and ideological changes in the latter part of the nineteenth century, however, meant that American culture became merely another product that could be mass-produced. As Robert Rydell and Rob Kroes explain, "Mass culture...means exactly that – and more. Mass culture means the mobilization of cultural and ideological resources on a scale unimaginable in a preindustrial society lacking mass transportation and communication facilities." The rapid growth of the American railway system, improvements in shipping, the expansion of the telegraph, and the rise of a national media in the forms of newspapers and magazines were the main facilitators of the new American mass culture that encompassed sports, large-scale fairs and expositions, the publication of "dime novels," and, eventually, motion pictures. Yet, the difference was more than simply one of scale. The growth of the audience for American cultural products from a few hundred or thousand to a national audience of millions was significant. More important was what this new mass culture meant. By the early 1900s, the United States boasted a network of culture industries that produced increasingly standardized entertainment forms for consumption within accelerating mass markets at home and abroad. It is equally apparent that these mass cultural forms were hardly value-free or neutral. They often expressed and conveyed ideologies of race, gender, empire, and consumption and played a pivotal role in the process of reconstructing the American national identity after the Civil War.[38]

Within the United States mass culture helped to spread the message about the nation's growing power and influence. This was perhaps nowhere better illustrated than at the first world's fairs hosted by America. At the Centennial Exhibition held in Philadelphia in 1876, and again in Chicago in 1893 with the World's Columbian Exposition, the United States announced itself as a world power. Traditional expressions of American culture, such as paintings, sculpture, and music, were certainly not forgotten. In a somewhat odd turn of events, some of the very same American artists who had been on display in Paris in 1867 were again shown in Philadelphia. This time, however, instead of being intruders into the European world of art they served as the standard bearers for American culture, prominently displayed among the classic works from the "Old World" sent by France, Great Britain, and Italy.[39]

The real stars of the fair, however, illustrated another potentially potent weapon in the nation's cultural arsenal – the manifestations of its rapidly increasing industrial power. Perhaps most symbolic of that power was what unexpectedly turned out to be one of the most popular "exhibits": the gigantic 700-ton Corliss engine that provided power for the fair's other buildings. In Machinery Hall audiences were introduced to new wonders: "typewriters, a mechanical calculator, Bell's telephone, Edison's quadruplex telegraph, machines for agricultural use and heavy industry – the cumulative impression of industrial power must have been the most stunning of all. And the United States, whose exhibits filled 80 percent of Machinery Hall, was at the center of progress." Seventeen years later, at the fair in Chicago, the United States decided to display the ultimate manifestation of that power by literally building a city within a city. The leading architects of the nation, including Louis Sullivan and Daniel Burnham, designed buildings that physically demonstrated the power and glory of America. The highlight was the so-called "White City," an imposing collection of neoclassical buildings – all painted white, of course – intended to inspire not simply wonder, but awe and respect.[40]

Machinery, technology, architecture, and art all helped to redefine the American nation for both the domestic and foreign visitors to the Philadelphia and Chicago fairs. If nothing else, the sheer size of the expositions emphasized the new mass culture of the nation, very nearly overwhelming the often-exhausted fairgoers. By the time of the Chicago fair, however, what often made the greatest impression on the masses was not the "White City" but the mass entertainment provided by what came to be known as the Midway Plaisance. Here, a weary visitor could find "German beer halls, Turkish bazaars, Algerian jugglers, Dahomean drummers, Egyptian belly dancers, the World's Congress of Beauty ('40 Ladies from 40 Nations'), balloon rides, wild animal shows, and ostrich omelets." At its center was the world's first Ferris wheel. It was hardly the "culture" the upper-class patrons might have desired, but "The Barnumesque eclecticism and 'exuberant chaos' of the midway provided visitors with an alternative to the beaux-arts neoclassicism of the Court of Honor [the White City], but it also offered a relief from the almost overwhelming complexity of the 65,000 exhibits of human progress displayed in the major exhibition halls." The fact that so many people wanted to see the "hootchie-kootchie" belly dancers (such as the perhaps mythical "Little Egypt") suggested to some that even the "lowest" forms of culture had their uses.[41]

The most famous example of American mass entertainment did not so much reconstruct a national identity as continue the century-long process of creating an identity for the United States. *Buffalo Bill's Wild West* show featured a man who was himself made famous through the readership of mass-produced dime novels – Buffalo Bill Cody. His show was indeed a wild mix of what its promoters called "historical authenticity" and outlandish showmanship. Formed by Cody and some business associates in the 1880s, the depiction of the "Wild West" was both garish and thrilling, eventually featuring a cast of over 200 performers ranging from ex-cowboys and Native Americans, to celebrities such as Annie Oakley, Wild Bill Hickok, and Calamity Jane. There were demonstrations of shooting accuracy and horse racing, but the climax of the shows were always the "reenactments" of battles between Buffalo Bill, cowboys, and the U.S. cavalry and war-bonneted Native Americans. The show was popular in the United States, but it was not until Cody took his troupe to Europe in 1887 that it became a certified phenomenon. The Prince of Wales, just as he did with the visiting boxer John L. Sullivan, made time to tour the Wild West encampment. Perhaps more startling was the appearance of Queen Victoria, who had not attended a public performance of any kind in twenty-five years. Other European dignitaries joined in the fun: "The highlight of the show came when several monarchs, including the Prince of Wales and the kings of Denmark, Greece, Belgium, and Saxony, hopped aboard the Deadwood Stagecoach with Buffalo Bill in the driver's seat and rode around the arena while the assembled Indians engaged in a mock attack." Following the enormous success of the shows in England, Cody's show embarked on a whirlwind tour through France, Spain, Italy, Germany, and Austro-Hungary.[42]

Beyond its entertainment value the show did have relatively distinct messages about America, its history, and its power. Some of this, as Rydell and Kroes argue, was purposeful: "The intention of Buffalo Bill's staging was certainly to make the story of the American West merge with the story of European expansion at a time when European colonization reached the far frontiers of its own empires." Other messages were interlaced with the sheer scale of the undertaking: mass publicity, mass communication, and, perhaps most important, mass transportation of the enormous troupe. All of this clearly illustrated the rapid rise of America as a modern, industrialized state. Rumors abounded that while touring in Germany Prussian military men took careful notes about the logistical undertaking required to move the show from nation to nation. As with the U.S. exhibits at the world's fairs Cody's retelling of the "settling" of the Wild West was also a paean to American technology and its usefulness in conquest and civilization. "The key to the whole affair was not the wild men and animals, the Indians, the frontier types, the bucking broncos and buffalo, but the revolver and the repeating rifles, two of the most innovative products of nineteenth-century industrial civilization in the United States."[43]

Thousands of other Americans went abroad in the nineteenth century with little or no thoughts about science, reform, or material gain. Tourists from the United States visited locales around the world (although primarily focused on Europe and the Middle East) with no interest in uplifting the native inhabitants, spreading American liberty, or serving as living advertisements for the American way of life. Instead of bibles and sporting equipment they carried little else but their luggage and their guidebooks, intent on soaking up a little foreign adventure and culture. Nevertheless, these roving bands of travelers brought with them a distinctly American view of their surroundings (and the people inhabiting them), and they were not always terribly shy about sharing their feelings. They bought souvenirs, interacted – in one way or another – with the locals, and often wrote about their experiences so that they served as the vicarious eyes and ears of the larger American public at home. These travelogues were sometimes tedious recitations of places visited and sights seen; some were fierce harangues about the burdens of overseas travel and/or the irritating people one encountered in this or that region of the world. One tourist, in particular, cast a more knowing eye on his surroundings and left us with an unmatched record of Americans (warts and all) who traveled the globe in the years after the Civil War.

Mark Twain had just turned thirty-one when, in December 1866, he set sail for a tour of Europe and the Holy Land. At the time, he was a minor celebrity. A year before he published the short story that brought him to national attention, "The Jumping Frog of Calaveras County," and based on the popularity of this work a San Francisco newspaper decided to send Twain abroad with the expectation that his wry observations on his travels would make for popular reading. The results of Twain's tour were published in 1867 in his book *The Innocents Abroad, or the New Pilgrims' Progress*. In many ways, his observations were a compendium of American stereotypes and denigrating comments about the "foreigners" he encountered. The Portuguese boatmen were a "swarm of swarthy, noisy, lying, shoulder-shrugging, gesticulating" humanity, "with brass rings in their ears, and fraud in their hearts." In Tangier, he was surprised to see the faces of several Moorish women without their veils and commented that "I am full of veneration for the wisdom that leads them to cover up such atrocious ugliness. They carry their children at their backs, in a sack, like other savages the world over." When in Paris he witnessed a ceremony where Napoleon III and Abdul Aziz, the sultan of Turkey, were riding together. The Turk suffered in comparison: "Abdul Aziz, the representative of a people by nature and training filthy, brutish, ignorant, unprogressive, superstitious – and a government whose Three Graces are Tyranny, Rapacity, Blood." While admiring the architecture of the fabulous churches and cathedrals in Italy, he had little good to say about the nation's people: "[W]hen the filthy beggars swarmed around me the contrast was too striking, too suggestive, and I said, 'Oh, sons of classic Italy, *is* the spirit of enterprise, of self-reliance, of noble endeavor, utterly dead with ye? Curse your indolent worthlessness, why don't you rob your churches?'"[44]

Yet, Twain could be equally harsh on what would in later years come to be known as the "ugly American." Commenting on his fellow passengers aboard the ship steaming across the Atlantic, the acerbic writer observed that "we have a poet and a good-natured, enterprising idiot on board," along with another "young and green, and not bright" individual who, upon landing in Gibraltar, proceeded to harangue British officials "with braggadocio about America and the wonders she can perform. He told one of them a couple of our gunboats could come here and knock Gibraltar into the Mediterranean sea!" At a French restaurant, his dining was disturbed by "the conduct of an American, who talked very loudly and coarsely." When the patron's behavior was noted by another guest, he exclaimed, "'I am a free-born sovereign, sir, an American, sir, and I want everybody to know it!' He did not mention that he was a lineal descendant of Balaam's ass; but everybody knew that without his telling it." Even American officials did not escape Twain's sarcasm. Upon meeting the "Commissioner of the United States of America to Europe, Asia, and Africa," he was disappointed to find that this individual was "a common mortal, and that his mission had nothing more overpowering about it than the collecting of seeds, and uncommon yarns and extraordinary cabbages and peculiar bullfrogs for that poor, useless, innocent, mildewed old fossil, the Smithsonian Institute."[45]

Twain's account of his travels is a remarkable document. While he constantly denigrates nearly every nationality with which he comes into contact, his admiration of European culture – its art, its architecture, its heritage – also manages to peep through the snide remarks. His embarrassment at the actions of many of his fellow Americans, however, reveals that behind the hubris was a deep uncertainty about exactly how his home country matched up with the older European civilizations. He almost seemed apologetic about America's comparative lack of culture: while Europe had breathtaking buildings and museums, the United States was stuck with the "mildewed old fossil" of the Smithsonian. As one scholar notes, *Innocents Abroad* has sometimes been called "'the American declaration of independence to Europe's superiority.' But this is not altogether accurate; neither is it quite fair to Europe, to America, or to Mark Twain." True, Twain would often dismiss the work of the European "Old Masters," but this was not simply cultural chauvinism: "In his heart he knows he is missing something and his knowledge sets up an inferiority complex within him and makes him angry – with others who perceive what he cannot perceive, and even more with himself because he cannot perceive it."[46]

Perhaps, but Twain himself would have the last word about the ultimate meaning of his tour:

> Wherever we went, in Europe, Asia, or Africa, we made a sensation, and, I suppose I may add, created a famine. None of us had ever been anywhere before; we all hailed from the interior; travel was a wild novelty to us, and we conducted ourselves in accordance with the natural instincts that were in us, and trammeled ourselves with no ceremonies, no conventionalities. We always took care to make it understood that we were Americans – Americans! When we found that a good many foreigners had hardly ever heard of America, and that a good many more knew it only as a barbarous province away off somewhere, that had lately been at war with somebody, we pitied the ignorance of the Old World, but abated no jot of our importance. Many and many a simple community in the Eastern hemisphere will remember for years the incursion of the strange horde of the year of our Lord 1867, that called themselves Americans, and seemed to imagine in some unaccountable way that they had a right to be proud of it.

And he was equally sure of his travel's impact: "The people stared at us everywhere, and we stared at them. We generally made them feel rather small, too, before we got done with them, because we bore down on them with America's greatness until we crushed them."[47]

At first glance it might reasonably be argued that these episodes, interesting though they may be, do not in any way provide evidence of a coherent or sustained effort in the field of cultural diplomacy on the part of the United States. In the most literal sense, this is true. Jefferson's moose, Douglass's speeches, the missionaries' bibles, baseball and boxing gloves, Wild West shows, and even Twain's acerbic commentaries were certainly not parts of a well-thought-out plan of American cultural conquest. Most of them had little or no direct connection with the American government and were often spur-of-the-moment undertakings. Nevertheless, these pioneers – seen in the larger picture of U.S. cultural diplomacy – established some important precedents that were reflected in the much more immense, and official, American efforts during the years following the Second World War.

Jefferson was one of the first Americans to grapple with arguments from abroad about America's supposed inferiority and to understand the diplomatic challenge that such arguments raised concerning U.S. political and economic power. His *Notes* served as the opening volley in what would become a steady stream of American propaganda after the Second World War that sought to simultaneously blunt anti-American attacks by the nation's enemies and secure a more positive opinion of the United States among all nations. If Jefferson's *Notes* exemplified the power of the word, his moose evidenced the power of the object. Written documents provided the foundation for both science and diplomacy. Rebutting Buffon's theories in his private correspondence was one thing, but with the publication of his first and only book Jefferson was attempting to reach a wider (and influential) audience both at home and abroad. Nevertheless, as the American diplomat quickly realized in the world of cultural diplomacy things mattered. Jefferson could argue until he was blue in the face; he could write volumes denying American degeneracy. But nothing could compare to solid evidence – a very big moose in this case. As Dugatkin observes, Jefferson "understood that in order to convince, you sometimes need to go with the tangible – things that people can hold, touch, feel, and smell."[48] The moose definitely fit the bill (at that point, one imagines, most certainly in the area of smell). Over 150 years later, America's cultural diplomacy flooded the world with tangibles – works of art, examples of technology, fashion – and even added taste to the list of senses, plying world audiences with soft drinks and snacks.

Douglass's impassioned speeches against the evils of slavery seem even less like cultural diplomacy than Jefferson's behemoth. After all, in criticizing slavery Douglass was taking to task nearly one-half of the states in the Union. As would be amply demonstrated during the Cold War, America's official cultural activities abroad very rarely spoke for, or about, all Americans. With such a polyglot nation to represent it would have been truly amazing had it done so. And Douglass's speaking tour through Great Britain was not the last time that the foreign audience would hear about an ugly blemish on the face of American democracy. At the height of the Cold War U.S. officials scrambled to explain to overseas observers exactly how the leader of the free world contained millions of black Americans who were not even allowed to vote.

American missionaries are equally difficult to tag as cultural diplomats. Like Douglass, they were unofficial representatives. They did not even represent a monolithic group, coming from different denominations and races and focused on different end results. In some ways, however, they did presage the growth and influence of what would be called much later in American history nongovernmental organizations (NGOs). The missionaries carried their bibles and their beliefs, but they also carried their own brands of Americanism and, unfortunately, they also brought their own brands of paternalism and racism in their desire to redeem the heathens. As such, they made stereotypical representatives of American culture. Unhindered by government dictates or direction, the missionaries, and the churches for which they served as representatives, were free to spread their own vision of Americanism. It is not terribly surprisingly that their Americanism often differed from what might have emanated from a U.S. government office of cultural diplomacy only in its lack of an official patina and, perhaps, its mode of delivery. Most American officials in the mid- to late nineteenth century were just as certain of American greatness, just as convinced that the United States had been ordained with a blessing of specialness, and just as committed to the idea of America's role of savior to the lesser peoples of lesser lands. By the time of the Cold War it was even more apparent that the U.S. government was hardly the only game in the cultural diplomacy town.

Perhaps the oddest cultural ambassadors of the nineteenth century (aside, perhaps, from the moose) were the first examples of a new phenomenon in the United States – mass entertainment. Spalding's baseball players and the great John L. were celebrities who could dominate headlines in ways in which statesmen and diplomats could only respond with equal amounts of awe and envy. What could these harbingers of the explosive growth of what pundits would refer to as "popular culture" in America possibly say on the world stage that was of any significance? Perhaps the ball players could attest to America's dedication to teamwork and adherence to established rules of conduct – while simultaneously serving as walking, talking advertisements for Spalding sports equipment. Sullivan's propaganda value was, as befit his gargantuan ego, even larger. An American held the most famous title in the entire world, heavyweight champion, and he delighted in exhibiting his strength, tenacity, and cunning in the manly art. It might be, as American elites sniffed, all part of a vulgar and low-browed culture of the masses, but American movies, TV shows, and rock music would later find important roles to play in America's efforts to reach the hearts and minds of those overseas masses. Sports figures continued to play a significant role in America's cultural diplomacy, from government-sponsored tours of the Harlem Globetrotters in the 1950s to baseball player Cal Ripken and figure skater Michelle Kwan serving as "sports ambassadors" in the years after 9/11.

Other forms of mass culture, such as world's fairs and Buffalo Bill's successful Wild West shows, indicated the ways in which entertainment could be used to both reshape the perception of America and its history, while simultaneously highlighting the role of the nation's technology, and the mass production capabilities of American industry built upon that technology. Although it might seem strange to include consumer items under the umbrella of American culture, we should keep in mind that the cultural products themselves were merely one part of the picture. Of equal importance was the message these products carried to the foreign audience. And steam engines, cookware, guns, and other consumer goods were also symbols of power, of creativity, and the benefits of a democratic and capitalistic nation where one's freedom to achieve wealth and fame was unlimited.

By the end of the nineteenth century American cultural diplomacy, in any sustained official sense of the phrase, had yet to come into being. For most of the 1800s, U.S. cultural relations with the rest of the world were handled by amateurs – a sometimes-inchoate collection of individuals and organizations acting with little, if any, government support or acknowledgment. All of them had messages to send and all of them, to one extent or another, believed that their particular message was important for shaping the American image abroad. As far as constructing a unified or consistent message, well, that was another matter. True, Thomas Jefferson battled the theory of American degeneracy while serving as ambassador to France, and the Department of State took a tentative step toward reaching out to a wider foreign audience by inaugurating the publication of the *FRUS* series, but these had been notable exceptions to the general lack of interest on the part of the U.S. government in engaging in cultural diplomacy. It took the right leader – or, rather, the right leaders – in the right place at the right time to slowly but surely move the United States toward the construction of an official apparatus designed to utilize American culture as part of the nation's foreign policy.

CHAPTER TWO

From the Cowboy to the Aristocrat: The Early Twentieth-Century Foundations of U.S. Cultural Diplomacy

Theodore Roosevelt was well aware of the importance of a good show on the international stage, and the year 1907 was filled with opportunities for international cultural relations. In April, Roosevelt gave the opening address at the Jamestown Exposition that celebrated the 300th anniversary of the first permanent settlement of English colonists in North America. The U.S. government went to great pains to invite foreign nations to participate and in his speech TR began with a "special greeting to the representatives of the foreign governments here present." He went on to lavish praise on the British, but also noted that "From almost every nation of Europe we have drawn some part of our blood, some part of our traits." And while much of his speech was a paean to the unique aspects of American history, he also spent a surprising amount of time talking about international relations. The core of his message to the foreign listeners was summed up when he declared that "the duties that most concern us of this generation are not military, but social and industrial."[1] Nevertheless, the old Rough Rider was not blind to the uses that displays of military power might have on the foreign audience. Also in 1907 Roosevelt announced the world tour of what came to be known as the Great White Fleet. The round-the-world tour of sixteen U.S. battleships was not, as Lori Lyn Bogle argues, simply a flexing of American military muscle but an example of TR's "sophisticated understanding of how political leaders shape public opinion." The Great White Fleet was the capstone of the president's understanding of the power of "naval pageantry and world's fairs... in his public-relations campaign for the Navy."[2]

Theodore Roosevelt's involvement with such "pageantry" was not because of his singular appreciation for and knowledge of culture. Indeed, even the largely forgotten James Garfield was at least as intellectually aware and immersed in high culture.[3] What sets him apart from the American leaders who preceded him (and from many of those who came after) was his understanding of the power and the possible uses of culture in constructing both his own cult of personality and an image for an America emerging on the world scene. As Richard Collin explained in his important study of Roosevelt, culture, and diplomacy, TR was a "master at creating political legends" even before he stepped into office. It was important that Roosevelt understood the power of image and representation – whether it was himself as Rough Rider or wielder of the big stick, or his nation as international peacekeeper and bastion of civilization – because "the expansion in early twentieth-century America was cultural rather than diplomatic." Collin argues that TR understood this and quickly established a "European-type salon in the White House" at which he could converse at length with American cultural figures and European diplomats about literature, history, and art. While famous for his bluster about "big sticks" and hemispheric policemen, Roosevelt realized that America faced a serious problem: it did not have the military force to simply take what it wanted or settle disputes to its liking. In addition, TR felt that his nation did not command much international respect, but he also believed that "a nation with a strong culture (and a common one) will be able to win more battles by diplomatic bargaining than by force of arms." Collin concludes, "More important than world economic domination is the emerging American cultural leadership, a phenomenon that has little to do with political imperialism."[4]

Three years before sending the Great White Fleet around the world, on April 30, 1904, President Roosevelt officially opened the Louisiana Purchase Exposition in St. Louis. Yet, as befit a world's fair that to a large extent celebrated American technology and industrial production, he did so from the White House via telegraph. Already running for reelection, Roosevelt postponed a personal visit to St. Louis until November because he did not want anyone to think that he was using the fair for political purposes. Once there, he declared it the "greatest Exposition of the kind that we have ever seen in recorded history."[5] For someone like the rambunctious president, who understood culture and power, he was not far off. The exposition in St. Louis was a celebration of American power and empire – both an explanation for the nation's success and a rationale for its recent rise to imperial status through its conquests in the Spanish-American War of 1898. And although the fair was seen by millions of Americans who swarmed the grounds, the over sixty foreign nations that were invited to participate were also intended to witness the announcement of America's rise to world power.[6]

The bases for that rise were abundantly evident on the fairgrounds in St. Louis. As if anointing royalty, the organizers set up individual "palaces" to highlight individual fields of endeavor. A wireless telegraphy tower, the latest in communication, was the centerpiece for electricity and machinery. In the palace of machinery sat a giant power plant that provided energy for the entire fair. Visitors to the palace for mines and minerals could pretend to be coalminers as they rode through a simulated mine. The transportation palace included "the latest developments in urban infrastructure developments, such as motor boats, cable cars, and above all, automobiles." Fairgoers who toured the palace for liberal arts were introduced to "how science and technology were used to produce manufactured goods from natural resources, thus providing ample evidence of human progress and its material manifestations." The overwhelming technology and industrial might on display clearly suggested that American greatness was no accident or happenstance of fate. The United States had quite literally made itself into the new world power.[7]

How to answer criticisms from at home and abroad about some of the costs of that rise to power was another issue facing the organizers of the fair. The apparent contradiction of the world's greatest democracy engaging in conquest and imperialism posed a significant dilemma. The United States gained an empire in the late 1800s, both through war with Spain and less bloody acquisitions of territories such as Hawaii. Somewhat to their surprise, the American conquerors did not always find themselves welcome guests. Such was the case in the Philippines where U.S. forces and Filipino nationalists engaged in a brutal conflict from 1899 to 1902. Critics at home and overseas chastised the United States for using its overwhelming power to crush the Filipino rebels; stories about the torture of prisoners did not help the American cause.[8] In St. Louis, American scientists worked to provide a rationale for what seemed to be a startling contradiction of everything their nation stood for.

As Robert Rydell notes, "The Louisiana Purchase Exposition featured the most extensive Anthropology Department of any world's fair." At first glance it might appear that what the scientists did in St. Louis was simply gather different "types" of humans – "pygmies from Africa, 'Patagonian giants' from Argentina, Ainu aborigines from Japan, and Kwakiutl Indians from Vancouver Island, as well as groups of Native Americans" – into "living ethnological exhibits." There was, however, a method to the apparent madness of this anthropological melting pot. By placing these "backward" peoples side by side with the trappings of American technology and power, the director of the Anthropology Department argued that visitors would be able to see "human progress from the dark prime to the highest enlightenment, from savagery to civic organization, from egoism to altruism." The suggestion, of course, was quite clear: human progress moved along a distinctly color-coded pathway, from the "dark prime" peoples of Africa, Asia, Latin America, and even North America, to the "enlightened" –

and whiter – inhabitants of Western Europe and the United States. If this were true, however, then why would the enlightened people of America risk lives and resources to expand into benighted areas such as the Philippines? American scientists made sure an answer was at hand by organizing the Philippine Reservation at the fair. The reservation (a telling name in itself, as it immediately reminded visitors of the recent "answer" to the Native American problem) involved shipping in over 1,000 Filipinos to serve as one of the "living ethnological exhibits." The Philippine Reservation was designed to show how the technological, industrial, military, economic, and ideological power of the United States could be transformative for the backward Filipino natives. Visitors first came face to face with a "typical" Filipino village, where the nearly naked savages lived in what appeared to be prehistoric squalor. As the shocked fairgoer moved on, they discovered another kind of "village," one where – under the tutelage and assistance of their American rulers – the Filipinos adopted Western dress, went to school, and, perhaps most important, learned the value of hard work on such new-fangled inventions as the sewing machine. Again, the overall message was inescapable – only through the uplift provided by the United States could these helpless people ever hope to progress beyond barbarism.[9]

Roosevelt, who was terribly impressed by what he saw in St. Louis, would soon have an opportunity to use the power of spectacle and culture that made the Louisiana Purchase Exposition such a hit at another fair held in France in 1907. It would involve Roosevelt in working closely with one of the non-state actors that made the Anthropology Department exhibits at the 1904 fair so instructive and useful – Mark Twain's "mildewed old fossil," the Smithsonian Institution. As such, the 1907 exposition illuminates a key moment in the relationship between the U.S. government and private entities in terms of pushing forward with an agenda for American cultural diplomacy.

In 1906 the French government issued an invitation to the United States to participate in the International Maritime Exposition scheduled to be held in Bordeaux the following year. One of the main themes of the exposition would be the centennial celebration of Robert Fulton's invention of the steamboat, and it therefore made sense that the United States would be an important (and eager) guest at the show. Initially, however, many in the U.S. government (and, eventually, the Smithsonian Institution) were less than enthusiastic about American attendance at the fair. When the invitation was handed to Secretary of State Elihu Root in late May 1906 a game of bureaucratic hot potato ensued. Root first approached the Department of Commerce and Labor. From there, Commerce and Labor passed the request on to the Smithsonian, where the response was tepid, to say the least. As the assistant secretary of the Institution explained, the Smithsonian certainly had enough materials, but the lack of any congressional appropriation was cited as a stumbling block. He did not stop there; in his opinion "the request should be discouraged on general principles, and also especially in view of the serious fire which has recently occurred at the Milan Exposition." The reference to Milan concerned a massive fire at its Universal Exposition in mid-1906 that destroyed between $2 and $3 million's worth of exhibition materials (none of the U.S. exhibits were damaged in the blaze).[10]

Despite the necessity of acting with some speed, the French invitation languished in diplomatic limbo for several months. When, by January 1907, the French ambassador had still received no official reply he went straight to Secretary of Commerce and Labor Oscar Straus. One can only imagine his frustration when Straus suggested that the ambassador approach Secretary Root about the exposition. Once Root got back to him, Straus explained, "the matter would have my sympathetic attention." And, so, back the French ambassador went to Root. Ambassador Jules Jusserand now pulled out all the stops. A "special honor to the genius of an illustrious American" – Robert Fulton, the inventor of the first steam-powered vessel – was planned. Jusserand asked that an American pavilion be constructed and noted that the other "Powers" – including Russia, Japan, Italy, Mexico – had already agreed to participate. Space on the exposition grounds had already been set aside; Jusserand even enclosed a preliminary sketch of his idea for the American building![11]

The round-robin began once again. Root contacted Straus asking him to reconsider the idea of U.S. participation at Bordeaux. Straus duly convened a meeting of bureau chiefs and Cyrus Adler, assistant secretary of the Smithsonian. The minutes of the meeting portray a group of men desperately trying to avoid commitments of any kind. The exhibit would cost perhaps $50,000, and Congress was unlikely to appropriate such a sum. Time was too short. Official after official declared that their bureaus had nothing of relevance or interest to contribute. Adler admitted that the Smithsonian could do an exhibit on the history of navigation in the United States, but the time frame was "prohibitive." Straus now asked Adler point blank whether it was possible to make a "fair showing" at Bordeaux. Adler responded that it was not feasible, although it might be possible to open up a small exhibit midway through the exposition. Straus, seeing an opportunity to pass the buck, immediately declared that the matter was settled. The Smithsonian would provide some "models" and the whole thing would be "fixed." Adler meekly agreed.[12]

The next day, Adler wrote Straus and started backpedaling furiously. The Smithsonian had examined the issue the previous year and lacking a congressional appropriation it was "impossible...to take part in the proposed Exposition." Even with an appropriation, it was "practically impossible" to assemble a worthwhile exhibit. Straus, apparently happy just to have the matter settled one way or the other, now explained to Root that he had promised Jusserand the subject would be given his "careful and sympathetic consideration. This I have done with the result as stated."[13]

President Theodore Roosevelt now entered the fray, with a letter fired off to Straus on the same day as the latter's report to Root. He was direct:

Straus was to "help out the State Department in having the appropriate action taken by Congress" for funding the Bordeaux exhibit. State would "manage" the affair, but TR was also clear that Root would need the "special assistance" of Commerce and Labor. Roosevelt did not stop there. Less than a week after giving marching orders to Straus, the president sent a special message to Congress requesting funds for the American exhibit in Bordeaux. He attached a memo from Assistant Secretary of State Robert Bacon in which Bacon requested $25,000 to support an American presence at the Exposition. He stressed the special focus of the exposition on the achievements of Robert Fulton and argued, "It would seem peculiarly regrettable if the United States should fail to signalize the coming occasion." He also argued for American "participation commensurate with that already announced to have been promised by Russia, Japan, Italy, Mexico, Belgium, and several other countries." The president stated that Bacon's recommendations had his "hearty approval." Roosevelt applied even more pressure by informing Congress that he had already agreed to send "one or more vessels to visit Bordeaux during the progress of the exhibition." Now, Roosevelt declared, it was time for Congress to appropriate funds so that "the Government of the United States may be enabled to be fittingly represented at Bordeaux."[14] Congress was suitably, if not entirely, convinced – it approved $15,000 for the American exhibit.

The obvious question is why would a president, even such an energetic specimen such as TR, become so personally and effectively involved in what was, by any standard, a relatively minor diplomatic episode? Quite simply, TR understood that an American exhibit in Bordeaux was not merely a flexing of American military might (indeed, just two American warships eventually visited the city, and they arrived after the exposition was over). Nor was it diplomatic posturing in order to cement the growing friendship between France and the United States (and the even closer friendship between Roosevelt and Ambassador Jusserand).[15] Instead, Roosevelt saw this as an opportunity to put a stamp on the American identity; to establish, through its exhibit, that the United States was a leader in science, technology, and engineering – in short, that America was the epitome of a modern (and modernizing) state. As Collin notes, Roosevelt grasped the idea that "In literature, art, politics, industry, and diplomacy, Americans were reaching out, looking for a new place in the world and a new set of accomplishments.... Americans were ready for grander leaps in 1900, and Theodore Roosevelt was ready to lead the new consciousness."[16]

The show in Bordeaux was, therefore, part of a larger initiative to represent the United States on the international stage. It soon became clear, however, that even with the funds approved by Congress no government agency was willing to take on the job. The Department of State considered exhibitions beyond its duties, and despite TR's very direct letter to Secretary Straus, the latter was already thinking of where to punt the ball. Employing the familiar Potomac two-step, Straus shuffled the project off to the Smithsonian. And thus the orphan exposition landed back at the Smithsonian's doorstep. This time, however, the Smithsonian seemed more receptive to the idea. The secretary of the Smithsonian informed Root that he was pleased to have the Institution handle the exposition. He raised some of the old concerns – the lack of time, the small congressional appropriation, the need for other departments in the government to cooperate in securing materials for the exhibit – but in the end he agreed that the Smithsonian would, for the first time in its history, "take charge of the preparation of a Government exhibit." He did not give any reasons for this change of heart, but it is not hard to posit some theories. When the French invitation to Bordeaux arrived in the United States in May 1906, the Smithsonian was without a permanent secretary. Thus, something of a leadership vacuum may explain the earlier hesitation about participating in the exposition. In addition, by the time Charles D. Walcott was selected as the new secretary the Smithsonian was under attack in the press. A *New York Times* editorial complained that the Institution's museum contained "great masses of uninteresting material" instead of artifacts and departments with more "universal interest." It concluded, "The American people desire a National Museum which shall be comparable, without apology, with the National Museums of England, Germany, and France." Walcott, who had been something of a science advisor to Roosevelt, was intent on raising the Smithsonian's profile both at home and abroad.[17]

Just as the *New York Times* hoped for a national museum to compete with those of the other great powers, the U.S. government also began to perceive the Bordeaux exposition as a competition for recognition. Even before things got started, the U.S. diplomat in Bordeaux was writing to warn that America might be left behind. Belgium and Uruguay had already appointed Special Commissioners; Greece, Brazil, Italy, Russia, and Mexico would also have official representation; unofficially represented would be England, Germany, Holland, Switzerland, Servia, Austria, Turkey, Japan, Sweden, Denmark, Portugal, Argentina, and Chile. In March 1907 Secretary Root and others in the Department of State wondered about the cost of building a separate American exhibit hall; Root also asked the American representatives in France, "What are the other nations doing?" The answers were direct. The United States could put all of its exhibits into the main exhibit hall being constructed by the French, but a "pavilion [is] important and advisable." Other nations were already lining up: Belgium and Russia had agreed to build their own exhibit halls. Greece, England, and Argentina would also be represented.[18] Such exchanges – and they continued throughout the planning and actual life of the exposition – suggest that for U.S. (and Smithsonian) officials, status and recognition were important and intertwined goals.

For, as competitive as both the Smithsonian and the U.S. government were about the American exhibit at Bordeaux, it was obviously not designed primarily for specific diplomatic purposes. There was no overt support of U.S. policies or attacks on other nations as one would see so blatantly exhibited during the Cold War period at world's fairs and other international cultural events. Instead, the design and contents of the American exhibit were subtly crafted to brand the rising power as a leader in science, technology, and engineering – the holy trinity of defining a modern nation. The building suggested the proud heritage of the United States by reconstructing a miniature White House. Pictures of the interior show a neat, well-organized, and informative exhibition space. Materials related to Robert Fulton and his accomplishments were on display, along with the very strong emphasis on the fact that it was an American who pioneered the use of steam for water travel. Also notably on display was the American work on the Panama Canal. Indeed, two pages of the catalog of the U.S. exhibition are taken up with photographs of everything from the construction work being done to the "quarters of the employees." (The latter featured shots of the "social parlor," "billiard and writing room," "dancing space," and "bowling alleys 100 feet long.") The centerpiece of the entire exhibition space, however, was a relief map of the projected canal that measured nearly 12 feet by 5 feet.[19] The focus on the canal was an interesting and effective means of demonstrating that the United States was not merely a modern nation, but a nation capable of modernizing the world.

In the end, despite all the complaints, the lack of money, the small amount of time, and the dilly-dallying of the U.S. government, the Smithsonian was able to put on a pretty fair show at Bordeaux. Jusserand was delighted to have the Americans in Bordeaux, and the French government awarded several "diplomas of honor" and "gold medals" to the U.S. exhibit. Once its success was apparent, the Smithsonian's attitude changed dramatically: other government departments, such as Treasury, Interior, and Commerce and Labor, had little or nothing to do with the good showing by the United States. Perhaps positioning the Institution for future assignments in this area, the Smithsonian representative at Bordeaux fumed that "The departments did absolutely nothing to help us in the matter," but then went on to lavish praise on the Smithsonian's efforts: "We did everything possible to suitably represent the United States Government at Bordeaux, and succeeded far beyond what we anticipated with the small appropriation and the limited amount of space and time available." And future opportunities were already in the wind. The same representative noted that "The President has recommended that we have a Commissioner and an exhibit in 1909 at Quito in Ecuador.... He also earnestly recommends that we take part in the Exposition in Japan in 1913."[20]

Both of those opportunities were in the years after Roosevelt left office, and the files at the Smithsonian suggest that its role in the U.S. participation at international expositions languished after Teddy stepped aside. Nevertheless, the American exhibit at the International Maritime Exposition is significant. It is certainly one of the earliest examples of a determined effort on the part of the U.S. government to create an image for the United States on a global scale. It marked the first time that the U.S. Department of State sought out and employed another agency – the Smithsonian – to design and construct an American overseas exhibit. And it marked the first time that the Smithsonian had been given complete charge of the American participation in an international exposition. As such, the show at Bordeaux provides an interesting bridge between the (mostly) non-state efforts at cultural diplomacy that took place during the nineteenth century and the full-fledged state programs of the post–Second World War period. The U.S. exhibit did not promote a specific diplomatic goal, nor did it look to simplistically flex the nation's economic or military muscle to awe and cow its international audience. It sought, instead, to promote an image of the United States in order to create a positive opinion of America as a modern nation (and one quite capable of modernizing other areas) in the minds of the foreign viewers. Roosevelt was a leader who understood that American power rested as much on the nation's reputation and image as on its Great White Fleet.

Although TR took a very important step in the development of U.S. cultural diplomacy, he did not leave much in the way of a permanent bureaucratic foundation for continuing the efforts begun in Bordeaux. The Department of State remained skeptical of any undertaking that smacked of culture, and even the Smithsonian seemed to lose much of its initial interest once TR was gone. It now remained to take the next logical step: to establish a central agency within the U.S. government to carry on a more sustained campaign of cultural diplomacy. That job fell to someone who could not have been more different from the old Rough Rider.

Woodrow Wilson is often lumped together with Teddy Roosevelt (and William Howard Taft) as one of the "progressive" presidents. Although Wilson and Roosevelt shared more similarities in their ideologies concerning government, business, and international relations than either man would have preferred to admit, personality-wise the two were nearly polar opposites. Whereas TR reveled in the "strenuous life," loved roughing it in the outdoors and the thrill of combat, and built an image of himself as a president who would not hesitate to wield the "big stick" of American military force to get what he wanted, Wilson was the quiet scholar, more at home in the classroom than the camp grounds, and committed to the proposition that ideals were more powerful than brute strength. In one important regard, however, the two men's thinking intersected: both believed that America had an important role to play in world affairs. They agreed, as well, on the proposition that the United States had to deal with problems concerning the international perception of their nation. Roosevelt took the first tentative official steps toward correcting those misrepresentations because of his desire to see America recognized as a modern (and modernizing) world force. Wilson would be prompted to more direct action as the United States was drawn into the horrific destruction of the First World War.

At least initially, Wilson appeared to be an excellent candidate to carry forward Roosevelt's first forays into official cultural diplomacy. Several personal characteristics suggested that he would be receptive to using American culture to reach (and teach) the international audience and paint a picture of the "real" United States. First and foremost, Wilson was a teacher. As president, he understood part of his job as "educating" those in need around the world. Surveying what he saw as the turmoil and chaos of Latin American politics, Wilson characteristically remarked, "I am going to teach the South American republics to elect good men!"[21]

Second, Wilson was a strong believer in the power of the "truth" – as defined by Woodrow Wilson. A colleague cited an example from Wilson's days as president of Princeton University that makes this point painfully clear:

> But Wilson was adept in using the steamroller, and never deviated from a course he thought right, or perhaps also advantageous. On one occasion he fell into an argument with a professor of the Princeton Theological Seminary with whom he was playing a friendly game of pool. The argument became so hot that, in order to end what had become dangerous disagreement, the professor remarked, "Well, Dr. Wilson, there are two sides to every question." "Yes," was the reply, "a right side and a wrong side!"[22]

Finally, Wilson certainly understood the power of culture. When the brutally racist film *The Birth of a Nation* was released in 1915, the author of the book on which the film was based, Thomas Dixon (who happened to be an old classmate of President Wilson), arranged a special showing at the White House. When director D.W. Griffith's paean to white superiority, African American perfidy, and the "heroics" of the Ku Klux Klan ended, Wilson was reported to have said, "It is like writing history with lightning. And my only regret is that it is all so terribly true."[23] One night later, the film was shown in Washington, DC, to a much larger audience that included a Supreme Court justice, at least one member of Wilson's Cabinet, and nearly ninety congressmen. If Wilson understood the impact of the film in terms of supporting his own well-known racial views, he was also made to understand how the relatively new medium of motion pictures could whip up emotions and controversy. The National Association for the Advancement of Colored People (NAACP) harshly condemned the film, made several efforts to secure injunctions against its showing in major American cities, and even organized boycotts when the film was shown in New York. Mary Childs Nerney, the NAACP's national secretary, summed up the organization's views when she declared,

> I am utterly disgusted with the situation in regard to 'The Birth of a Nation.' As you will read in the next number of the *Crisis* we have fought it at every possible point....The harm it is doing the colored people cannot be estimated. I hear echoes of it wherever I go and have no doubt that this was in the mind of the people who are producing it.[24]

Yet, all of these factors did not, at first, combine to push his administration to take the next step of creating a permanent official agency to handle America's cultural relations with the world. Wilson was faced with such numerous foreign policy crises during his first few years in the presidency that such an action was never even seriously debated. There were constant problems with Mexico, U.S. military interventions in both Haiti and Santo Domingo, and, of course, the brewing troubles in Europe that eventually boiled over into the First World War. With America's belated entry into that conflict, however, the conditions were ripe for the establishment of the first governmental office dedicated to the art of propaganda.

Just one week after America entered the First World War, President Woodrow Wilson issued an executive order creating the Committee on Public Information (CPI). The CPI was, and remains, a controversial topic. For its defenders, it was a necessary adjunct to America's military efforts that sought to sustain support for the war at home and counteract insidious German propaganda abroad. Others came to believe that the CPI was itself a monstrous propaganda machine that whipped up a nationalistic frenzy in the United States while simultaneously acting as a means of intimidating and silencing domestic opposition to the war.[25] For everything that the CPI was, or might have been, there is no denying that it served as the first official federal office dealing with propaganda, public diplomacy, and cultural diplomacy.

With three brief sentences, President Wilson ordered the creation of the CPI with Executive Order 2594 in April 1917. It merely announced the committee's establishment and noted that it would be composed of the secretaries of state, war, and the navy as well as one "civilian" – the journalist George Creel, who was charged with the "executive direction" of the CPI. Not a word was said about the committee's charge, duties, or goals. Over the next two years the CPI busied itself with "selling" the First World War to the American people through a dizzying array of posters, pamphlets and booklets, movies, slogans, and public speakers. These efforts on the domestic side are covered in numerous scholarly books and articles primarily due to the fact that it was the home front activities of the CPI that generated the most criticism and controversy. For the purposes of this study, however, we focus our attention on the lesser known – but vitally important to the history of U.S. cultural diplomacy – actions taken by the CPI abroad.[26] In fact, the short lifetime of the CPI proved to be a crucial watershed moment in the history of U.S. cultural diplomacy, and many of the ideas and actions of Creel's committee abroad served as precursors to programs and agencies developed during the interwar and Cold War years.

Just how important the foreign work of the CPI was is indicated by Creel himself, who devoted nearly one-half of his 1920 book, *How We Advertised America*, to "the foreign section" of his committee. As Creel dramatically declared in the opening pages of his semi-memoir, "It was in this recognition of Public Opinion as a major force that the Great War differed most essentially from all previous conflicts. The trial of strength was not only between massed bodies of armed men, but between opposed ideals, and moral verdicts took on all the value of military decisions." For Creel, the work of the CPI was not in the line of crude propaganda or manipulation of public opinion: "It was a plain publicity proposition, a vast enterprise in salesmanship, the world's greatest adventure in advertising." In short, it was simply a matter of telling the truth to the world. And Creel made sure that "Every conceivable means was used to reach the foreign mind with America's message." By the time the First World War came to a close, the CPI operated in over a dozen foreign nations in Europe, Latin America, and the Far East, utilizing an impressive array of information tools to get America's message to the world. As one study notes, "Never before had the mass cultural resources of a nation been mobilized on such a scale."[27]

According to one early work on the CPI, the committee's "mission" overseas was to "convince the people of the world" of three main ideas: "America could never be beaten"; "America was a land of freedom and democracy"; and, finally, "thanks to President Woodrow Wilson's vision of a new world and his power of achieving it, victory for the Allied arms would usher in a new era of peace and hope." The emphasis on Wilson was central to the CPI's work: "the main object was to convince all the world that hope for the future lay in Wilson alone." Yet, Creel realized that "simply telling the truth" was not as easy as it might sound. In contrast to some nations, "the United States had no subsidized press service with which to meet the emergency," and therefore had to rely on the CPI to carry America's message to "the peoples of the Allied nations that had to be fired by the magnitude of the American effort," "to the neutral nations, poisoned by German lies," and "into the Central Powers" that needed to be made aware of "the ideals of America, the determination of America, and the invincibility of America."[28]

The work of the CPI overseas was compromised not simply by the limitations of American media in reaching outward, but also by the kind of news that did make it to foreign lands:

> The volume of information that went out from our shores was small, and, in what was worse, it was concerned only with the violent and unusual in our national life. It was news of strikes and lynchings, riots, murder cases, graft prosecutions, sensational divorces, the bizarre extravagance of "sudden millionaires." Naturally enough, we were looked upon as a race of dollar-mad materialists, a land of cruel monopolists, our real rulers the corporations and our democracy a "fake."

Americans, he concluded, were "at once the best-known and the least-known people in the world." It was little wonder that Creel lamented, "It was a task that looked almost hopeless. The United States, alone of the great nations of the world, had never conducted a propaganda movement."[29] With the establishment of the CPI, America entered the propaganda game.

The workings of the CPI overseas quickly revealed two important issues that would have repercussions for America's cultural diplomacy efforts in the decades after the First World War. First, the "message" was not the same for every nation. Telling the truth about America was not as straightforward as it might seem due to the different situations being faced in various nations and the differing initial conceptions (or, as Creel and his associates preferred, misconceptions) about the United States that existed in each individual nation. Second, the work of the CPI was constantly challenged by a number of factors, including domestic suspicions about and criticisms of any program that smacked of "propaganda," bureaucratic fights between the CPI and other U.S. government agencies, misunderstandings of the foreign audience Creel and his followers were trying to reach, and controversy over government censorship.

Not surprisingly, the vast majority of the CPI's overseas work took place in war-torn Europe. By the end of the First World War Creel's representatives conducted propaganda efforts in Denmark, Switzerland, Italy, Sweden, England, France, the Netherlands, and Russia. All of this, of course, was in addition to the propaganda directed toward the German enemy. The CPI's messages, and the purposes behind those messages, differed widely, however. Some of these nations were America's allies in the conflict; others were less involved or neutral. As the *New York Times* reported in early 1918, the CPI's work abroad would

> have for its purpose the spreading among the neutrals of the truth about America's role in the war, the informing of the people of Germany what the United States is fighting for, and lastly, and most important, bolstering up the morale of our Allies by a thorough knowledge of what this nation is doing and plans to do to help them.[30]

For America's allies, as Creel explained, the message focused on the military side of the U.S. involvement in an effort to address the "war-weariness [that] had sapped ardor and enthusiasm." In France, for example, the CPI utilized its wire and press services to ensure a steady stream of news that sought not only to portray the United States in the best possible light but also to emphasize its contributions to the actual fighting against the German enemy. Lecturers were sent to French industrial plants to talk about the American troops and supplies that were pouring into Europe and to "stem the unrest constantly cropping up." To give the French audience a firsthand view of Americans fighting in the war, French journalists and publishers were invited to the front lines to see the Yankees in action. Films depicting the U.S. forces fighting on the front and disparaging the German enemy were readily supplied to French theaters and other venues.[31]

Another ally, Italy, presented a different situation that resulted in a different approach by the CPI. In Italy, unlike in France or England, Germany spent significant resources to counter American propaganda, and U.S. officials there recognized the success of the German effort in spreading fear and uncertainty. This effort was assisted by the fact that Italian forces suffered a series of embarrassing military fiascos that shook the willpower of the nation's civilian population. In addition to this war-weariness, the American CPI representative in Italy confronted a population that was not only "uninformed" about America's goals and actions in the war but also "highly skeptical" about U.S. intentions during and after the conflict. Therefore, in addition to the usual propaganda output about America's military actions and assistance to its allies, the CPI in Italy also had to do a bit more in terms of creating a favorable image of the United States and its people. Charles Merriam, one of the CPI directors in Italy during the war, later claimed that his organization's activities were not designed to "advertise America but to help win the war," but his actions demonstrated that the two aims were not so easily separated. The usual assortment of films, press releases, and lectures touting America's military prowess were supplemented by efforts that seemed orchestrated largely to curry favorable public opinion about the United States. A special message from President Woodrow Wilson to the Italian people in May 1918 was given wide circulation by the CPI. Although Wilson noted the military alliance between the United States and Italy, the speech focused on the "personal and intimate ties" that "bound" the two nations together and stressed the goal of protecting the "rights of the weak as well as of the strong." Another attempt to emphasize those "intimate ties" was the CPI-sponsored visit of over twenty wounded U.S. soldiers of "Italian extraction, who were honored in their home towns" in Italy. As the war was nearing its conclusion, the CPI organized a visit by Italian journalists to America, where they met with President Wilson at the White House before embarking on a tour of the United States. Wilson declared that "we are not here in the service of Italy. We are not here in the service of America. We are here in the greatest of all services … the service of mankind," and then assured the Italians that they were "going to have a chance to see everything there is" in America. It is little wonder that Merriam eventually changed his tune about the goal of the CPI work in Italy:

> The work of the Committee on Public Information in Italy shows the great value of international publicity. The simple work of systematically and vigorously sowing the facts proved to be of great political and military significance…. Italy was won, however, not merely by military facts, but by American idealism.[32]

As Creel made clear in his story of the CPI, another factor determined the precise makeup and content of the American propaganda in Italy: the

Italian people. Not only were the people of Italy "almost childishly eager for American news," but their "childish" proclivities were also demonstrated by their fascination with colorful objects. "More peculiarly than any other people, the Italians loved picture-cards and little gimcracks of all kinds," and the CPI made sure that they were inundated with picture postcards, small flags and ribbons, pins, and posters.[33] Not for the last time would the character of American cultural diplomacy be determined by the ethnic and racial stereotypes concerning the intended audiences.

It was in those nations farther removed from the actual military contest that the CPI moved away from standard propaganda techniques and toward something that served as a clear predecessor of later U.S. efforts in the field of cultural diplomacy. For many of these nations, America's accomplishments on the field of battle were far less important than clear concepts about the postwar world, their own place in that new world, and what the United States – now a full-fledged member of the great powers club – would do after the war to end all wars. In many of these countries the CPI confronted governments and peoples that were not simply ill-informed about America and its intentions but also harboring deep suspicions about the United States that sometimes bordered on outright anti-Americanism.

Spain was one such nation. A long history of conflict with the United States, highlighted by Spain's humiliation in the Spanish-American War less than twenty years earlier, left many of that nation's officials and people with a less-than-glowing picture of the American people. As the king of Spain declared in early 1918, "the American brain ran more to making motor-cars and money." This animus was compounded by other more immediate factors. A recent trade embargo imposed by the United States caused tremendous resentment in Spain, and this in turn helped to further fuel a very strong strain of pro-German sentiments among the Spanish people. Finally, as one historian concludes, "It would be difficult to imagine a less promising environment for the CPI than Spain in 1917. To begin with, about two thirds of the country's inhabitants were illiterate peasants or laborers, apathetic about politics and indifferent to the war." Therefore, instead of deluging the Spanish people with films about American heroism in battle, the CPI's activities concentrated on convincing the Spanish audience that the Allies were certain to win the war and that a closer postwar relationship with the United States would provide tangible benefits. As one CPI representative argued, "Spain wants to bet on the winning horse," and the CPI's job would be "convincing Spain that, by God, we are going to win this war, and that if she is going to get on the bandwagon, it's time for her to start" by demonstrating that "the Allies and the Allies *only* can butter their bread, save their face, preserve the monarchy, and prevent sheer anarchy." The CPI's film program was geared to advertising American agricultural and industrial prowess, with shorts about the U.S. rail system and making cars and beer. Lecturers concentrated on the "Spanish-American cultural ties," and, once again, President Wilson was prominently featured in news stories and pamphlets with a particular emphasis on his plan for the League of Nations.[34]

As in Spain, the CPI confronted an old and deeply entrenched anti-Americanism in Latin America. And, here again, the Americans were faced with audiences that were less interested in the immediate military conflict than in the contours of the postwar world – most notably, their relationship with a United States that had grown significantly in its power and influence. To be sure, the CPI made certain that the message concerning the inevitability of an Allied victory was hammered home in press releases, posters, and films. Nevertheless, American propagandists in Latin America quickly realized that their neighbors in the western hemisphere were more concerned with learning more about the United States. The Chilean people, for example, were "much more interested in information about America itself" than the war in Europe, and the CPI official in that nation therefore "requested the New York headquarters to stop sending stories of individual exploits on the American battle front." One film, unfortunately titled *Pershing's Crusaders*, even had the effect of whipping up more anti-Americanism when it was shown in Mexico City – appearing less than two years after General John Pershing led American troops into Mexico in 1916 in a fruitless search for Pancho Villa. (The film was quickly retitled *America in the War*.) The CPI "received from the southern republics requests for information about the economic, social, educational, or political phases of our national life," and responded with a barrage of pamphlets, news stories, photographs and posters. A "reading room" in Mexico City was established where the Mexican people could "look at pictures or read books, periodical literature, and pamphlets – all in Spanish – dealing with our war efforts or merely with news from the United States." Films were extraordinarily popular and included "animated cartoons, weekly current events, and longer films." As it had done in Italy, the CPI invited twenty Mexican reporters and newspaper editors to tour the United States.[35]

In addition to some of the normal challenges – existing and effective German propaganda, a largely illiterate population, and relative indifference on the part of the general population toward the war in Europe – China also posed special problems for the CPI. As Kazuyuki Matsuo notes in his study of the CPI's work in China, "Some Chinese intellectuals realized the dualistic nature of America's propaganda. On one side, America said that she was a friend of oppressed nations. On the other side, America was the friend of the powers that tormented China." In addition, no American newspapers had established offices in China and so the CPI had to turn to a local American journalist and publisher to start the propaganda campaign from scratch. In addition to the usual stories about the war, America's military victories, and speeches from Woodrow Wilson, the CPI in China concentrated on placing informational pieces on the United States in Chinese newspapers and, in particular, magazines. These stories included news about "American history, the development of industry, the role of women in society, disappearing child labor in factories, and other contemporary topics that were believed to be representative of American progress." Through connections with American missionaries and their schools in China, the CPI also provided short publications for Chinese schoolchildren. However, film proved to be a futile method of reaching the Chinese population. Although nearly 150 films about America were sent to the nation, the Chinese typically made up only about 2 percent of the audiences for the English language productions. All of these efforts had only a minimal impact on the Chinese. As Matsuo concludes, "In spite of this apparent American 'victory' of the information war, however, the Chinese attitude toward the war was curiously non-responsive." Part of this was due to widespread illiteracy, but much of the resistance to the American messages had to do with what many Chinese intellectuals saw as "America's dualistic role in China. America said it was the greatest friend of oppressed nations and preached equality and liberty. Yet, the same country was friendly to the Peking regime – a suppressor of rebels and liberals." In addition, "America's insistence on Chinese domestic peace and her alliance with England was a sign of America's ignorance of 'what is at stake in China'." All of this made numerous educated Chinese "skeptical about America's intention and idealism."[36]

As CPI officials tangled with adjusting their approaches and messages to fit audiences spread across the globe, they also confronted numerous other obstacles to success – some of which would seem very familiar to America's cultural diplomats in the years after the Second World War. One immediate problem was that the CPI was working from ground zero: there had never been an office such as this in the federal government and, of course, there were no "professional" propagandists or cultural diplomats to staff this new organization. Not surprisingly, given Creel's background, many of the earliest recruits for the CPI came from the world of journalism. Others, such as Edward Bernays, were leaders in the relatively new field of public relations. Ernest Poole, who worked primarily on the foreign audience side of the CPI, was a novelist who won the very first Pulitzer Prize for fiction in 1918. Famous American artists and illustrators such as Charles Dana Gibson contributed their talents to many of the posters and other illustrated materials produced by the CPI. While this new federal office and these amateur propagandists were given relatively free rein for their activities within the United States, their work abroad meant that they were often forced to rely on cooperating with other American officials and institutions who had already staked out their territory in the realm of U.S. foreign relations.

In particular, the CPI often butted heads with the Department of State. Relations between the heads of these organizations, George Creel and Secretary of State Robert Lansing, got off to an almost immediately rocky start. As Christopher Howard notes,

"Tensions between the older, more conservative Lansing and Creel were evident from the very beginning. In his diary, Daniels [Josephus Daniels, Secretary of the Navy] related how Lansing had insisted that the memo creating the CPI be rewritten on State Department letterhead and that Lansing's be the first signature. These tensions had not eased by the end of the war. As late as December 15, 1918, Wilson's friend and advisor 'Colonel' Edward House wrote in his diary: 'I told him (Wilson) that a "head-on collision" was about to occur with Creel on the one side and with Lansing on the other…I told him Lansing's dislike for Creel was only equaled by Creel's dislike for Lansing.'"[37]

That decidedly unpromising beginning was often reflected in the acrimonious relations between CPI and State officials overseas. The appointment of the famous New York suffragist Vira B. Whitehouse to serve as the CPI representative in the neutral nation of Switzerland in 1917 clearly illustrates the lack of a professional working relationship between the CPI and State. In his book on the CPI, Creel devoted an entire chapter to Whitehouse's efforts in Switzerland and lauded her for her success in spreading the American message. However, he also noted that "It can be said truthfully that never at any time did Mrs. Whitehouse receive the assistance to which she was entitled." He attributed this partly to the sexist viewpoints of the American diplomats in Switzerland but also mentioned that even before she arrived a "wretched canard" had been printed in U.S. newspapers declaring that Whitehouse would be undertaking diplomatic duties. Creel knew where the rumor came from – Lansing. Upon hearing of Whitehouse's appointment, the Secretary of State issued a scathing denunciation of Creel, the CPI, and Whitehouse to the press. Both Creel and President Wilson overrode Lansing's concerns, but the stage was set for Whitehouse's reception in Switzerland. Once in Bern, Whitehouse found she was on her own: "Unable to secure proper offices, lacking an office force, and compelled to work under every inconvenience," she soldiered on as best she could. The most complete study of Whitehouse's time in Switzerland concludes that the State Department officials on site "claimed no knowledge of her appointment nor of the very existence of the CPI." While the staff of the American legation "tried to entertain her," they also made it crystal clear that "she would expect no help from them." In short, "the State Department personnel's obstructionism suggests an understanding that her appointment was an infringement on their licenses."[38]

In at least one other case, the tensions between State and the CPI exploded into open warfare. In November 1917, Edgar Sisson arrived in Petrograd, Russia, to serve as the head of CPI operations. His timing was unfortunate as the Bolsheviks had just taken power, the nation was still in turmoil, and State Department officials – both in Russia and in Washington – had not developed clear or consistent policies to deal with the new reality. As one study of the CPI's activities in Russia concluded,

Though it was not at first apparent, this situation created a void in which the functions of the American embassy were assumed more and more by the Creel Committee, the American Red Cross, and, to a minor degree, the YMCA. Yet there was little or no coordination between the activities of these agencies and those of the American diplomatic corps in Russia. In truth, they often conflicted.

This was nowhere more in evidence than in September 1918 when Sisson convinced Creel and President Wilson to release to the public what became known as the "Sisson documents." These documents purported to show that both Lenin and Trotsky were, in fact, paid agents of the German government, thereby discrediting the entire Bolshevik government. Lansing was furious that the documents were released without any discussions with the U.S. diplomats in Russia or the Department of State in Washington, DC.[39]

In addition to clashing with State, the CPI also had to contend with other domestic critics who questioned its entire enterprise. In general, those who criticized the CPI were dubious about its effectiveness (particularly in terms of its cost), skeptical about the reliability of "news" from the CPI, and very suspicious about anything that smacked of "propaganda." A *New York Times* editorial from July 1917 labeled Creel's organization "The Committee on Public Misinformation" and criticized the CPI for exaggerating reports of German attacks on U.S. transport ships. The editorial continued, "Americans will never pardon expanded, adorned, exaggerated, and untruthful accounts of conflicts in which our forces may be engaged." It also roasted Creel, concluding that "it is evident that in his present position he is out of place, that his abilities, whatever they may be, are misapplied, misdirected." His background in journalism, "where emotion and imagination count for much and accuracy is of minor importance, has evidently disqualified him for the service he has been called upon to perform." The Wilson administration's choice of Creel was simply "a blunder." Less than a year later, Congressman Allan Treadway (also referring to Creel's organization as the "Committee on Public Misinformation") strongly criticized the millions of dollars being spent on the CPI's efforts and charged that "The misinformation that the public is receiving through the so-called Committee on Public Information will fill a very large volume, not only of printed matter but of photographs."[40]

Disturbed as they were by the CPI's work on the domestic front, others were also unnerved by what they saw as an illegal expansion of the CPI's authority by engaging in activities abroad. In early 1918, one member of the House of Representatives wanted a full investigation into the CPI's "policy of sending American Commissioners abroad to spread propaganda." He questioned the cost of the operation and its legal authority. Overall, he had come to believe that "this committee is assuming more authority than has been delegated to it by Congress. Congress was never informed of the propaganda, and it seems to me that the Committee of Foreign Relations of

Congress should have been consulted before Americans were sent abroad to present the American point of view."[41]

In addition to the misunderstandings at home, the CPI also managed to create unintentional consternation among the foreign audiences it addressed with its public diplomacy. Although the CPI propaganda in each nation was tailored to fit that particular nation's attitude toward the war – ally, neutral, or even enemy – there is little to suggest that Creel's representatives undertook any substantive studies of the history, culture, or people of the countries in which they operated. The propaganda messages, therefore, could often have impacts that went far beyond the main goals of increasing American prestige or pushing these nations to support the Allies. In his study of the CPI's actions in Spain, Gregg Wolper argues that although America's propaganda concerning its war aims was largely successful, such "success, however, had a price." The emphasis on Wilson and his vision of a democratic world "raised unrealistic expectations," particularly among the Spanish people whose "disheartening experience with a weak and inept parliamentary system had left them suspicious of all forms of representative government." The CPI's constant trumpeting of Wilson's ideal of self-determination also encouraged the "separatist movements in Catalonia and the Basque provinces" to push their agendas with "renewed vigor." The result was a classic case of mixed messages as the demands for self-determination in some regions of Spain served to destabilize the nation and "undermined Spain's ability to establish a stable, liberal democracy. The pursuit of one Wilsonian goal thus hampered the achievement of another."[42]

Finally, the issue of government censorship sometimes caused friction – and set the stage for even bigger battles after the Second World War. Although Creel would later claim that the CPI simply oversaw "voluntary censorship" on the part of American publications and movies sent abroad, Rydell and Kroes are emphatic in arguing that "This was inaccurate." In fact, "Magazine publishers had to submit copy to CPI censors weeks before publication deadlines; books intended for export had to pass muster before military intelligence officials, and CPI officials collaborated with the U.S. Postal Service to censor mails." It was in its censoring of American films, however, that the CPI really hit its stride. Anything from supposedly injurious portrayals of the U.S. military to the showing of matters deemed "objectionable" concerning the nation's history or current social, political, or economic problems were quickly identified by CPI and military officials – and just as quickly cut from the reels sent abroad. Films that might bother our French or British allies, or inflame anti-Americanism in Latin America, came in for special attention. Just how much censorship was exerted is difficult to assess, but "In July 1918, 17,779 feet of film was deleted by motion picture producers who had to comply with the recommendations of the CPI censorship team or find themselves without access to overseas export markets." That increased to 82,230 feet of film in August 1918.[43]

The relatively short life of the CPI's overseas activities makes it difficult to draw meaningful conclusions about its successes and failures. In December 1918, Creel announced that the foreign work of the CPI would end on January 1, 1919. Shortly thereafter Congress cut off all funding for the committee. Nevertheless, it is clear that the CPI – particularly its work overseas – was significant. Recent studies of the committee's foreign work suggest that the CPI was a precursor of later developments in America's use of "soft diplomacy" to achieve its international goals. One historian argues that Creel's organization was "America's first large-scale experiment in what would become known as 'public diplomacy'." In his work on Whitehouse's actions in Switzerland, Tibor Glant claims that "Her propaganda work was nothing short of what we now call cultural diplomacy."[44] What the CPI might have done in the postwar world is, of course, unknown. As Frank Ninkovich notes, "the guillotinelike suddenness with which Congress abolished the CPI ruled out any possibility of following up on wartime cultural activities."[45]

What is clear, however, is that the CPI stands as the first government organization detailed to take American words and images overseas in an attempt to sway public opinion and increase the international support and admiration of the United States. In terms of the means it used to achieve those goals – and the many problems it faced in meeting its objectives – the CPI also served as a clear precursor to America's efforts in the field of cultural diplomacy in the years to come. Certainly many of the individuals who worked with the CPI abroad recognized the importance of this new form of diplomacy. One historian aptly summarizes the conclusions of America's Pulitzer Prize–winning propagandist Ernest Poole:

> Of all the reasons given for continuing our publicity in Latin America, however, Ernest Poole presented most of them. He stated that if we were entering an era of more and more open diplomacy, in order to make the policies of this government understood abroad, we would have to use the legitimate methods of publicity to reach widely the great masses of people in other countries with the significant facts about the life and purposes of this nation.... He stated that to gain abroad agreement with our foreign policies we would have to gain the good will of the world, and arouse a friendly interest in all aspects of life and work in the United States.[46]

What Poole could not have realized at the time was that it would be nearly twenty years before the U.S. government would reenter the field of cultural diplomacy – but he might have been pleased to know that when it reemerged its first target was Latin America.

During the First World War, officials from the CPI identified Latin America as a region where America's reputation was disastrously negative. Its efforts to counteract Latin Americans' suspicions about their northern neighbor were not only multifaceted but also sporadic and short lived. In addition, attempts to tell the "truth" about the United States confronted one seemingly intractable problem. Latin America's recent experiences with Theodore Roosevelt and, in particular, Woodrow Wilson, convinced many in the area that they already knew the truth about the giant to the north: that it was militaristic, expansionistic, and arrogantly racist. The facts certainly seemed to support that conclusion. By the time the First World War came to a close: the United States, in just two decades, seized Puerto Rico and Cuba during the Spanish-American War and continued to treat these holdings as virtual colonies; Teddy Roosevelt, according to his own account, "took" Panama from Colombia while Congress debated; Woodrow Wilson initiated two military interventions into Mexico and sent U.S. troops to occupy Haiti and Santo Domingo. Roosevelt called the Colombians "dagoes," while Wilson paternalistically promised to "teach the South Americans to elect good men" and his secretary of state, William Jennings Bryan, blithely expressed surprise that the "niggers" of Haiti could speak French. It would take more than a few government-sponsored films, posters, and lecturers to convince Latin America that the United States could be a trusted ally.

As Ninkovich explains, however, during the 1920s the U.S. government did not even attempt to pick up the tattered remains of the "guillotined" CPI. Any ideas about having the federal government reinvigorate a sustained effort in cultural diplomacy ran up against a "general distrust of the centralization of power brought about by the war" and a "fear of government meddling" that "turned out to be even more relevant in the case of cultural policy."[47] A confluence of events – some domestic, some on the international scene – eventually prodded the United States to hesitatingly pick up the CPI's fallen banner and set the foundations for the "golden age" of cultural diplomacy that took place in the years after the Second World War.

While the experience with the CPI drove the federal government from the field of cultural diplomacy during the 1920s and early 1930s, the shock caused by the nearly apocalyptic destruction of the First World War suggested to some private groups within the United States that cultural engagement with the other peoples of the world was more necessary than ever in order to increase international understanding and avoid such cataclysmic conflicts in the future. Perhaps not surprisingly, considering the long history of antagonism between the United States and Latin America and the simple matter of geographic proximity, Latin America was an early target for these unofficial cultural diplomats. In his detailed study of inter-American cultural relations, J. Manuel Espinosa catalogs the interwar efforts by schools, museums, and private philanthropic and cultural groups. Slowly, but steadily, U.S. professors and university students made their way to Latin America to study and interact with colleagues. The Institute of International Education, established in 1919 with support from the Carnegie Endowment, supported some of this travel as well as exchanges between U.S. and Latin American universities.[48]

Librarians in the United States also saw the possibilities and benefits of cultural relations with Latin America. As an official of the American Library Association (ALA) proclaimed shortly after the First World War, "America as a whole may not be internationally minded. But the librarians of America are so minded." Working with various foundations during the 1920s and 1930s, the ALA adopted a "missionary justification for their international interests" by arguing that "the printed word remained a primary vehicle of cross-cultural communication." By the 1930s, the Association had in place "a comprehensive set of cultural programs including visits, fellowships, library training, and exchange of publications." In his comprehensive study of the ALA's international work, Gary Kraske goes so far as to identify such efforts as part of the "origins" of America's cultural diplomacy.[49]

These private efforts were plagued with problems. Just as with the earlier efforts of the CPI these programs encountered varying amounts of suspicion from the Latin American audience. As Kraske notes, it was sometimes difficult for the ALA to convince their Latin American counterparts of the benefits of working with representatives from the United States: "an Anglo-Saxon partner whose program was formulated on democratic principles and reciprocity among equals but which had a history of economic and military domination."[50] Coordination was also a factor that limited the effectiveness of these early attempts at cultural diplomacy. With numerous individuals, universities, foundations, and organizations it was inevitable that despite some successes there was never any overall cohesion or coherence. In addition, the working relationship with U.S. government representatives in Latin America proved difficult to say the least. Despite the fact that these were private initiatives, they all, to one extent or another, depended on State Department officials to help facilitate their work. The noted historian Samuel F. Bemis vented his exasperation over State's lack of interest in assisting U.S. professors who arrived in Latin America to lecture and establish relationships with scholars in that region:

> Visiting professors who went out had to depend on the good will and welcome they might merit, or receive, in the connections which they themselves established without official assistance. They might be introduced to a Latin American audience by the Rector of the University, or by the janitor! The State Department shrank from imparting to the Good Neighbor Policy the imputation of cultural propaganda, even for the innocent purpose of actively assisting cultural exchange by private educational endowments.[51]

Funding was another consistent problem. Private efforts were often hamstrung by a lack of money. The ALA was a good example: "Inevitably, its enthusiasm always outdistanced its resources." Even with grants provided by the Guggenheim Foundation, the Carnegie Corporation, and the "bottomless pockets" of John D. Rockefeller, Jr., many of the programs operated on endless reserves of passion and dedication coupled to finite financial support.[52] The uncertain nature of funding obviously limited the ability of these private cultural ambassadors to construct coherent, sustained, and far-reaching programs.

American cultural diplomacy was at a crossroads by the early 1930s. The private efforts of the 1920s reflected the "liberal cultural perspective" that the "achievement of world peace and prosperity depended not so much on the expansionist dynamics of capitalism as on the common properties of human intelligence." This ideology was now coming into conflict with the "pessimistic climate of the 1930s, with a tendency toward cultural nationalism and the aggressive employment of cultural policy for political ends." As Ninkovich concludes, "Were it not for a threatening international environment, there would have been little inclination to tamper with the system as it then stood."[53]

Many scholars working on the history of U.S. cultural diplomacy echo the notion that the "threatening international environment" of the 1930s finally spurred the American government to become a more active participant. The main tenets of this argument are that the confluence of anti-Americanism in Latin America, the need for Latin American markets and resources by the United States that was mired in the midst of the Great Depression, and – most ominously – the successful penetration of Latin America by German (and, to a lesser extent, Italian and Japanese) propaganda masquerading as cultural diplomacy convinced American officials that leaving America's cultural diplomacy in private hands was inefficient and ineffective. The U.S. government, however reluctantly, picked up the gauntlet flung down by the fascists.[54]

More recently, historian Justin Hart has taken exception to the argument that the U.S. effort in public diplomacy beginning in the late 1930s was simply "a weak and largely inept response to the formidable operations of Nazi Germany." Certainly fears of fascist penetration of the New World provided additional impetus to the American government's interest in this new (at least for the United States) form of diplomacy. Hart, however, argues for a broader conception that fits the American experiments with cultural diplomacy during the 1930s and 1940s into what he refers to as a "fundamental transformation of U.S. foreign relations during that period." That transformation, the result of several interlocking factors, pushed U.S. policymakers to consider their nation as the next hegemonic world power. This hegemony would not, however, be based on older, cruder notions of what constituted "power" – the United States would achieve its goals by "avoiding costly, atavistic exercises in military conquest" or engaging in the dying practice of colonialism. How to do so meant solving a dilemma: "how to manage without ruling, or perhaps how to rule without managing." Hart argues that "Americanization" – the spreading of American ideology and culture – was the "antidote to colonialism." By the time the Second World War came to a close, "that sense of ideological mission became not only the rationale for a predetermined set of foreign policies but an actual component of foreign policy itself, as image became a crucial tool of empire."[55]

Whether the impetus for the U.S. government's foray into culture as part of its official diplomacy in the 1930s and the Second World War came from immediate concerns about hemispheric security or from a more far-reaching understanding among American diplomats of culture's increasing role in establishing their nation as a new and improved hegemon, there is no denying that these initial efforts constituted the beginnings of a permanent place for cultural diplomacy in America's foreign policymaking bureaucracy. Not surprisingly, these early attempts focused on picking up where the private sector had already established a foothold, in Latin America.

In his 1933 inaugural address, President Franklin Roosevelt announced the beginning of what came to be known as the Good Neighbor Policy. In brief, the idea behind the Good Neighbor was to improve relations between the United States and Latin America. This involved political actions, such as declaring a policy of nonintervention in Latin American nations (and the end of the unpopular and costly U.S. occupation of Haiti), as well as assurances of a more reciprocal economic relationship. For some in the Roosevelt administration, however, improving the reputation and image of the United States in Latin America would involve a heavy dose of cultural initiatives. Sumner Welles, who some historians credit with being the chief architect of the Good Neighbor Policy, stated in 1935, "In Latin America there is a frank skepticism as to the existence of interest here in the things of the mind and of the spirit. There is admiration of our capacity for organization and achievements in industry and business, but open incredulity of our interest in literature, music, art, and philosophy."[56] A year later, at the Pan American Conference for the Maintenance of Peace in Buenos Aires, Argentina, the "U.S. government for the first time committed itself to a policy of official sponsorship of international educational and cultural exchange" with the other republics of the Western Hemisphere.[57]

Franklin Roosevelt's precise role in both the establishment of the Good Neighbor Policy and his government's new foray into cultural diplomacy is still debated by historians. Born into a world of wealth, prestige, and power, FDR struck some as a patrician dilettante whose understanding of the complexities of foreign affairs was sometimes embarrassingly thin. Roosevelt certainly did not help matters with some of his remarks about his new policy toward Latin America, such as his statement in 1940 that fairly dripped with paternalism: "Give them a share. They think they are just as good as we are, and many of them are." These occasional gaffes aside, Roosevelt was certainly no newcomer to the byzantine world of international relations. He served as Wilson's assistant secretary of the navy for nearly eight years and always evidenced a healthy interest in diplomacy. Perhaps most important for a president overseeing a new cultural thrust in America's foreign policy Roosevelt was also a consummate master of image and public relations. Soon after assuming the presidency of a nation reeling from economic disaster Roosevelt took to the relatively new medium of radio and began a series of what came to be known as "fireside chats" with the American people. He understood the power of words and the importance of gaining the audience's trust. All of this was on display at the 1936 conference in Buenos Aires. Despite his physical limitations caused by polio, Roosevelt undertook the arduous journey to Argentina and became the first sitting president to visit South America. He was at the top of his form, hobnobbing with Latin American rulers and enjoying the cheers from the people who were eager to embrace his idea of a new and improved relationship. And given Roosevelt's understanding of the power of radio it was no surprise that U.S. officials at the conference called for the "use of radio broadcasting in the service of peace."[58]

Despite Roosevelt's support and an awareness on the part of U.S. officials that cultural diplomacy might have a more important role to play in the nation's foreign relations, "U.S. cultural diplomacy did not exactly get off to a roaring start" after Buenos Aires.[59] The reasons were clear and familiar. Rhetoric was a fine start, but without the bureaucratic mechanisms to translate words into action there was little likelihood of a dramatic change in the government's role in cultural diplomacy. There was still no single and specific office within the Department of State to deal with cultural matters – and, in fact, there was still resistance on the part of veteran diplomats to including culture as a tool in the nation's diplomacy. Even when, in 1938, the Department created the Division of Cultural Relations it was immediately made clear that the primary function of this new office was to coordinate any ongoing and new private initiatives in cultural diplomacy. As one U.S. official explained to Congress, the Division would exist to "assist the foundations and universities in this country" in carrying out their international cultural activities. The rather tepid nature of this first step in creating a bureaucratic home for U.S. cultural diplomacy can be explained by a number of factors: by emphasizing the coordinating nature of the Division, the primary source of funds for the efforts would come from private hands, thus sidestepping possible congressional criticisms about cost; by keeping the focus on private efforts, State avoided contending with long-standing concerns about government involvement in anything that hinted at cultural endeavors; and the reliance on domestic institutions to carry out the work also helped to allay concerns, both at home and abroad, about cultural diplomacy being a cover for propaganda.

The Division of Cultural Relations was small, poorly funded, and operated on a global scale. Perhaps more troubling for some of the traditionalists in the Department of State, the division's head consistently emphasized that he was interested in "genuine cultural relations," and would not allow his organization to become a "diplomatic arm or a propaganda agency."[60] The events of 1939–1940, however, convinced Roosevelt and others that a new direction for America's cultural diplomacy – particularly in Latin America – was necessary. In 1939, Germany's invasion of Poland initiated another great war in Europe. By May 1940 German troops marched into France and in just a few short weeks crushed the French armed forces. In Latin America, Germany used these successes to expand and increase its propaganda output. Roosevelt initially assured the American people that he would keep the United States out of this new wave of destruction and death, but by 1940 it was becoming clear that his nation was being pulled into the whirlpool of war.

It was surely no coincidence that just two months after Paris fell to the Nazis Franklin Roosevelt announced the establishment of an entirely new agency – the Office for the Coordination of Commercial and Cultural Relations between the American Republics. (In a little less than a year, the name was shortened to the Office of the Coordinator of Inter-American Affairs – henceforth, the abbreviation OCIAA will be used.) What was surprising was that this new office was not part of the Department of State; it was designed to report directly to Roosevelt. Another surprise was the person selected to be its director – Nelson A. Rockefeller, grandson of the legendary oilman John D. Rockefeller and a Republican. As Darlene Sadlier points out in her recent study of U.S. cultural diplomacy in Latin America, Nelson Rockefeller brought two important strengths to the new job. First, he was well acquainted with Latin America through both his business interests and philanthropic efforts. Second, Rockefeller was uniquely qualified for a position focused on cultural activities. He sat on the board of the Metropolitan Museum of Art and became president of the Museum of Modern Art in New York in 1939. In particular, he had a "passion for Latin American art."[61]

Rockefeller (perhaps setting a trend for future American billionaires) also developed a passion for politics and in 1940 saw his opening. On the same day German forces marched into Paris, Rockefeller met with Roosevelt's influential advisor, Harry Hopkins, and pushed for a "'vigorous program' of cultural, education, and scientific exchange" in Latin America. Shortly after the meeting, Hopkins passed along a memo (perhaps written by Rockefeller himself) to Roosevelt setting out the dangers and opportunities existing in Latin America. The note began by emphasizing the important economic contacts with the southern republics that were threatened by the war, but strongly argued that a program of cultural and educational efforts should be "pursued concurrently with the economic program."[62]

Once in his new position Rockefeller wasted little time in putting the cultural side of his plans into effect and during the next few years his agency helped to "stimulate what became a near craze for Pan-Americanism." The cultural tidal wave from the United States that hit Latin America during the years of the Second World War dwarfed any previous efforts. Recognizing the power of cinema, Rockefeller's organization worked with Hollywood to not only ensure a steady stream of films into Latin America but also make sure that those films contained the right messages. One of the first steps taken by the OCIAA was to work closely with the film industry's production code office to try and make sure that the "stereotypes of Latin Americans as greasers, bandits, and prostitutes were simply replaced with another, less obvious stereotype of a light-skinned, urbane people." Disney representatives were sent to Latin America to gather ideas for some cartoon shorts. This resulted in two of the most famous products of the American cultural offensive – *Saludos Amigos* and *The Three Caballeros* – both designed to press home the message that the United States and Latin America were friends and should work together. Music was another weapon in the cultural arsenal, and radio was used to fill the Latin American airwaves with works ranging from symphonies performed by American orchestras to jazz. In 1941, the OCIAA sponsored a Latin American tour by the renowned composer Aaron Copland.[63] Perhaps reflecting Rockefeller's special interest (and influence) American art also made its way to Latin America, beginning with a sparkling exhibit of some of the country's best-known modern artists, including Georgia O'Keeffe and Edward Hopper, organized by the Museum of Modern Art that traveled through Mexico, South America, and Cuba.[64]

While the OCIAA certainly succeeded in bringing greater enthusiasm, focus, and resources to the program of U.S. cultural diplomacy in Latin America, problems were already popping up before the Second World War came to a close. Some, such as complaints about the federal money being spent on such frivolous activities during wartime and the old bugaboo about having the government involved in cultural matters at all, were all reiterated during the war years. Ironically, however, it was the very success of Rockefeller's office that began to put into sharper relief one of the primary issues surrounding America's use of culture as a tool of its diplomacy. As described by Justin Hart, "The debate that would emerge over the next several years pitted purists, who viewed intellectual exchanges as an almost post-national exercise in reducing strife through a meeting of minds, against policymakers, who sought to deploy 'culture' as a tool of U.S. foreign policy."[65] And it appeared that the policymakers were winning the fight.

The Department of State had always been reluctant to embrace the idea of cultural diplomacy, only somewhat grudgingly accepting the creation of the Division of Cultural Relations. An awareness of the power of the fascists' combination of culture and propaganda as well as the prestige and resources allocated to the OCIAA began to alter State's views. In 1941, the department clipped Rockefeller's wings by pressuring Roosevelt into issuing an order that from that point on the OCIAA would not only have to keep State informed about its activities but also have to seek the department's approval before initiating any new programs. By 1943, nearly all of the OCIAA's cultural programs were transferred to the Division of Cultural Relations, and in 1944 Rockefeller himself was in the Department of State, working as assistant secretary for Latin American affairs.[66]

Although the threats posed by Nazi Germany and Imperial Japan might not have been the initial impetus for all of this new official interest in cultural diplomacy, it is clear that, as had occurred during the Civil War and the First World War, the Second World War spurred the U.S. government to more seriously consider the establishment of specific agencies to utilize the nation's culture to inform the world of American ideals and intentions and to counter the propaganda emanating from the Axis powers. Two months before the attack on Pearl Harbor, the writer Archibald MacLeish was named as the first director of the newly created Office of Facts and Figures (OFF). The work of the new agency seemed deceptively simple, as President Roosevelt explained: its purpose was "facilitating the dissemination of factual information to the citizens of the country on the progress of the defense effort and on the defense policies and activities of the Government." MacLeish, however, had a broader view of his office's work that went beyond giving facts and figures to the American people, and he almost immediately began to speak of "the strategy of truth" for combatting what he believed to be the insidious propaganda from Germany and Japan. When the United States joined the war in December 1941, the OFF became a smaller version of the old Committee on Public Information, producing posters and films in support of the war effort.[67] Although the office was in operation less than a year, it set the stage for the next step in formalizing a program of cultural diplomacy that went beyond the confines of Latin America.

The Office of War Information (OWI) was established in June 1942, largely in response to criticisms of MacLeish's approach which centered on the idea that government agencies such as the OFF should "provide sufficient information to enable citizens to form judgments of their own." His "critics insisted that Americans needed to be motivated to think and act in unison, to fight the enemy, and to achieve specific ends." Roosevelt's executive order setting up the OWI made clear this new and expanded vision when he laid out the primary objective: "Formulate and carry out, through the use of press, radio, motion picture, and other facilities, information programs designed to facilitate the development of an informed and intelligent understanding, at home and abroad, of the status and progress of the war effort and of the war policies, activities, and aims of the Government." Not only was Roosevelt more specific in denoting the means by which the information would be spread, but he also enlarged the information base by including not merely "defense efforts and defense policies," but also the "aims" of the United States in the Second World War. Finally, and perhaps most important in terms of the increasing use of cultural diplomacy, the OWI was given the task of reaching audiences both in America and abroad.[68]

In fact, a series of events quickly led the OWI to spend most of its time and resources on "selling" the war and America to the foreign audience. Very soon after the United States joined in the war effort the OWI found itself enmeshed in the same sort of arguments that resulted in the elimination of the OFF. Members of the OWI's Domestic Branch began to complain about what they saw as efforts to censor their attempts to "present the unadorned facts of the situation to the American public"; instead of illustrating for the American people the "fundamental, complex issues of the war" – even if these sometimes did not present the United States in glowing terms – they now felt compelled to engage in "manipulation and stylized exhortation." In January 1943 a number of writers for the Domestic Branch tendered their resignations in protest, declaring "the activities of OWI on the home front are now dominated by high-pressure promoters who prefer slick salesmanship to honest information....They are turning this Office of War Information into an Office of War Bally-hoo."[69] Congress, always ready to take advantage of controversies with U.S. information programs and displaying signs of rebellion against the older New Deal politics, sprang into action: "an increasingly conservative Congress, tired of the liberal-leaning tracts released by the Bureau of Publications, slashed almost all funding for the OWI's domestic branch."[70]

The virtual elimination of the OWI's domestic work, however, was an unintended windfall for its overseas activities. Many of the same tensions that essentially crushed the Domestic Branch of the OWI were present in the Overseas Branch. Here, too, as Allan Winkler explains, "The liberal propagandists again sought to convey their vision of the meaning of the war and again faced ever increasing resistance from others in the administration." The OWI's grasp of the power of culture as a weapon in the war, however, trumped those concerns. Ben Cherrington, the first chief of State's Division of Cultural Relations, summarized the importance of culture: "Culture in all its aspects must be utilized as an instrument of the one commanding purpose of the nation – victory over the enemy....Too fine a line could not be drawn between sheer propaganda and education in the best sense of the term. Friends must be won and held, the enemy frustrated, divided and conquered." The fine line between "unilateral propaganda" and "reciprocal cultural cooperation" would become "increasingly blurred."[71] Examining OWI's use of libraries and film provides useful examples of just how "blurred" the line could become.

In mid-1943, in collaboration with the Department of State and the American Library Association, the OWI established the first of what was to become a "far-flung system of overseas libraries" in the American Embassy in London. Citing increased interest in Great Britain about its new wartime ally as a motivating factor in establishing the library, the OWI was also quite clear about exactly what it had in mind: "It should be a reference and circulating library and information center, not *a publicity and propaganda agency*." Yet, when the first director of the library (a professor of history from the University of Pennsylvania) arrived at the U.S. Embassy in London, it was obvious that the original intentions would not be served. The new American library should be a "high-powered mechanism" that served as an information outlet, "not a cultural institute." In her study of the OWI library project, Pamela Spence Richards concludes that "the American library in London was initially designed to be a U.S. government-controlled channel of current information to the British communications industry." The focus would be on technical and industrial publications. While it eventually contained nearly 20,000 books, documents, newspapers, and magazines, and served over 1,000 people a month, the first OWI library was "not one of its more glamorous and conspicuous operations."[72]

Despite the rather limited vision employed at the London library, OWI officials were undaunted and quickly made plans to expand their operations into Australia, New Zealand, South Africa, India, and Spain. (The OWI eventually operated libraries, small and large, in other nations including Egypt, Portugal, Turkey, China, Lebanon, Syria, and even Russia.) Even the director of the London library recognized the potential: "These outpost libraries were born of the war ... but it seems clear that they are likely to be just as valuable in peace .... The O.W.I., by very practical and factual efforts, has carried the importance of libraries and books to the people and has raised them to a new and honorable position." He and others in the OWI (and the American Library Association) grasped "the growing importance of American materials to the man in the street." Yet, there were obvious changes taking place that moved the libraries from mere dispensers of data to centers for understanding American culture. Many of the first librarians were women, with backgrounds in both library science and U.S. information activities. The rather amorphous nature of their work was readily apparent – they were fully trained by the OWI in such things as "self-defense, psychological warfare, and infiltration techniques," while being told that "none of this applies to you librarians; your job is to tell the truth." This they attempted to do, through their work as reference sources in the libraries where they "answered questions on America's race problems as candidly and willingly as those on agricultural production," and as professional mentors for what were often poorly trained and demoralized local librarians.[73]

In the realm of film, the OWI initially rested its hopes on the already-well-established movie industry in Hollywood, relying on the studios to "respond with patriotic enthusiasm to wartime needs." Disturbed that popular films were not reacting seriously enough to the call for help in the information war, the OWI vacillated between employing "the club of censorship" and the "carrot of unconquered markets." What the OWI wanted was quite clear as it "urged Hollywood to trumpet the idea of America as a 'melting pot' of 'many races and creeds' who 'live together and progress'." Although the movie industry promised to do so, it became apparent to OWI officials that "propaganda was too important to be left solely to Hollywood," and so the agency embarked on production of its own documentary series entitled *American Scene*. In his study of the series, Dean Kotlowski notes that there were specific guidelines for the proposed films. They would emphasize "American Character" ("especially the blending of realism and idealism"); the forms and functions of the U.S. government;

America's technical and industrial achievements; "social reform;" and, perhaps as a direct tie-in with the OWI libraries, the American "free library system." There were also certain topics that were completely off-limits. Social reform was a fine topic, but any films on the subject "should not over-emphasize the evil at the expense of the measures taken to correct it." In particular, any discussion of America's race situation should "avoid showing segregation...and not deal too lengthily with sharp contrasts between the conditions of majority and minority peoples." The emphasis should be on portraying "mixed groups, but without self-consciousness." Other taboos were American "opulence" or anything else that might be cited as examples of "crass American materialism." Finally, nothing that gave an "impression of American political or economic imperialism" would be allowed.[74]

Even before the *American Scene* series, the OWI had dabbled in the making of documentaries, most of which, such as 1943's *The Autobiography of a Jeep*, focused on the war effort and American know-how. Despite the fact that these films often met with very favorable receptions overseas, the OWI intended the new series to concentrate on telling the "truth" about America and its people. Much of the focus was on the diversity of the American population. And although they were OWI productions, they still relied heavily on the expertise that only Hollywood and other show business professionals could provide. The Swedish actress Ingrid Bergman narrated *Swedes in America*, a film that accentuated the positive impact of immigrants on the American nation. Famous composer Aaron Copland provided the musical score for *The Cummington Story* that focused on European refugees settling into a small Massachusetts town. For one of its key productions, *The Town*, the OWI selected Josef von Sternberg to direct. Von Sternberg, already a legend for his work in German cinema (including the 1930 classic *The Blue Angel*), was given the task of making a short film about "a town awakening to its responsibilities in a nation at war." Released in 1945, *The Town* echoed the sentiments from earlier documentaries that emphasized the ethnic diversity of a small town in Indiana. It also focused on religious freedom, the American work ethic, the role of education, the power of democracy, and in its closing shots a reference to the important work being done by the town's young men in liberating Europe. It was, in short, the portrayal of "America as it was, or at least how the OWI's filmmakers wanted it to be." Although it celebrated diversity, there were no references to racial segregation and included one solitary shot of an African American man browsing through a book in the local library.[75]

Was the work of the OWI in setting up libraries and producing documentaries – as well as using radio broadcasts, publishing magazines and pamphlets, producing posters, distributing news stories, and many other forms of disseminating information – propaganda? Or was it simply "telling the truth about America"? Or was it using American culture to "sell" America to the world? In truth, it was a little bit of all of these things.

The frenetic activity engendered and accelerated by the Second World War meant that while information and cultural activities achieved a more prominent role in the nation's diplomacy, the precise nature of that role was left relatively undefined. Clashes between those who believed that culture should merely be a means to educate the world's masses about the soul and spirit of the American nation and people, and those who felt that culture and propaganda were nearly inseparable tools to achieve more definite political and economic ends, continued throughout the war years. And although the somewhat confusing mushrooming of new federal offices – the OCIAA, the OFF, the OWI – suggested that the government was now in control of cultural and information activities conducted abroad, the reality was that U.S. officials still relied quite heavily on the input and expertise provided by private individuals and groups. Very often, the only point of agreement between the state and non-state participants in America's cultural diplomacy was that it was a vital new tool in international relations.

While the first issue of exactly what America's cultural diplomacy was supposed to accomplish would continue to plague U.S. efforts for years to come, by the time the Second World War came to an end in 1945 it appeared that the American government – in particular, the Department of State – was intent on solving the question of who should be in charge by achieving what Ninkovich calls "the politics of institutionalization." The years 1944–1945 witnessed an acceleration of the process of making cultural diplomacy more "official" – with the U.S. government moving away from its traditional role of simply coordinating the cultural activities undertaken by the private sector and instead taking on more and more of the responsibilities and activities historically left to these nongovernment actors. President Harry Truman cemented the alliance between the various "information" and "cultural" wartime activities when he "transferred to the State Department many of the mass media functions of the two wartime propaganda agencies, the Office of War Information and the Office of [the Coordinator of] Inter-American Affairs." As usual, Truman minced no words in proclaiming, "The nature of present-day foreign relations makes it essential for the United States to maintain informational activities abroad as an integral part of the conduct of foreign affairs."[76] By 1945, the United States was the preeminent world political, economic, and military power. Yet, it faced a world reeling from the destruction of a second world war in three decades. It also confronted the rising power of the Soviet Union that already had its own official government office (the Comintern) to spread the word among the peoples of the world about the militarism and materialism of what remained of "western culture" and the inevitability of communist success. In such an environment, "U.S. officials increasingly viewed the cultural programs as a tool of empire to be used to facilitate American hegemony."[77] In the new Cold War world there was less and less need for "amateurs" in running America's cultural diplomacy. Such programs would now be left to the professionals.

CHAPTER THREE

The Truth about America

The Dutch audience that filled the Metro-Goldwyn-Mayer Studio in Amsterdam in May 1951 was unsure about exactly what it was to see that night. It had been promised an evening of entertaining films focusing on sports in America, all provided by the U.S. embassy as part of its cultural relations program. The proceedings got off to a rough start. The featured film of the night was *Princeton Football 1950*. It appeared to be a promising choice. The embassy's information officer was a Princeton graduate, and the university's team was an unstoppable juggernaut that year, going undefeated and ranked in the top ten in many national polls. Perhaps the film would impart the vigor and vitality of America and its dedication to good sportsmanship. The Dutch, however, were unfamiliar with the game and could only conclude that it was "a kind of rugby football, that could be played with so many liberties, that it looked like a kind of struggle rugby." And while the Princeton grad could take obvious delight in watching his school's team destroy the opposition, the audience ended up sympathizing with the victims and concluded that the Princeton team, which "seemed much stronger" than its opposition, was a bit of a bully. All was not lost, however. A second film feature delighted the Dutch audience. Certainly the participants in the "sport" highlighted in the presentation were more evenly matched. The film focused on fights between monkeys. The animals were provided gloves and then allowed to whale away on each other. A newspaper report the next day could hardly contain its enthusiasm, claiming that the monkeys "showed a marvelous training and overshadowed many matches of human beings." The embassy's information officer finally admitted defeat and summed up the Dutch opinion: "Princeton had no opposition and the boxing monkeys were better than the football."[1]

In the years immediately after the Second World War the United States engaged in a battle of words, ideas, and images with its communist opponents as part of the Cold War. The battle, as many U.S. officials noted, was not confined to the usual fields of politics, military dominance, or economic might but was at its core a battle for the "hearts and minds" of the world's people. Not surprisingly, propaganda – which had been a controversial issue for American society since the days of the Committee for Public Information during the First World War – was suddenly seen as not simply more palatable but absolutely necessary for the nation's survival in the struggle against the Soviet Union (and, later, Red China). What had previously been rather ad hoc efforts at "information," with an inordinate focus on Latin America, now became official and permanent parts of the nation's foreign policy bureaucracy. In order to counter the vicious and slanderous lies about the United States emanating from the well-established propaganda machinery of the Soviets, it was necessary to tell the world the truth about America.

As the bizarre incident with the boxing monkeys suggests, however, the use of American culture as part of that propaganda effort was still finding its way. Trying to tell the truth about America through cultural means was a tricky thing. What *was* the truth, and how did foreign audiences that might know little to nothing about the United States perceive it? Although U.S. officials might be very clear in the messages they wished to convey through displays of American culture, how could they be sure that the audience was receiving that message? As the films shown in Amsterdam revealed it was difficult to figure out what to show the foreign audience and how it would be understood. The Dutch might have liked boxing monkeys, but American officials would be hard-pressed to explain how battling simians assisted in telling the truth about America.

The year 1945 was a tumultuous, but significant, period for the development of American cultural diplomacy. The new president, Harry Truman, made it clear that international information and cultural affairs were to henceforth be the responsibility of the Department of State. To head the effort, Truman named William B. Benton as assistant secretary of state for public affairs; Benton would also be in charge of the Office of International Information and Cultural Affairs and the Interim International Information Service. The selection of Benton represented more than simply a reshuffling of personnel. The man he replaced, Archibald MacLeish, was a Pulitzer Prize–winning poet who espoused the use of art and culture as an international language of peace and understanding. Benton was something entirely different. By the time he began his work in State Benton was a millionaire many times over. He made his fortune working in the field of advertising and thus knew how to tailor messages to sway audiences. Benton was also a strong supporter of the power of education, serving as a vice president of the University of Chicago and chairman of the board for the *Encyclopedia Britannica*. He seemed to be a perfect choice to lead America's cultural diplomacy in a new direction – as a means to sell America to the international audience and gain their support for U.S. policies.[2]

He also understood, as did a growing number of other U.S. officials, that America was not the only nation willing to employ culture to win hearts and minds. Although more recently Nazi Germany and Imperial Japan infamously included music, art, literature, film, and other cultural genres to spread their influence, in truth they were relative newcomers to the game. As early as the late 1700s, France used its cultural products as a tool of its diplomacy. Even when French dominance in the field of art and other cultural achievements waned in the mid-1900s – along with its great power status – the nation's distinguished heritage was still proudly waved to the world: "Cultural prestige had become a substitute for power."[3] The British long believed in the power of culture in terms of uplifting and educating the masses at home, but by the mid-1930s they were taking steps to formalize the use of culture as part of the nation's foreign policy. In 1934, British policymakers, fearful of the rising power of Germany and that nation's use of culture as propaganda, responded with the creation of the British Council. The new organization was charged with spreading British art, literature, language – and power – around the globe.[4]

By the time the Second World War came to a close, however, U.S. officials focused their attention on Soviet propaganda and the Russian use of culture as a means of diplomacy. The Soviets embraced their own brand of cultural diplomacy long before the Second World War. As one scholar notes, the new communist state "adopted classic instruments of foreign policy," but also saw to it that "an entire network of so-called 'cultural' organizations was implemented" as early as the 1920s. The purpose was to have culture serve not as strictly "political propaganda;" this "cultural diplomacy was aimed at the dissemination of a positive and controlled image of Soviet life." Throughout the 1920s and 1930s the Soviet Union invited writers, artists, and scholars to visit and lecture. In addition, carefully selected Russian cultural and intellectual figures were sent abroad. Following the Second World War, the Soviets accelerated these efforts. According to historian Rosa Magnusdottir, they soon discovered that "their preferred propaganda methods were no longer working." Early on, particularly in war-scarred Europe, the Soviet Union "seemed to be winning the propaganda war...where anti-Americanism was one of its main strategies." Almost immediately, however, they confronted the fact that "the increased appeal of consumerism and the increased weight of American propaganda" put them on the "defensive." Ironically, like their counterparts in the United States they adopted culture as a means of "telling the truth about socialism at home and abroad."[5] Not surprisingly, telling that story often dovetailed nicely with painting a grim picture of American culture (or, more precisely, lack thereof).

Benton and his associates in the Department of State clearly perceived the danger. Echoing sentiments that stretched all the way back to Jefferson's defense of American culture, they understood that while the "appeal of consumerism" was undeniable so, too, was the belief among many nations of the world – both friend and foe – that the United States still languished in a cultural and artistic backwater. All of this played into the hands of communist propaganda that portrayed Americans as money-mad war mongers who valued the dollar above the beauty of art. As one official put it, "The United States has demonstrated its superb ability to manufacture tanks, airplanes, guns, and all the other implements of war....The United States must demonstrate that it also has an interest in and a vigorous movement in the fields of art, music, and allied fields." Benton wholeheartedly agreed, arguing that American culture sent abroad could result in "a favorable effect in foreign countries. It is the sort of thing which helps to counter the propaganda which tries to label us as cultural barbarians."[6]

Benton's experience in advertising, however, led him to discern another value in the display of American culture overseas. The actual exhibits or performances were entirely secondary to the primary goal: to "serve the kind of purpose that music serves on a radio program: to attract the customers who are then more numerous and more responsive to the sales story." (And Benton knew the power of music. In 1939 he was a member of a group of businessmen who purchased the Muzak Corporation which produced what has become world famous as "elevator music."[7]) He was not the only official to grasp the connections between culture, advertising, and the power to persuade. One of his associates bluntly stated the case: "Art we believe helps nations understand and support us, just as some of the biggest industries in the United States believe art helps advertise their products and gain peoples [sic] support." Art could serve as a similar tool in ensuring that the United States would be "understood and respected in the world today so that our foreign policy will be supported and followed by the nations of the world."[8]

As had many previous purveyors of American cultural diplomacy, Benton and his associates firmly believed that they were not engaging in simplistic or misleading propaganda. Even in viewing culture as a somewhat crass advertising gimmick, they steadfastly clung to the idea that it was absolutely necessary to attract the "customers" so that they could learn the truth about America. Just as America's informal cultural diplomats discovered in the nineteenth century, however, it often proved difficult to find simple, well-defined truths in such a heterogeneous society.

As noted in Chapter Two, the Department of State, even before the Second World War came to a close, was moving toward not only a more permanent cultural diplomacy bureaucratic structure within the department but also more control over the makeup, direction, and purpose of the international cultural efforts. Instead of serving as merely the coordinating and financing body for the activities of private organizations and individuals, the department would take a more active role in setting up and directing America's cultural diplomacy to ensure that the proper messages were being sent to the right audiences. The scattershot efforts of the 1930s and the Second World War would no longer suffice. There was little doubt among U.S. officials that some of those efforts had been successful, but leaving much of the control over such an important undertaking in unofficial hands also resulted in some embarrassing debacles. Many in the Department of State could recall the disaster that occurred in 1941–1942 when Orson

Welles was recruited to work his magic by producing some fascinating and popular documentaries on Latin America that could be shown to audiences in the United States. Perhaps they should have known that Welles, still best known for scaring the daylights out of many Americans with his radio version of *War of the Worlds* in 1938, could be a bit of a loose cannon. When it was all over thousands of feet of film were shot for a never-released production entitled *It's All True*, department officials were howling over the large amounts of money sunk into the project, and charges were being leveled at Welles that his lack of attention to the details and purpose of the work (his attention being directed elsewhere at wild parties and chasing Brazilian beauties) amounted to almost criminal neglect. Others argued that the biggest problem was that Welles simply didn't get it: he concentrated much of his attention on the poor, black population of Brazil instead of creating a toe-tapping celebration of salsa music and the stereotypical "happy" Latino. Whatever the real story (which is still being debated by scholars), the experience with Welles left a bad taste in the mouths of many State Department members, many of whom came to believe that this was what happens when you leave such important work to the amateurs.[9]

It was, therefore, quite appropriate that one of the first major U.S. undertakings in cultural diplomacy after the Second World War would be an entirely "in-house" affair. In 1946, the Department of State initiated its boldest foray into cultural diplomacy to date. Using money left over from some of the wartime propaganda and cultural initiatives, State purchased seventy-nine oil paintings from various art dealers and an additional thirty-five watercolors from the American Federation of Arts and began to plan for the overseas exhibit of what came to be known as the *Advancing American Art* collection. The name aptly described the nature of the collection itself as well as State's intentions. This was no retrospective of American art; the works leaned heavily toward the more recent, modern form of painting. There were a few names that might have been recognized by the public at large, such as Georgia O'Keeffe, but only gallery owners and museum curators would have known most of the other artists – Yasuo Kuniyoshi, Marsden Hartley, Arthur Dove, and Milton Avery, for example. Yet, these were the men and women leading the charge in American art and the collection represented a premier gathering of the works by those who were truly advancing American art.[10]

This was a conscious decision on the part of the Department of State. It was influenced by the reaction to another exhibit of American art that went overseas in 1946 and by reports from its representatives abroad. In June 1946, the National Gallery of Art took the lead in responding to a British request for a grand show of American art. Working with several other museums, the National Gallery assembled a massive show of nearly 200 paintings. If the U.S. museums hoped to overwhelm by sheer numbers, they were sadly mistaken. Although there were a few polite comments sprinkled throughout the British press, more typical was the devastating review that declared, "There is a lot this exhibition might have done – had the actual show not been poorly chosen and inadequate, poorly publicized and poorly hung." Many of the critics focused on the lack of modern art, noting that less than 30 of the 200 paintings were from the twentieth century. One fumed that "with the twentieth century the selection stopped being a selection and became a grab-bag of everyone who could pull a string." A French reviewer, however, had the last word: the "modern section was truly catastrophic."[11]

If the American exhibit in Great Britain was even more evidence of the need for professional cultural diplomats to handle things, it also supported what the Department of State was hearing from its personnel in the field: the international audience, particularly in Europe, wanted to see America's modern art. During Rockefeller's heyday in the 1940s, numerous reports came back to Washington from American representatives in Latin America clamoring for more of the kind of modern art exhibits being put together by the Museum of Modern Art. Now, as some art connoisseurs began to suggest that America's modern painters were beginning to supplant the French as the artistic vanguard "artists and art critics abroad are interested in knowing what the modern schools in America have accomplished."[12] Benton and his associates would give the people what they wanted.

Recognition of America's rising prestige in the world of art was one explanation for the rather brash name of the new collection, but the paintings and watercolors were also designed to advance a political agenda. Benton made this clear when he argued that exhibits such as *Advancing American Art* would "also make an impact among Communists overseas because they illustrate the freedom with which and in which our American artists work." In case the message was not clear enough, another official in the Department of State put it a bit more directly: "Only in a democracy where the full development of the individual is not only permitted but fostered could such an exhibition be assembled." *Advancing American Art* was nothing less than a cultural broadside leveled against the stifling dictatorship of the Soviet Union, where even artists found themselves forced to toe the official party line and paint within the confining lines of the form known as "socialist realism." Moreover, it was a message directed with laser-like precision at a very specific audience: the exhibit would find its mark with the "artistically literate groups who constitute the opinion-forming public in many foreign countries."[13]

While officials from the National Gallery of Art silently fumed over being pushed aside, the Department of State worked successfully to smooth over any concerns that the private art world might have about an "official" art show being sent overseas. Several notable figures representing American artists, art critics, and museum curators were consulted about the makeup of the collection. The influential American Federation of Arts was brought on board when State purchased the watercolor collection from the group. Finally, the department capped off its domestic campaign by having the first showing of *Advancing American Art* at the Metropolitan Museum of Art in

New York. The reviewers' responses were almost embarrassingly effusive in their praise. One waxed poetically that "this time we are exporting neither domestic brandy in imitation cognac bottles nor vintage non-intoxicating grape juice, but real bourbon, aged in the wood – what may justly be described as the wine of the country."[14]

Despite the accolades from the domestic critics, U.S. officials were still noticeably nervous about what the foreign reception might be. Before being sent abroad, the collection was split, with the oil paintings heading off for a European tour and the watercolors shipped off to Latin America. At the first stops for what were now two *Advancing American Art* shows – Paris and Cuba – the reviews were overwhelmingly positive. Even the French critics, normally reticent to recognize American art as anything but a pale imitation of the far superior works of their fellow countrymen, had to admit that not only were the paintings "interesting" and "vigorous," but also had "not been directly influenced by the European styles." For Benton and other officials, however, the real test of the exhibition as a tool of foreign policy came in Prague, Czechoslovakia. The eastern European country was already a Cold War battlefield. Although the nation considered itself an independent state, Winston Churchill included it as being on the communist side of the Iron Curtain in his famous speech given just the year before *Advancing American Art* arrived. It was in Prague that American cultural diplomacy engaged in its first face-to-face battle with the Soviets. The United States scored first, with the Czechs flooding in to see the art exhibit and the critics raving about the "creative vitality" of the paintings. Almost immediately, the Soviets struck back, hustling to get a massive exhibit of Russian paintings shipped to Prague. It was nearly twice the size of the American show and U.S. officials on the scene complained that the Soviet exhibit "copied the Dept's in presentation, related events, such as concerts and lectures, posters, location and announcements." In fact, the Soviets literally bombarded the Czechs with culture using aircraft to drop free tickets to the Russian exhibition over the city. The Russians were clearly aware of the intended message of artistic (and, by implication, political) freedom demonstrated by the modern art in the *Advancing American Art* show and countered by arguing that at least the socialist realist art could be "understood by the simple spectator." Despite these efforts, however, the Americans won this first round. As a leading Czech newspaper put it, "the two exhibitions could not be spoken of in the same breath since the American was obviously the product of genuine artistic creative ability while the other portrayed 'popular state art'."[15] Perhaps letting the nation's culture tell the truth about America might really be the most effective propaganda.

Even before leaving for Europe and Latin America, however, there arose a few hints of the storm to come. Newspapers owned by the conservative media mogul William Randolph Hearst lampooned the modern art in the exhibit, often using the word "lunatic" to describe the paintings and watercolors. More ominously, some reports suggested that if the art was bad the artists were worse. Some stories dropped hints about the "left-wing artists," while others were more emphatic in claiming that many of the people represented in the show were members of communist organizations. As Taylor Littleton and Maltby Sykes note in their history of the collection, these charges were enough to raise some eyebrows about a show funded and sponsored by the Department of State, but the key ingredient in the attacks was the "assertion, accompanied by ridicule, that the pictures selected for 'Advancing American Art' set forth a distorted and disfigured portrait of the American scene, particularly since the exhibit contained no examples of art which depicted the nation's values and traditions in recognizable forms."[16] Such an argument was critical for it strongly suggested that not only were the works of art failing to tell the *real* truth about America but that they might, in fact, be telling an entirely different – and un-American – story.

Although the stories in the Hearst newspapers did not delay the sending of the art overseas, they did create a small fissure in the wall of official and unofficial praise for *Advancing American Art*. Others would soon apply their own wrecking balls and destroy the exhibit – and, very nearly, the U.S. government's involvement in cultural diplomacy. In late 1946 and early 1947, just as the exhibition enjoyed success overseas, at home the blows came fast and furious. Organizations representing American artists who worked in a more traditional format were outraged that a show of "American art" was composed entirely of modern works. *Look* magazine picked up on the murmurings of discontent and published a piece provocatively entitled "Your Money Bought These Paintings." While the short article was not entirely negative, the pictures of the modern paintings soon caught the eyes of other critics. The radio commentator Fulton Lewis became positively apoplectic in a tirade against both the art and the fact that the U.S. government spent taxpayers' dollars to send it overseas. "If that be American art," he righteously concluded, "God save us."[17]

A number of congressmen smelled blood in the water. Congress was already brewing up campaigns to find communists in America; just a few months after the *Look* article and Lewis's screed, the House Un-American Activities Committee (HUAC) would begin its infamous hearings on communist infiltration of Hollywood. In such an atmosphere, *Advancing American Art* was readymade for a political savaging. Following up on the earlier attacks, several congressmen repeated some of the same charges: it was unconscionable for the U.S. government to spend tax dollars on paintings and watercolors, particularly so when the artwork itself was completely unintelligible to the average viewer. More and more, however, the attacks focused in on the political backgrounds of the artists. One request to Benton was patently obvious about the intent of these inquiries: "I am particularly anxious to know what information you had regarding the Communistic background and Communistic affiliation of the various artists." The attacks sharply divided the Department of State, with some officials counseling a full-fledged retreat from the art program before Congress turned its attention on other aspects of the department's cultural diplomacy and information activities. Others, with Benton in the lead, tried to stem the tide by accentuating the value of the art exhibit as a tool of the nation's propaganda and pointing to the recent successes in Latin America and Europe. Even Benton, the super-salesman, could not successfully deflect the charges of communist influence among the artists. He was forced to concede that more than a third of the painters' names had come up in HUAC hearings and a handful were reported to be "members of the Communist Party."[18]

It was up to President Harry S. Truman and Secretary of State George Marshall to administer the fatal blows. Truman, already under attack by Republicans in Congress, understandably avoided the communism issue and focused instead on the quality of the art. In a letter to Benton Truman fumed that the paintings were "the vaporings of half-baked lazy people" and declared that there were "many American artists who still believe that the ability to make things look as they are is the first requisite of a great artist." The works in *Advancing American Art* were "no art at all." (Later reports suggested that Truman, after seeing the *Look* article, sneered, "If that's art, I'm a Hottentot.") All of this was more than enough for Secretary Marshall. Just two days after Truman's furious letter Marshall froze any further showings of the collection in Latin America and Europe. When Congress cut funding for the department's cultural and information programs, the secretary declared that there would be "no more taxpayers' money for modern art." He ordered the exhibits (then in Haiti and Czechoslovakia) to be packed up, shipped home, and disposed of by auction. In the summer of 1948, bids were submitted for the paintings. A collection conservatively valued at nearly $100,000 was auctioned off for a little less than $6,000, with at least one painting going for the rock bottom price of $6.25. *Advancing American Art* had gone as far as it was going to go.[19]

The *Advancing American Art* debacle certainly staggered the proponents of cultural diplomacy in the Department of State. They were completely taken aback by the savage attacks at home and quickly realized that the sad end of the art exhibit might very well mark the end of the use of culture as a foreign policy tool. Some, however, also recognized the central issue raised by the destruction of the collection. The works of art were sent abroad to tell the truth about America – to quite literally show the foreign audience the nation's commitment to freedom of thought and expression while, not coincidentally, setting the cultural manifestations of that freedom in vivid contrast to the state-controlled "culture" of the Soviet state. Yet, by telling one truth *Advancing American Art* unwittingly revealed another: that the freedom of thought and expression suggested by the paintings could face some chilling limitations in the Cold War United States. Few U.S. officials appeared to grasp the ultimate irony that involving art and politics created a blade that cut both ways.

It soon became clear that Congress, having dismantled the art program, now had its sights set on eliminating most – if not all – of America's information and cultural programs. Republicans gained a majority in Congress after the 1946 elections and immediately made their views on such programs crystal clear. The negativity had several sources. Some congressmen believed that the wartime propaganda programs had been far too favorable to Roosevelt and the liberal ideas of the New Deal. Others, who could recall the criticisms leveled at the CPI during the First World War, worried about any government program that involved itself with cultural affairs or the dissemination of information. For many in Congress, however, it simply came down to dollars and sense: the programs were costly and, with the Second World War over, completely unnecessary.[20]

One program, in particular, came in for especially brutal attacks. The Voice of America (VOA) started broadcasting on the radio airwaves in February 1942. Quickly rolled into the overall structure of the OWI, the VOA stated that its goal was to simply relay news about the war whether that news was "good or bad." Originally put together by individuals such as John Houseman, who had deep experience in theater and popular radio working with Orson Welles, the broadcasts were not always so cut and dried. In place of a dull recitation of news stories, Houseman livened things up by having the news "performed" by individuals who became the voices of world leaders, generals, and the American public. Many of the broadcasts were directed at the enemy as part of an effort to demoralize and confuse America's opponents. There was also a certain amount of editorializing on the early VOA transmissions. Many of the initial employees were strong supporters of both the New Deal and what they perceived as the anti-fascist crusade of the Second World War. This sometimes led to conflict and criticism as in 1943 when a VOA broadcast "criticized harshly Allied dealings with newly appointed Marshal Pietro Badoglio, the prime minister of Italy, referring to the fascist party leader as 'a moronic little king'." The press in America claimed that the VOA was subverting U.S. war strategy and even President Roosevelt stated, "The commentary should not have aired."[21]

After the "moronic little king" fiasco the VOA took on more of a straightforward reporting of events, and by the end of the war employed over 3,000 people broadcasting in over forty languages around the world. As the Second World War came to a close, however, it appeared to many in the United States that its days were numbered. One of the largest news services in the United States, the Associated Press, abruptly ceased its cooperation with the VOA in early 1946 arguing that its association with the government agency would harm its credibility: "the government cannot engage in newscasting without creating the fear of propaganda which necessarily would reflect on the objectivity of the news services from which such newscasts are prepared." The United Press service quickly followed suit. When Republicans gained a majority in Congress following the November 1946 elections, the problems increased. Intent on cutting the federal budget, some congressmen zeroed in on information programs such as the VOA. Arguments for slashing the VOA's budget, or eliminating it entirely, were aided by charges that many of the wartime information agencies were riddled with subversive elements – extreme liberals or, even worse, communist sympathizers. The radio program was a prime target: "The VOA was also singled out as a security risk because it employed aliens."[22]

In an ironic turn of events, however, the Cold War fears that fueled some of the attacks on America's information and cultural programs during the years 1945–1947 also served to rejuvenate and expand those very same activities. When President Harry S. Truman issued what would become famous as the "Truman Doctrine" in March 1947, he not only officially inaugurated the Cold War with the Soviet Union but also spurred renewed interest in the use of culture as a weapon against communism. Although he never mentioned the Soviet Union by name, anyone who heard or read Truman's forceful speech to Congress knew exactly what he meant when he declared that the world was now faced with a choice "between alternative ways of life." And he made clear the role that the United States must play in that battle: "to support free peoples who are resisting attempted subjugation by armed minorities or by outside pressures." Congress responded by overwhelmingly approving aid packages to two nations threatened by such "subjugation" – Turkey and Greece. Secretary of State George C. Marshall asked Congress to go farther by arguing that American power and security rested "not only on our economic and political and military strength, but also on the strength of American ideas – on how well they are presented abroad." Coming at the same time as he was administering the final blow to the already mortally wounded *Advancing American Art* show, Marshall's newfound embrace of culture and information programs was evidence of just how much – and how quickly – things had changed. Two months later, Representative Karl Mundt introduced a bill "providing legal authority for the State Department to distribute overseas publications and films, administer international exchanges of college students and professors, and operate the VOA." In January 1948, the United States Information and Educational Exchange Act (more popularly known as the Smith-Mundt Bill) was signed into law. As Nicholas Cull concludes, "Large-scale U.S. information overseas had legislative authority at last."[23]

Despite this success, supporters of cultural diplomacy were cognizant of the fact that "legislative authority" did not obscure the fact that America's international cultural program still faced serious difficulties. Many officials in State had never fully subscribed to the value of cultural diplomacy, seeing it as at best a meaningless and insignificant gesture toward international understanding or, at worst, a worthless drain on important resources that was also a lightening rod for political attacks. The question for its supporters was how to maintain the nation's cultural activities overseas without incurring the wrath of a variety of domestic critics. In short, how could it continue to use culture to tell the truth about America without America noticing? Fortunately for the advocates of cultural diplomacy a laboratory for continuing the experiment already existed.

Since occupying the western half of Germany and a portion of Berlin in the Soviet-occupied eastern half, U.S. officials from both State and the military engaged in a sustained program of "re-education," which was more popularly known as "de-nazification." As political scientist Cora Sol Goldstein explains, "To combat the 'warped German mentality,' Germans had to be taught new moral and political categories by which make sense and organize their views of reality." The Office of Military Government for Germany, US (OMGUS) therefore "waged a 'war of ideas,'" in occupied Germany by putting forth a steady stream of pro-democratic and anti-Nazi propaganda, combined with censoring what it felt to be less acceptable expressions of politics and culture. At first, however, "OMGUS did not regard the fine arts as a means of re-education, and its cultural policy ignored the potential usefulness of art as a political instrument." There were occasional forays into the use of art, including a 1946 showing of some of the paintings stolen by the Nazis during the war. Then came the *Advancing American Art* disaster and thoughts about using American art – particularly anything remotely modern in nature – fell off the radar.[24] Just five years later, however, a large U.S.-sponsored art exhibit featuring the works of some of America's best-known modern artists opened in West Berlin. Why such a show took place at all is actually quite understandable. How it came about provided clear evidence that the Department of State had learned its lesson about getting involved in the culture business.

Just as the Soviet use of cultural diplomacy spurred the growth of the parallel U.S. efforts, so it was in divided Germany. Goldstein argues that the Russians, already old pros at the propaganda uses of culture, pushed forward with an extremely aggressive program in postwar Germany that simultaneously portrayed the USSR as an incubator for artistic development and the United States as a cultural degenerate. The latter aim was assisted by similar Nazi propaganda put forward during the 1930s and the Second World War. As one U.S. official in West Germany explained, there was now a "real danger that American advice and influence would be ineffective if Germans were not enabled to realize that America was more than a nation of lady wrestlers, bloody strikes and boogie-woogie fiends such as Hitler had portrayed." Surveys conducted by the U.S. military authorities in western Germany consistently found that the German people considered the Americans culturally inferior. As one historian notes, "The only exception to that rule was avant-garde art, especially abstract expressionism." And at a 1950 meeting between U.S. military officials and representatives of the West Berlin government and cultural sector the Germans specifically requested an "international exhibition of modern art," with "special enthusiasm for an exhibit of American moderns." Thus, it came to pass that at the Berlin Cultural Festival in September 1951 an exhibit of nearly seventy American paintings went on display. At least fifty of the works of art represented the nation's modern artists. Particularly ironic was the fact that thirteen of the artists in the show had also been in the recently demolished *Advancing American Art* collection.[25]

The fact that the show was in West Berlin where the U.S. military could more effectively put a lid on press coverage obviously helped to deflect the criticisms that doomed the earlier State Department–sponsored exhibit. More important in explaining why there was no congressional outrage, no fulminations from Fulton Lewis, no snarky comments from Harry Truman was the fact that the 1951 exhibit was successfully portrayed as a completely private effort. The wounds from the disastrous *Advancing American Art* experiment were still fresh and sensitive. Almost as soon as the U.S. military officials in West Berlin forwarded the German request for American modern art to the department, State representatives started searching for ways to pass off this political hot potato. Ironically, just a few years after deciding that professional diplomats should take charge of America's cultural diplomacy the Department of State now did a complete about-face. The request was handed to a group of museum curators to make the selection of the paintings for the show. State contacted the American Federation of Arts (AFA) to provide direction and handle the installation of the exhibit. Funding was provided by a grant from a private philanthropic organization. The Department of State would limit its participation to "observation" and facilitating the shipment of the artworks overseas. In West Berlin, the show proved popular with the German audience. The art program was back in private hands. For the remainder of the Truman presidency, the Department of State was more than happy to let the AFA, the Museum of Modern Art, private funding organizations, and even the Smithsonian Institution handle the more controversial aspects of America's cultural diplomacy.[26]

Just because it shied away from modern art did not mean a complete retreat by State from the cultural field, however. Libraries of American books, inaugurated by the OWI during the Second World War, soon spread elsewhere and proved quite popular. To counteract Hollywood films that department officials believed often presented a sensationalistic and misleading portrayal of American society, State oversaw the production and distribution of hundreds of documentary-style films about American life. Mobile projection units were sent out to ensure the widest possible audience and by 1950 it was estimated that over 125,000,000 people around the world saw the films. "The content of the newly produced films was determined by the State Department policy experts, who were guided by reports from special film officers and other information personnel attached to U.S. embassies and consulates." And State worked closely with the VOA which began to expand its programing to spread news about American life, and music, to friends overseas and also to penetrate the Iron Curtain.[27]

The Smith-Mundt Bill of 1948 that helped to stave off the elimination of the VOA and other parts of America's cultural and information programs abroad also reinforced the role of individual Americans in the field of cultural diplomacy. During the 1800s, individuals and groups of "average" Americans served as unofficial cultural ambassadors overseas. The 1948 legislation blurred the lines by giving the Department of State the task of overseeing officially sponsored exchange programs that sent American students and professors abroad, while inviting foreign visitors to the United States. In fact, this particular aspect of the Smith-Mundt Bill expanded on an effort that had been under way since 1946, when Senator William J. Fulbright set in motion what would become one of the most famous components of America's post–Second World War cultural diplomacy.

American-sponsored exchange programs were not exactly new. Earlier in the century, after the Boxer Rebellion in China, the U.S. government set up a mechanism for having Chinese citizens come to America for an education. Following the First World War, another such program was established with Belgium and part of the program of cultural relations with Latin America during the late 1930s also included an exchange initiative. Yet, the program established by Senator Fulbright was "markedly different from its country- and region-specific forerunners by virtue of its global potential and its attempts to organize educational exchanges between America and the rest of the globe." Fulbright's idea was to use wartime "surplus" to fund an exchange program that would send Americans abroad and bring foreign visitors to the United States. The surplus he identified was the tremendous amount of Lend-Lease supplies that had been provided to America's allies during the Second World War. With the end of the conflict, millions of dollars of these materials lay in foreign lands. The Fulbright Act, introduced in 1945, called for "authorizing use of credits established through the sale of surplus properties abroad for the promotion of international good will through the exchange of students in the fields of education, culture and science." Therefore, nations that purchased the surplus goods (usually for a fraction of their actual value) would see those funds used for the student exchange program. It seemed an ideal arrangement. The program would require no additional funds from Congress, the surplus property problem would be eliminated, and, so it was hoped, "international good will" would ensue. In August 1946, President Truman signed the Fulbright Act.[28] The 1948 Smith-Mundt Bill expanded the scope of such exchanges by making the program truly global and not limited to only those nations that purchased the surplus war goods.

The exchange program became one of the most publicized of America's cultural diplomacy efforts. Stories and photos featuring the smiling faces of students, teachers, and other technical experts immersing themselves in different cultures became a staple of America's public diplomacy. In her study, Liping Bu explains what the program was designed to accomplish: "The exchangees or foreign students, as the foreigners were called, were encouraged to learn about American values and democratic ideals while Americans abroad were encouraged to spread American concepts and ways of life." Yet, since the program was coordinated by the Department of State there were natural suspicions that "mutual understanding" might not be the foremost priority for the U.S. government. Indeed, William Benton made the intent of America's cultural efforts quite clear when he argued that such programs were designed "to support United States foreign policy in its long range sense and to serve as an arm of that policy." As with nearly every phase of the nation's cultural diplomacy, there was a conflict: "The government's principal interest in educational exchange was to achieve short-term political objectives whereas educators were more interested in the long-term educational goals." In the main, the short-term goals predominated: "How effective was the attempt to separate educational programs from political propaganda? Not very. Some scholars noted that, with the Cold War dominating international relations, 'educational exchange was massively overshadowed by the information program and reduced, administratively, to a "media service" thereof. Information received the major share of the budget and the bulk of attention.'"[29]

Both at home and abroad the exchange program faced obstacles. The effort to establish a Fulbright exchange with Australia is illustrative of some of these issues. Although there were many Australian scholars and students who wished to come to the United States for additional training, the Australian government worried about the "politicization" of the program. Almost from the beginning of formal discussions between the United States and Australia in 1947, the latter nation expressed its concern that "The United States naturally expects to hold a dominant position in implementing the programme." American officials were exasperated by Australia's failure to simply ratify the agreement and chalked it up to a "suspicious and hostile" attitude toward what Australia perceived as "American economic imperialism." After a good deal of negotiations, the two governments finally signed off on a Fulbright exchange program in 1949. Alice Garner and Diane Kirkby, in their study of the workings of the program, argue that although many of the Americans involved (and some of the Australians) saw the exchanges – particularly the bringing of Americans to Australia – as part of a larger effort of the anti communist campaign, the resistance from the Australian government and academia kept it from becoming completely "distorted or politicised." Nevertheless, it was always a battle between the "goals of 'mutual understanding' enshrined in the Fulbright program" and "the more limited unilateral goals of US foreign policy."[30]

The other half of the program – bringing "exchangees" to the United States – faced a quite different difficulty. One study of these foreign visitors concluded that they came away with four "salient features" of America and its people: "(1) America's ascendancy as a world power, (2) America's grand size and wealth, (3) American emphasis on science and technology, and (4) America's big heart." This did not translate to entirely positive views, however. Many visitors expressed "reservations centering on America's lack of maturity and experience in global leadership." Although there was a great deal of rhetoric in America about its commitment to the basic "tenets of American democracy," foreign exchangees found "little indication of the deeply emotional faith in it as a model for other peoples which was typical in former times." In particular, they were concerned about the race problem and the nation's "preoccupation with the 'Red Scare'." American society moved far too fast, "with an orientation toward the kind of force and violence exhibited by Hollywood movies." Richard Pells concludes that "the chance to travel around the country and meet the people did not necessarily make the visitors more favorably disposed toward America. On the contrary, the experience often confirmed their worst fears about the United States." There was no doubt that America was a land of plenty. "Yet even America's affluence was subject to European criticism."[31] Despite these problems, and with the consistently vocal support of Senator Fulbright, exchange programs continued to be part of America's cultural diplomacy long after the Cold War ended.

The last years of the Truman presidency, from 1950 to 1953, witnessed another turn in the history of American cultural diplomacy. Some months after the defeat of the Democrats in the election of 1952, former secretary of state Dean Acheson remarked to an audience, "Korea came along and saved us." Historians have long interpreted what Acheson meant by this somewhat cryptic statement. After all, how could the Korean War, a messy, inconclusive conflict that cost the lives of over 50,000 Americans, be seen in a positive light? Some have suggested that Acheson meant that Korea "saved" Truman's anti communist foreign policy by providing an example of communist aggression that could be used to argue for increased military spending, military assistance to America's allies, and covert activities by the newly established Central Intelligence Agency. All of that had been recommended in the influential National Security Council Study Number 68 (NSC-68) – often called the "blueprint for the Cold War" by scholars. The communist invasion of South Korea provided a vivid rationale for instituting the policies called for in NSC-68 in the name of national security.

Yet, NSC-68 contained another recommendation that attracted significantly less attention as the war in Korea ground to an unsatisfying cease-fire and sparked a tremendous jump in the American defense budget. In addition to military responses to growing Soviet power, the document argued for the "[d]evelopment of programs designed to build and maintain confidence among other peoples in our strength and resolution, and to wage overt psychological warfare calculated to encourage mass defections from Soviet allegiance and to frustrate the Kremlin design in other ways." In addition to the conflict in Korea, another ominous development spurred renewed interest in America's information programs – including cultural diplomacy. In 1950 the Soviets unleashed what came to be known as the "Hate America" offensive, a propaganda campaign that simultaneously painted the United States in the harshest and most unflattering terms possible while presenting the Soviet Union to the rest of the world as a champion for peaceful coexistence. Culture, as always, played a large role in the Soviet effort.[32] Thus, Korea and the growing intensity of the Cold War that it symbolized also came to the rescue of America's cultural diplomacy.

The U.S. response seemed straightforward enough. Edward W. Barrett, a former journalist who took over as assistant secretary of state for public affairs in 1950, laid out the strategy in his 1953 book, aptly titled *Truth Is Our Weapon*. The goal was not to "sell America." Instead, the United States was trying:

> To bring about a fuller understanding of America, its life, its government and its ideals – including faults as well as virtues – because we are convinced that America stands up well under examination and that knowledge of this nation fosters respect for it and confidence in it. We try to present a really balanced picture of America.[33]

Indeed, by 1950 Barrett oversaw the development of a comprehensive propaganda program by the United States. Naturally enough, it was named "The Campaign of Truth."[34] As American officials during the Truman years had already discovered, truth and culture did not always make for compatible bedfellows.

In his analysis of "The Campaign of Truth," former United States Information Agency (USIA) official Richard Arndt argued that "Culture or education did not appear in Barrett's program." Blatantly anti communist and pro-American propaganda replaced earlier ideas about the use of culture as a weapon of diplomacy: "Information had boldly taken over culture's kingdom."[35] There is a certain amount of truth in this interpretation, but the reality was far more complex. Although straightforward propaganda did gain the ascendancy in the Department of State's "information" programs of the early 1950s, it did not mean that its involvement in cultural diplomacy came to an end. For example, relying more heavily on private actors, State participated behind the scenes in several important showings of American art, including the 1951 exhibit in Berlin. In 1952, the department made the momentous step of formally accepting an invitation to sponsor the U.S. exhibit at the prestigious Venice Biennale. With the AFA or MOMA serving as the public faces for the overseas cultural efforts, other showings of American art traveled to France, India, and the Far East.[36]

Arndt's analysis also works from a more limited definition of "culture and education." As we have seen, America's cultural diplomacy did not always involve the fine arts – or even what might be liberally categorized as "culture." And it did not initially involve any government sponsorship. As Frederick Douglass and other abolitionists suggested in the mid-nineteenth century, there was one issue in the culture of the United States that was not only of high interest to the foreign audience but also one where the ideal and the reality of the truth about America met head to head: racism. During the Cold War, African Americans and the segregation, bigotry, and violence they faced became inextricably involved in American cultural diplomacy in ways that were often frustrating, sometimes controversial, and always problematic for the U.S. government.

Unlike the vast majority of America's cultural diplomacy efforts in the Cold War period, the programs and approaches dealing with America's race issue developed not only because of the need to counteract communist propaganda but also because of loud and sustained criticisms within the United States. For the Soviets, America's civil rights problem was easily and frequently exploited to slam the United States on the international stage. The ease resulted from the fact that the Russians did not really need to search very deeply for incriminating evidence, nor did they have to wildly exaggerate the situation. Anyone who read American newspapers or magazines in the years after 1945 could easily find racist statements, racial stereotypes, news about African Americans being denied voting rights and access to public facilities (including schools), and shocking stories about violence, including the brutal beating and blinding of Isaac Woodard, a black veteran of the Second World War, by a South Carolina policeman in 1946.[37] That all of this took place quite openly and publicly in the nation that proudly proclaimed its leadership of the "free world" provided a propaganda goldmine for the communists. In their study of the foreign press coverage of America's race problem, Richard Lentz and Karla Gower cite one typical example: "*New Times* (Moscow) sketched a devastating (and generally accurate) picture of the 'thralldom' of black Americans: They were 'paid less than whites for the same kind of work,' barred from public accommodations and from voting in many states, subject to lynchings, and so on. 'Black slavery,' it summed up, 'virtually still exists in this highly developed country'." Eschewing any subtlety at all, a cartoon in *Pravda* showed "Uncle Sam with pockets full of atom bombs strangling a chained negro on whose back he rides."[38]

It was also clear that the Soviets were simply giving the world's people what they wanted. From around the globe, U.S. officials and private travelers remarked on the intense interest in America's race problem. In much of Europe, discrimination against African Americans was considered "a permanent blot on our character." For citizens in Asia and Latin America, the prejudice and violence exhibited toward black Americans was particularly troubling, and the Soviet reports simply illuminated in the harshest way possible a central question: If the United States treated African Americans as second-class citizens at home, how could it position itself as the champion of people of color abroad?[39]

The loudest voices making the connections between America's domestic racial problem and its Cold War diplomacy, however, came from African Americans.[40] African American organizations such as the NAACP, individuals, and the influential black press combined to hammer away at the U.S. government's lack of movement on the civil rights issues. More troubling for American diplomats, however, was that one tactic coming to the fore was to link the miserable U.S. race situation with Cold War policies and suggest that discrimination against African Americans was having a real and decidedly negative impact on the nation's image abroad. Here, the African American protest at home dovetailed nicely with the troubling reports the Department of State received from official and unofficial sources abroad and the merciless barbs of communist propaganda.

The initial responses from the Department of State and other U.S. officials to the intertwining of the domestic racial situation and Cold War diplomacy bordered on righteous indignation. When the President's Commission on Civil Rights solicited input from the department regarding the impact of America's treatment of its black population in 1947, Secretary of State George C. Marshall provided a classic example. Yes, Marshall agreed, there were "isolated incidents" of racial discrimination against people of color from abroad traveling in the United States and, with breathtaking understatement, also agreed that discrimination and violence against African Americans was "alluded to frequently in the foreign press." Then, ignoring the fact that much of the communist propaganda on the issue came directly from American media sources, Marshall declared that "much of the adverse publicity abroad given to our civil rights record" was simply a communist lie. America, he argued, actually "represents a truly remarkable achievement" in the field of civil rights, but the communists insisted on jumping all over "instances of violations and discrimination" and created "embarrassment out of all proportion to the actual instances of violation." Commission officials were flabbergasted, but in their final report simply reprinted a Department of State memo that tepidly admitted that the civil rights problem could have an "adverse effect" on the nation's diplomacy.[41] However, as the Cold War accelerated abroad – particularly with the eruption of the war in Korea in 1950 – and African Americans became increasingly vocal in their demands for civil rights, naïve arguments about how the communists were maliciously distorting America's "remarkable" record on race relations simply could not be sustained. In this environment, U.S. officials came up with new approaches that they hoped would effectively silence the critics both at home and overseas.

For many years prior to the Second World War, organizations such as the NAACP and much of the African American press lambasted the Department of State for its "whites only" hiring practices. Leading black newspapers labeled State the "lily-white club." Most of the African Americans working at State held low-level positions such as cleaning people or drivers. There was even less of a chance of an African American serving abroad as a U.S. diplomat. Both the Democrats and Republicans, angling for the black vote, appointed one or two African Americans to some of the less desirable overseas postings – Liberia, Haiti, Madagascar, the Canary Islands. These quickly became known as the "negro circuit" and the handful of blacks who managed to pass the bureaucratic gauntlet in State to become part of the Foreign Service began – and ended – their careers in these posts. By the time the Second World War came to an end, only one African American served as the head of a U.S. mission overseas – as the minister to Liberia; none had ever served as a U.S. ambassador. All of that began to change in 1948–1949.[42]

In 1948 the Truman administration announced that Edward R. Dudley would be the new U.S. minister to Liberia. Dudley was certainly more than qualified for the position. During the past few years he worked as a lawyer with Thurgood Marshall in the NAACP and also did a brief stint as the legal aide to the governor of the U.S. Virgin Islands. In some ways, however, Dudley's appointment continued the trend of making "token" gestures in order to garner black votes. The 1948 election was going to be a close one and naming a well-known NAACP lawyer to Liberia might swing a few important black votes toward Truman. As the evidence makes clear, however, Dudley was put in Liberia because that nation (with its heavy production of rubber and strategic location) was becoming more important to U.S. policy in Africa. Naming Dudley, therefore, would kill two political birds with one appointment: gain the support of African Americans at home and signify to Liberia (and all of Africa, it was hoped) that the United States would now be taking a more active interest in affairs on that continent. In early 1949, after Truman's reelection, Dudley was named the first African American ambassador. If U.S. officials believed that Dudley would simply be a useful "public face" for America in Liberia they were sadly mistaken.[43]

Dudley quite capably represented U.S. interests in Liberia, but he also had another agenda – breaking the "negro circuit" and securing more, and better, opportunities for African Americans in the American diplomatic bureaucracy. In a report to the Department of State, the new U.S. ambassador to Liberia argued that naming African Americans to other posts around the world would have tremendous benefits. At home, it would provide "a splendid opportunity to refute the oft repeated charge that the President's appointment of a Negro Ambassador to Liberia is so much 'Window Dressing'." Dudley also believed that such appointments could have benefits abroad: "in view of the great problems facing our country in winning the Colored peoples of the world to our side, particularly in Asia, now is the time for our government to demonstrate that it does more than assign only one of its negro citizens to another Negro country." They would also serve as living rejoinders to communist propaganda that sneered about America's laughable attempts to solve "the Negro problem by the single appointment of a Negro Ambassador to Liberia." Although Dudley never secured an appointment elsewhere for himself, a 1986 study of his work in Liberia credited him with starting a "silent revolution" that slowly eroded the walls around the "lily-white club" and ended the rigid segregation of the "negro circuit." By the time he left Liberia in 1953, Dudley secured appointments for other African Americans who had been sent to Liberia to posts in Switzerland, France, Portugal, Denmark, India, Great Britain, and Italy.[44] Dudley's actions also prodded the Department of State to more deeply investigate the value that African Americans might have in the battle against communist propaganda. Officially and unofficially, black Americans might profitably serve as cultural ambassadors to show the world the truth about American race relations.

At first glance it might appear odd to refer to the African American diplomats sent abroad during the years of the Cold War as "cultural ambassadors." Yet, the record makes clear that in addition to their extraordinarily high qualifications for such positions (indeed, they were quite often much more qualified than their white peers in the Department of State), African Americans were also chosen to serve as symbols of America's dedication to civil rights and equality. The very fact that they were appointed as U.S. diplomats would put the lie to Soviet propaganda about the mistreatment of black Americans. Yet, Dudley's "silent revolution" in Liberia also moved U.S. officials to consider the profitable uses that might be made of other African Americans in the nation's cultural diplomatic battle with the communists.

In many ways, Dudley initiated the efforts that began to slowly tear down the walls of discrimination in the Department of State. There were others in the Department, however, who agreed with Dudley's assessment concerning the diplomatic value of not only appointing more African Americans but also making sure that they were dispersed beyond the strangling confines of the old "Negro circuit." Chester Bowles, serving as the U.S. ambassador to India, explained to his superiors in Washington that he "would like very much to have top notch Negro Foreign Service Officers assigned here." Terrific damage was being done to America's reputation because of the race issue. Having more African Americans in the U.S. mission in India would lead to more fruitful dialogue since Indians seemed to "open up much more freely to an American Negro than they will to others." The very fact that they would serve as official U.S. representatives would "help us combat to a certain extent the feeling in India about the Negro problem in the U.S." When Dudley's push for a greater range of assignments resulted in some African Americans being sent to India, Bowles was ecstatic: "The Negroes we have had have done us a world of good." In Washington, Assistant Secretary of State for Near Eastern, South Asian, and African Affairs George McGhee agreed with Bowles that the race problem was hurting the United States with people of color around the world and was happy to assist Dudley "regarding the important problem of Negro assignments in the Foreign Service." Another State official recognized the significance of having African Americans serve around the world: "it is heartening to know that this great democracy of ours does practice some of the things it preaches."[45]

Appearances, however, could be deceiving. The United States certainly did consistently jump atop the international soapbox to proclaim its dedication to equal rights for all. Putting those words into practice in the Department of State proved to be quite another matter and suggested, as the *Advancing American Art* debacle did just a few years earlier, that telling the world the truth about America was more complicated than it might seem. While the African American press justifiably celebrated the successes of Dudley and other black diplomats, the reality of the situation regarding the Department of State and civil rights was quite another matter. First and foremost, it is clear that while some officials in State supported Dudley's efforts, the department, by and large, still remained a "lily-white club." By the time Truman left office in 1953 Dudley remained the only African American serving as an ambassador. Two other African Americans had been appointed to the prestigious Foreign Service; less than 60 of the over 8,000 Foreign Service personnel serving overseas were black. Nearly half of those still worked in the posts traditionally referred to as the "Negro circuit."[46] A handful of high-profile appointments did not change the fact that African Americans still faced an uphill struggle securing a place in America's foreign policy making bureaucracy.

Perhaps more troubling was the fact that many in the Department of State firmly believed that the biggest impediment to hiring more African Americans was not the department's rigid and racially charged bureaucracy, but African Americans themselves. A 1949 memorandum, telling entitled "Countries to which an Outstanding Negro might Appropriately be sent as Ambassador," clearly laid out what the author saw as two interconnected problems. First, the memo argued that most nations around the world would resent the appointment of a black U.S. ambassador. All of Latin America (including, somewhat amazingly, Haiti) would exhibit "initial hostility" to an African American. "Arab" nations would regard such an appointment as an "affront." Asia was basically dismissed without further discussion. Even in Europe, only the Scandinavian nations were "highly civilized and enlightened and generally without the race prejudice found in other places." There were some tantalizing options, such as Romania or Bulgaria: "the appointment of an outstanding Negro as Ambassador to one of the iron curtain countries should serve to counteract the communist propaganda that Americans are guilty of race discrimination." The irony of all of this was quickly revealed by the author's use of the term "outstanding Negro." In the entire memorandum only one African American was identified as meeting the "outstanding" benchmark – Ralph Bunche.[47]

In perhaps the strangest twist of all, it was Bunche himself who most clearly illuminated the contradictions revealed by using African American diplomats as examples of the truth about America's civil rights problem. In 1949, Bunche was offered the position of assistant secretary of state for Near Eastern, South Asian, and African affairs. He had already served a brief stint in the Department of State during the Second World War, but by 1949 had turned all of his attention to his work with the United Nations. To the surprise of the Truman administration, Bunche flatly refused the job. President Truman personally met with Bunche to try and change his mind, but to no avail. When asked why he was turning down such a prestigious foreign policy making position, Bunche was unequivocal. His work with the UN was more pressing, he told reporters. But to the chagrin of the White House, a report in one of the leading African American newspapers, headlined "Bunche Blasts D.C. Jim Crow," revealed an equally important factor. Bunche stated in the story, "I have bucked segregation long enough in my lifetime. I do not intend to inflict it unnecessarily on my children," by living in the racially segregated city of Washington, DC.[48] The Truman administration hoped that naming Bunche to such a high-profile position would tell the truth it wished the world to know: that African Americans were already making significant progress in the field of civil rights and that stories to the contrary were simply pernicious rumors spread by the Soviets. Bunche, however, knew better, for he actually lived the truth of racial discrimination in America.

While the Department of State continued to be a less-than-inviting environment for African Americans, this did not deter officials at State from feeling quite free to tell the world all about black Americans. The Voice of America regularly pumped out stories such as the "Increasing Job Opportunities for Negro Women." Features on prominent ("outstanding"?) African Americans such as the author Richard Wright, singer Marian Anderson, and, without the slightest hint of irony, Ralph Bunche were aired. Publications, such as the Russian-language *Amerika*, carried articles rebutting communist propaganda about the treatment of African Americans. To ensure that its diplomats overseas could deal with the always-awkward questions about the race issue, State provided "Negro Notes" that highlighted the progress made by African Americans. The high point was reached with the 1951 publication of *The Negro in American Life*. Full of pictures, charts, and stories, this extremely polished magazine was designed for the mass audience. It offered a history of African Americans, admitting that the past had indeed been filled with racial injustice. More recently, however, "the twentieth century, for Negro and white Americans alike, has been one of notable progress." Prominent African Americans such as Louis Armstrong (and, again, Bunche) were featured. It ended on a remarkably upbeat note, with a picture of a white and a black family in a typical housing project: "These neighbors in a housing project, like millions of Americans, are forgetting whatever color prejudice they may have had; their children will have none to forget."[49]

State also considered the more direct use of some prominent African Americans by sending them abroad on government-sponsored speaking or performing tours. By 1952, one official suggested sending "one or two outstanding [that word again] negro intellectuals" abroad. Bunche was once again deemed to be adequately outstanding, but also mentioned were the journalist George Schuyler and the academic Rayford Logan. A suggestion that would gain more traction under the Eisenhower administration was to send sports figures, such as Jackie Robinson. In response, another member of the department argued that sending intellectuals would not have the same impact as sending someone like a labor leader: "we would be able to send him down *as a labor leader* and not *as a negro*. We don't have to play the negro issue. It will be played for us."[50]

Part of the problem in "playing the negro issue" by sending popular African Americans overseas as cultural ambassadors was that some of the most prominent black Americans in the world did not seem to want to play along. Certainly the most famous African American intellectual was W.E.B. Du Bois. Du Bois was a towering figure within the U.S. civil rights movement, a powerful voice within the NAACP, and a world-renowned author. In recognition of his international visibility the U.S. government accepted him as one of three members of the NAACP who attended the 1945 conference that established the United Nations. By the 1950s, however, Du Bois had worn out his welcome. The NAACP unceremoniously fired him in 1948 after his long and acrimonious battle with the organization's leader, Walter White. Of more concern for U.S. officials were Du Bois's increasingly vocal attacks on America's Cold War policies – particularly its support of its colonialist allies in Europe and its failure to recognize racism as a problem of international dimensions. When he turned out the publication *We Charge Genocide* in 1951, the break with the U.S. government was beyond repair. The document chronicled the consistently brutal treatment of African Americans. What distressed American officials, however, was his objective: to have the report submitted to the United Nations where it would be debated and, Du Bois hoped, pressure would be brought against the United States to reform its miserable civil rights record. That, as far as the Department of State was concerned, cemented the growing suspicion that Du Bois was not simply dangerous, but also a communist. Although he had been prominently featured in some of the propaganda issued by State in the late 1940s, by the early 1950s his name virtually disappeared from the publications and news stories put out by State. Du Bois no longer told the preferred truth about African Americans. In 1953, the U.S. government revoked his passport.[51]

Du Bois was not the only noteworthy African American providing their own retelling of "The Negro in American Life." The famous entertainer Josephine Baker, who scandalized audiences in the United States in the 1920s with her revealing attire and suggestive performances, gained worldwide fame after moving to Paris; she later became a French citizen. By the 1950s, however, Baker was persona non grata for Department of State officials not due to the sexual content of her act, but for her increasingly vocal assaults on racism in America as she traveled around the world. The department often alerted U.S. posts in foreign nations where Baker was to perform so that they could be ready to counter her accusations. As with Du Bois, Baker was liberally tarred and feathered as a communist and during the 1950s she was a frequent target of FBI investigations and had to run a gauntlet of harassment from the Immigration and Naturalization Service on each occasion that she traveled to the United States. Baker was a "notable Negro"; unfortunately, for American officials she sounded the wrong note in telling the truth about

African Americans. So, too, did the multitalented Paul Robeson. During the 1920s and 1930s he exploded on the American entertainment scene starring on Broadway in musicals and serious dramas, in films, and on recordings where he could highlight his extraordinary singing ability. Yet, even as he became one of the nation's most popular performers during the Second World War, Robeson's words and actions were already raising red flags for the U.S. government. He was a staunch supporter of the Republican cause in the Spanish Civil War. In addition, he spoke out loudly and frequently on the rights of labor and the dismal plight of African Americans in his country. He supported Du Bois in his efforts to get the damning *We Charge Genocide* report before the United Nations. Perhaps most troubling was his travel to the Soviet Union and his praise for the communist dedication to racial equality. By the late 1940s and early 1950s the FBI already decided that Robeson was either a Soviet patsy or a full-fledged communist supporter. As with Du Bois, the Department of State made sure that Robeson's application for a passport was denied. Robeson, like Du Bois and Baker, might still make noise, but the U.S. government was determined to make sure that at least he could not make waves abroad.[52] Given these kinds of loose cannons among African Americans perhaps, at least for now, the Department of State should handle the race issue without the use of African American middlemen to make sure that the foreign audience received the officially approved truth about blacks in America.

During the years of the Truman administration the cultural diplomacy of the United States proceeded by fits and starts. Public and congressional criticisms, vocal elements within the Department of State who were still dubious about any involvement with cultural activities, combined with uncertainties about precisely what kind of activities were available and effective, meant that the promising beginnings during the 1930s and the Second World War inched forward only incrementally during the late 1940s and early 1950s. What is also painfully obvious about these early Cold War attempts is that try as they might, U.S. officials often found themselves confounded in their goal of telling the truth about America. On paper, it seemed such a simple idea: the United States, unlike the communists, would not rely on naked propaganda. It would, calmly and clearly, tell the world the truth about American culture.

There was nothing calm, or particularly clear, about the initial forays into truth telling. Art, it was thought, would speak a universal language to the world about America's cultural maturity and leadership. Modern art would take things one step further by serving as a vibrant reminder that in the United States, at least, freedom of expression was a hallowed right. *Advancing American Art* quickly blew all of the talk about goodwill among people right off the easel. Although the exhibit turned out to be a hit with audiences in Latin America and Europe, it also turned into a publicity nightmare for the Department of State when it discovered that it was not the communists who portrayed the modern art collection as a false symbol of American democracy, but loud and significant members of the domestic audience. Congressmen, conservative art groups, and the media jumped on the art show as a waste of money and an example of government overreach into the field of culture. More damaging, however, were the complaints about the art and artists: they were most definitely *not* representative of America. In fact, some suggested, both the paintings and the painters might be something much worse – tools of communist propaganda. With little fanfare, the Department tossed the art away and from that point on mostly relied on the private sector to provide foreign audiences with examples of American culture.

Even the Voice of America, which was supposed to relay the unvarnished truth to the world – "good or bad" – found itself embroiled in political controversy when the "truth" it told did not sit well with government officials or the American media. Where was the line between information and propaganda? Should such an important task be left to the government or remain the purview of private news sources? Finally, could an organization that employed "suspect" individuals – liberals, possible communists, foreigners – really be counted on to tell the truth about America? The same held true for the poster child for "mutual understanding," the exchange program. Was understanding, or simply the direct transmission of political ideology, the main purpose? And how did one control what the foreign visitors saw in the United States? Showing the good and the bad sounded like an admirable goal, but what happened when the bad outweighed the good?

Even more problematic for any efforts to tell the truth about America was the race issue. Although recognizing that the Soviets made significant use of anti-American propaganda centered on the plight of African Americans, State mostly stuck to its guns right through the early 1950s by insisting that black Americans were making terrific progress, that the promised land of equality for all was right around the corner, and that any suggestions to the contrary were the result of communist machinations. Yet, the various attempts to utilize forms of cultural diplomacy to put forward the correct version of the American civil rights story merely served to accentuate the yawning gulf between the official "truth" and the reality. The tepid attempts at desegregating the Department of State and Foreign Service and using "token" appointments of African Americans overseas to advertise the nation's commitment to equality merely highlighted the deeply engrained racism within the American foreign policy making bureaucracy. Official complaints about the lack of "outstanding Negroes" revealed more about the state of race relations in the United States than anything the Soviets might have come up with as propaganda. The single "outstanding" African American they finally identified, Ralph Bunche, knew the score and humiliated the Truman administration by refusing to work in segregated Washington, DC. Other efforts at reframing the race issue in America for the foreign audience were equally futile. For every glowing story about "the progress of the Negro" that came out of the Department of State's information factory, there were other less flattering stories in American newspapers and magazines about the denial of voting rights and educational opportunities or even about savage attacks on African Americans. Every idea about using "prominent" African Americans abroad as cultural ambassadors for the United States was trumped by the voices of the likes of Du Bois, Baker, and Robeson. It seemed impossible in such an atmosphere to tell the truth about America – or, at least, the truth the U.S. government wanted the world to hear.

By 1953, and the election of the Republican Dwight D. Eisenhower as president, it was clear that for America's cultural diplomacy to move forward some changes had to take place. How could (or should) the U.S. government continue its cultural efforts abroad? If State, now gun-shy after the *Advancing American Art* fiasco, was unwilling to actively participate, should a new government agency be established? Or, should America take a step back and return cultural activities to the control of the private sector? In 1953, all of those questions would be answered as the Soviets began a full-fledged cultural offensive and the Eisenhower administration decided that it was time to fight fire with art, dance, ballet, music, and theater. America was poised to enter the golden age of cultural diplomacy.

CHAPTER FOUR

The Golden Age of Cultural Diplomacy, 1953–1961

During the darkest years of the Cold War in the 1950s the American public became accustomed to seeing the battle between the Free World and communism depicted through maps. Newspapers, magazines, and the U.S. government used a rather simplified cartography to depict American successes, failures, and challenges. Some, as during the Korean War, were straightforward depictions of the lines of battle arraying U.S. forces against the North Koreans and Chinese communists. Others presented a more global battlefield, color coded to impress upon the American mind the enormity of the ongoing struggle: the United States and its allies might be represented by the purity of white; the communist empire, almost inevitably, portrayed in a garish blood red; and those nations that had yet to make up their minds were denoted (as suspected communist sympathizers within the United States were) as pink. Maps were an important way in which the American people came to perceive the dangerous postwar world, replete with tiny missiles and tanks, stars and stripes, hammers and sickles, and star bursts representing areas of conflict.

In 1955, however, the American public was treated to a new geographical depiction of the Cold War in an article in the popular magazine *U.S. News & World Report* entitled "Art and Entertainment: Latest 'Cold War' Weapon for U.S." In place of armaments, or flags, or colors denoting nations' political allegiance there were simply large, capital letters imposed on various countries. An accompanying legend explained the meaning of the marks: An "A" stood for art exhibits; "B" was for ballet; "C" denoted concerts; a "D" meant drama; and, finally, an "M" was for musical comedies. This provided some guidance, but to understand what all of this had to do with the worldwide battle against communism the reader needed to dig into the accompanying article. What the map represented was the global cultural offensive being launched by the United States. In truth, the article revealed, it was really more of a counteroffensive: America was "making up for lost time" against the Soviets who were in the midst of a "big cultural drive" of their own. In this effort the U.S. government was pulling no cultural punches, sponsoring overseas tours of plays, musicals, symphony orchestras, dance companies, and even art shows. The report concluded that Americans should take pride in the fact that "judging by audience reaction" the government's cultural efforts were "doing very well in the world-wide battle developing between American and communist artists."[1] Left unsaid in the gushing review was the fact that these efforts represented something entirely new in the history of America's cultural diplomacy: for the first time, cultural initiatives were not merely being supported by the U.S. government, but actually embraced as essential tools of diplomacy. The 1955 article was nothing less than the announcement of a golden age for the nation's cultural diplomats.

It seems odd to some that the burst of cultural diplomacy initiated in the mid-1950s should come at the hands of President Dwight D. Eisenhower. As Kenneth Osgood explained in his study of U.S. propaganda programs during the Eisenhower years, "One might expect a battle-hardened soldier and fiscally conservative politician like Eisenhower to...balk at plans to spend taxpayers' money on cultural attractions." Yet, Osgood and other scholars have amply demonstrated that Eisenhower was perhaps the perfect person to resurrect the cultural diplomacy programs from the morass of indecision and backtracking created during the Truman years. At about the same time that *Advancing American Art* was being thoroughly shredded by Congress, Eisenhower appeared before a House subcommittee to argue the case for cultural programs. He urged the United States to provide funds to send exhibits and information that would be "readily comprehended by the people" abroad. Eisenhower did not, however, wish to limit the category of "culture" to the fine arts. The people of the world should know all about Americans – their "ice boxes, radios, cars, how much did [they] have to eat, what they wear, when they get to go to sports spectacles, and what they have available in the way of art galleries and things like that." Yet, Eisenhower very clearly understood the value of "art galleries and things like that." As had Americans since the time of Jefferson, Eisenhower believed that the world's understanding of the United States and its people was seriously distorted. In a letter to his brother, he complained that,

> Europeans have been taught that we are a race of materialists, whose only diversions are golf, baseball, football, horse racing, and an especially brutalized brand of boxing. Our successes are described in terms of automobiles and not in terms of worthwhile cultural works of any kind. Spiritual and intellectual values are deemed to be almost nonexistent in our country.[2]

When Eisenhower took office in 1953, it was immediately evident that a change was coming in terms of America's cultural diplomacy. As Laura Belmonte argues, the new president "accorded information activities – both overt and covert – the same stature as military, economic, and diplomatic operations."[3] Nevertheless, Eisenhower had to confront the fact that America's cultural diplomacy was still teetering by 1953. Neither Truman nor Secretary of State Dean Acheson evidenced much interest in the value of culture as a tool in the Cold War. Acheson's attitude was indicative of deeper currents of mistrust and suspicion in the Department of State, where many officials continued to believe that the cultural programs were an ineffective waste of time and resources. When *Advancing American Art* crashed into the iceberg of congressional wrath in 1946–1947, any pretense of an officially sponsored art program seemed to sink with it. After that, State was happy to pass off anything dealing with the fine arts to private sector professionals. Trying to deal with the race issue seemed to be more trouble than it was worth, particularly when so many people in the department were of the opinion that the civil rights situation was really not that bad. There had been some discussions about using African American sports figures and entertainers as cultural ambassadors, but with the press and the world seemingly more interested in troublemakers like Du Bois and Robeson it seemed safer to just let sleeping dogs lie. Telling the truth about America via culture was tougher – and more unpopular at home – than even its most ardent supporters imagined.

In addition, at the precise moment Eisenhower entered the White House with a new and clearer emphasis on cultural diplomacy Senator Joseph McCarthy was reaching the pinnacle of his destructive efforts to ferret out the communists he was certain were eating away at the bowels of the American government. By the time Eisenhower was inaugurated, McCarthy had turned his fire directly on the cultural programs overseas, arguing that he had discovered another nest of communist traitors. The Voice of America, already a veteran of congressional assaults, was the target of his first attacks. Now wielding the chairmanship of the Senate's Committee on Government Operations, McCarthy, assisted by his two most trusted investigators – Roy Cohn and David Schine – had no trouble finding people ready to accuse the VOA of malfeasance – or even worse. The VOA had long been a hotbed of internal strife, and when McCarthy went looking for complaints he found employees and former employees willing to vent. Secretary of State John Foster Dulles was well aware of the trouble McCarthy could cause and, unlike Eisenhower, had only a limited interest in the information activities of his department. In short order, Dulles threw some VOA officials under the bureaucratic bus and hoped that their sacrifice would satisfy McCarthy's appetite for attention.[4]

McCarthy, however, was just getting started. Next on his cultural hit list were the popular libraries that had been established overseas with the help of the American Library Association. Citing the need to investigate these libraries in order to root out "waste, subversion, and any left-wing library books," McCarthy unleashed his trusted bulldogs – Cohn and Schine – on unsuspecting U.S. embassies and information centers in France, Germany, Austria, Greece, Italy, Great Britain, and Yugoslavia in early 1953. Historian Kenneth Osgood summarizes the impact. Cohn and Schine:

> announced that they had found 30,000 procommunist books in the stacks. In the ensuing scandal, books by communists and "fellow travelers" were purged from the libraries and in some cases burned. The State Department issued strict orders banning anything remotely controversial from the information centers.... Before McCarthy's onslaught, approximately 120,000 books had been sent to the U.S. information centers each month. This number fell to less than 400 at the height of these investigations. McCarthy destroyed, virtually overnight, the liberal image of the United States and the goodwill fostered by the information centers. The list of banned authors was truly stunning: "Thomas Paine, Albert Einstein, Helen Keller, Henry David Thoreau, Charles Beard, W.E.B. DuBois [*sic*], Jean-Paul Sartre, Ernest Hemingway, Arthur Miller, and Upton Sinclair" were among those targeted as representing un-American thinking.[5]

All in all, it was not an auspicious start for any sort of revitalization of America's cultural diplomacy. Perhaps most disturbing for the proponents of the cultural programs was the perception that Eisenhower was giving in to McCarthy's tactics and allowing what little there was in terms of a program to be systematically destroyed. Ironically, it was the Soviet Union that gave the new president the excuse he needed to completely reshape America's approach to culture as a Cold War tool. At the exact moment that McCarthy was busily ransacking America's cultural programs, the Soviet Union was reaching the pinnacle of what came to be known as its "cultural offensive." Edward Barrett's *Truth Is Our Weapon* appeared in 1953 and alerted both the American government and its people to the danger coming from the East. Barrett warned that the Soviets, beginning in 1950, started sending tens of thousands of their artists and intellectuals abroad to serve as "unofficial" ambassadors:

> Little noted by Americans, the Soviet began, in late 1950, an ambitious intensified "cultural offensive" through use of such unofficial emissaries. It became an offensive to prove conclusively that the West, particularly the war-minded U.S., was without culture, while the peace-loving Soviet Union was virtually becoming the Athens of the Twentieth Century.... The impression gained by many millions who witnessed the performances or heard them by radio was that any nation having such skilled musicians and such delightful ballet hardly seemed a warlike monster. And maybe there was truth, they thought, to the talk that the Americans were too preoccupied with war preparations to indulge in such pursuits.

Barrett concluded with a somber assessment of what this meant for America. The Soviets, he claimed, had spent one and half billion dollars on their cultural efforts. "If America spent a comparable percentage, it would total roughly sixty-seven times the current cost of the Voice of America and all related U.S. information activities." Lest his readers miss the main point, Barrett hammered it home in no uncertain terms:

> Such is the propaganda mechanisms of America's self-styled enemy. Its output is cold, calculated, and virulent. It steals such terms as "peace" and "democracy" and distorts them. It is seemingly bound by no budgetary considerations.... On one point there can be no doubt: Malenkov, like Stalin, endorses fully the words of Lenin that 'propaganda is of crucial importance for the eventual triumph of the Party.'[6]

The Soviet understanding of the power of culture was accelerated by a change in leadership. On March 5, 1953 (just one month before the Cohn-Schine invasion of Europe) Joseph Stalin passed away. The man who emerged as his successor, Nikita Khrushchev, seemed to grasp the possibilities of cultural diplomacy more fully than Stalin. In her study of American and Soviet uses of culture in the Cold War, Cadra Peterson McDaniel notes that "For the Soviet leadership, the arts played a crucial role in foreign policy and were assumed to be an instrumental weapon in spreading Communist ideology. Khrushchev and his generation considered the global success of Soviet culture of monumental importance. Khrushchev, in particular, praised the Soviet system for making him a cultured individual." Indeed, culture was to be a powerful force in the worldwide communist revolution: "The arts' ideological role was further evidenced in comments by Soviet leader Nikita Khrushchev who stated that '[t]he press and radio, literature, art, music and cinema and theater are a sharp ideological weapon of our Party. And the Party sees to it that that weapon should be kept ready for action at all times and strike telling blows at our enemies.'"[7]

Eisenhower might have been timid in dealing with McCarthy's reckless attacks, but his own understanding of the power and usefulness of propaganda and cultural diplomacy, combined with the increasingly visible and threatening Soviet cultural offensive, pushed him to take dramatic action almost as soon as he entered office in 1953. Although Eisenhower deeply respected Secretary of State Dulles, he was also keenly aware that Dulles wanted his department free of the cultural programs. The assaults on the VOA and the overseas libraries cemented Dulles's view that such efforts provided easy targets for congressional critics. Eisenhower's solution was to propose a completely new government office to handle all information and cultural activities. In August 1953, the United States Information Agency (USIA) was created.[8]

As scholars who have looked at the history of the USIA concede, the name of the new agency was a bit misleading. It did not, for instance, hold a monopoly on information activities overseas – the Central Intelligence Agency and the military, for example, kept a hold on their own overt and covert propaganda operations. In addition, although a separate agency in name, USIA remained closely tied to the Department of State. Dulles and other officials in State might have been relieved to rid themselves of the problematic cultural programs, but they did not want the new agency to be a completely independent player. As Osgood notes, "In deference to Dulles's wishes, Eisenhower required that the USIA act according to policy guidance developed by the State Department. The USIA was subordinate to the Department of State and was initially excluded from permanent representation on both the NSC and the OCB [Operations Coordinating Board]."[9] Despite these limitations, the USIA represented a tremendous step forward for America's cultural diplomacy.

The basic goal of the USIA remained unchanged from earlier U.S. activities in the informational and cultural fields: to tell the truth about America and its people. A few months after Eisenhower set up the agency the National Security Council (NSC) met to formalize the USIA's goals. Much of it must have sounded very familiar to the handful of State employees who witnessed the information programs during and immediately after the Second World War. The agency would show the world's people that the "objectives and policies of the United States are in harmony with and will advance their legitimate aspirations for freedom, progress, and peace." And, of course, it would also work toward the goal of "unmasking and countering hostile attempts to distort or to frustrate the objectives and policies of the United States." There were also, however, distinct hints about the new cultural thrust of the USIA. It would achieve its mission by "depicting imaginatively the correlation between U.S. policies and the legitimate aspirations of other peoples in the world." The only specific suggestion the NSC had to make in regard to how to do so was by directing the USIA to illuminate "those important aspects of the life and culture of the people of the United States which facilitate understanding of the policies and objectives of the Government of the United States."[10] In this way, the NSC report made it quite clear that the cultural programs would not exist for their own sake simply to create international goodwill. Henceforth, culture would serve policy. With this directive in place, it was obvious that things were about to change for the nation's cultural diplomacy. Unlike the timidity and frustration that led to only incremental cultural efforts during the Truman years, the USIA, with Eisenhower's support, was now given its marching orders and acted quickly to greatly expand both the scope and array of programs used to reach the international audience and achieve America's aims and simultaneously blunt the Soviet cultural offensive. The Russians might be able to mount their charges to the strains of Tchaikovsky or bombard foreign audiences with the Bolshoi Ballet. As the map in the

1955 *U.S. News & World Report* indicated, the gloves were now off and the United States was prepared to mount its own cultural offensive.

Yet, despite all that was new about America's cultural diplomacy under Eisenhower many things remained the same. Although the USIA was understood by much of the American public (and the wider world) to be the main force behind the nation's overseas cultural efforts, this was only partially true. While the Department of State was more than happy to have the new agency handle the politically ticklish art program, it remained a significant player in the cultural field. Dulles might have been less than enamored with the use of music, art, or theater as diplomatic tools, but many officials working under him still believed that not only could culture be an important weapon, it could also be effective. In addition, the fact that the Soviets were so blatantly using their own cultural products as propaganda tools forced even the most reluctant cultural diplomat to reconsider the idea that the USIA should have a monopoly in the field. Thus, while the agency handled many exhibitions (including the art program), State remained a primary force in the performing arts – music and theater, for example.

To make matters more complicated, neither the USIA nor the Department of State wanted to be in direct control of the cultural products sent overseas. Perhaps still stinging from the *Advancing American Art* disaster, both offices looked for assistance from the private sector – to provide both artistic integrity and, even more important, distance themselves from any domestic criticisms concerning government involvement with the arts. The solution arrived in the form of the American National Theater and Academy (ANTA). Established in 1935, ANTA's primary mission was the "advancement of interest in the drama throughout the United States of America by furthering in the production of the best plays." It gradually spread its interests into other fields – musicals and ballet, for instance. ANTA was no stranger to working with the government. During the 1940s and early 1950s, it often assisted the Department of State in ensuring U.S. participation in international drama festivals and had been the primary organizing force for the Berlin Cultural Festival in 1951. In 1954, State signed an agreement with ANTA that gave the organization the responsibility "to choose artists or to handle the numerous details regarding contracts, performance spaces, programs, travel arrangements, and schedules that would require attention." State and the USIA would provide the financial backing, ask for particular programs for particular regions, make suggestions as to the artists included in the programs, and handle things like advertising the events and setting up supporting events (lectures, for example) in the foreign nations.[11]

Despite the veneer of private direction of the overseas cultural programs provided by ANTA, it was clear from the beginning that the USIA and State exercised ultimate power in terms of both the content and purpose of America's international cultural efforts. Lisa Davenport, in her study of the jazz component of the cultural program, argues that "The State Department maintained final authority in approving all musical and dramatic selections and advocated the 'utmost discretion in the selection of artists'." By 1957, a "rating system" was in place that "helped assess the integrity, personal attributes, musical abilities, and 'Americanness' of artists proposed for American tours." The USIA was active in "determining what types of artists would perform and which themes performers would emphasize."[12]

If the U.S. government hoped that this arrangement would eliminate the controversies associated with past cultural programs, this proved to be a futile hope. As we shall see, domestic attacks continued unabated and conflict between State, the USIA, and private cultural organizations revealed anew the problems inherent in using culture as a means to tell the world the truth about America. In particular, one truth – civil rights in America – remained, as one report put it, the nation's "Achilles heel." Nevertheless, with Eisenhower's blessing the United States embarked on a full-frontal cultural assault utilizing classical music, jazz, modern and traditional painting and sculpture, books, opera, theater, dance, and even sports that would climax in 1958 and 1959 with the largest – and most controversial – cultural efforts yet undertaken.

At least initially, State and the USIA concentrated their efforts on examples of "high" culture – classical music and dance were two areas that attracted a great deal of attention. Perhaps this was due to the fact that two of the strongest elements in the Soviet cultural arsenal were the classical works of great Russian composers and dance, particularly ballet. As Danielle Fosler-Lussier noted in her study of music and American cultural diplomacy in the Cold War, the members of ANTA's Music Advisory Panel typically tried to be fair in evaluating projects, but on the basis of their personal preferences they steered musicians away from popular music. In 1955, for instance, the panel agreed that "show tunes and folk music should be discouraged, as there are no standards by which to judge 'light music' except 'charm,' and charm is hard to judge, and is not international in its acceptance."

Classical music also better fit the needs of American diplomacy, since the aim of the cultural program was to demonstrate to the world that the United States was also a leader in the field of arts. While much of the music played by America's symphonies and orchestras was European in origin, Fosler-Lussier makes a critical point about its value: "Crucially, the European tradition of classical music was imbued with social prestige – and its prestige was more widely recognized than the numbers of listeners would suggest."[13]

The U.S. government wasted no time in launching an impressive assault by some of America's finest orchestras. The Philadelphia Orchestra was one of the first to go abroad, landing in Europe in mid-1955 and hitting all of the cultural hotspots in France, Austria, West Germany, and elsewhere. On the other side of the world the Symphony of the Air performed throughout the Far East, including Japan, South Korea, and Hong Kong. Soon afterward, it was announced that the New York Philharmonic would follow the trail blazed by the Philadelphia Orchestra and play throughout Europe. In 1956, there would be even more tours by the New Orleans Philharmonic, the Los Angeles Philharmonic, the Symphony of the Air (this time to the Middle East), and the biggest bombshell of them all – the Boston Symphony Orchestra would become the first American orchestra to play in the Soviet Union. It eventually performed to enthusiastic audiences in Leningrad and Moscow.[14]

Since dance was a high-profile part of the Russian cultural weaponry, U.S. officials put this art form high on their own performing arts agenda. However, dance was a somewhat trickier proposition. First and foremost, the Soviets simply had more firepower. The Bolshoi Ballet was world renowned as the finest ballet company in the world. Even the lesser-known Moiseyev Dance Company made an impressive splash when it performed in London in 1955. As one reporter noted, "The Igor Moiseyev Ensemble from Moscow exploded in London this November like an A-Bomb." In addition, as Naima Prevots observes in her study of American dance and cultural diplomacy, the panel of music experts working under ANTA was reluctant to send some of the more avant-garde American dance companies abroad. Hesitant to confront the Russians on the ballet front and too timid to sponsor dance groups that appeared *too* modern, the dance portion of America's cultural diplomacy certainly faced its share of challenges.[15]

Despite these problems, dance played an important role in the early stages of the new U.S. cultural offensive. In fact, one of the first large-scale programs mounted with support from the U.S. government was the sending of the José Limón Company on an extended tour of South America in late 1954. The effort was notable because so many of the initial programs were directed at Europe and, in some ways, could be seen carrying on the initiatives begun during the 1930s and 1940s in Latin America. Much more publicity, both at home and abroad, came from the Asian tour of the Martha Graham Company from late 1955 through early 1956. Graham was a leader in the development of American modern dance, and she was also no stranger to negotiating with the U.S. government to help sponsor the overseas journeys of her dance troupe. In her insightful work into the foreign tours of Graham's dance company in 1955 (and again in 1974), Victoria Phillips Geduld astutely describes the political and diplomatic purposes U.S. officials hoped the Asian trip would address. The company's long trip through Asia carried it through Burma, India, Indonesia, the Philippines, and several other nations in the region. As a tool of cultural diplomacy in an area being wracked with revolution and anticolonialism (the tour came on the heels of the French defeat in Vietnam in 1954), Graham's dance repertoire seemed perfect: "Because the Department of State sought to repair relations after the war and create alliances in Asia to promote American political ideologies, Graham's work was particularly useful: demonstrating cutting-edge ingenuity, Graham's dance modernism fused Asian aesthetics with the distinctive characteristics of the American landscape." American officials were also convinced that Graham's modern dance would play well with important elites in Asia since, "Traditionally, Graham's works had been received by the intelligentsia, and thus neatly suited the State Department desire to engage elites with high art." During the successful and popular Asian tour, Graham and her dancers worked closely with Department of State officials to publicize the performances and mingle with the Asian elites who attended.[16]

While appealing to elite audiences abroad with classical music and dance was certainly a primary aim of much of America's initial attempts at cultural diplomacy under Eisenhower, U.S. officials quickly discovered that another more "popular" form of American culture could also be a potent weapon. Jazz became a staple of American cultural diplomacy during the late 1950s, largely because of the foreign demand for this uniquely American art form. Requests from U.S. posts around the world poured into the Department of State and the USIA requesting jazz music and performers. Jazz, however, was problematic for America's cultural diplomats. A main purpose of the nation's cultural diplomacy was to demonstrate to other nations that America had class and taste; that it was more than the Hollywood version of the nation that emphasized crime, drinking, and illicit activities. Jazz musicians and their audience, however, seemed to relish their "outsider" reputation. Movies emphasized the less savory aspects – music played in dark, smoke-filled clubs populated by less than reputable males and openly sexual women. Equally troublesome for many Americans was the fact that jazz was often referred to as "colored music." While a number of white jazz musicians plied their trade, for the public at large jazz remained largely the domain of African Americans. And as U.S. officials discovered during the late 1940s and early 1950s utilizing black Americans as cultural ambassadors could prove troublesome to say the least.

Eventually, however, American policymakers came to see jazz as a valuable Cold War weapon. Although the music did not fit the aura of high-class sophistication that these officials tried to create through sending examples of "fine culture" abroad, jazz was an undeniably *American* music. As Kenneth Osgood explains,

> The problem, the *New York Times* pointed out in a front-page story, was that there was nothing uniquely American in the traveling performances by orchestras and ballet troupes. Jazz music, on the other hand, was America's "Secret Sonic Weapon," a truly American product with great propaganda value, "for to be interested in jazz is to be interested in America."[17]

The fact that Soviet officials consistently denounced jazz, at the same time that many Russians clamored for the music, was just icing on the propaganda cake. The communist government denounced modern Western art forms as an assault on the "purity of Soviet art," and singled out jazz as "bedlam from the decadent West." This did not stop the Russian people from listening, however. According to Lisa Davenport, American jazz entered the Soviet Union via radio broadcasts on the VOA while "Soviet jazz musicians also smuggled jazz records into the country from Western and Eastern Europe and traded jazz records on the black market."[18]

In addition, the fact that many of the top jazz performers were African American (and that many of the jazz groups were integrated) meant "the State Department could try to undermine the prevalent belief that the United States was nothing more than a nation of segregationists."[19] This became especially important as racial tensions in the United States continued to increase during the Eisenhower years following the Supreme Court's controversial 1954 decision ordering the desegregation of American public schools, the arrest of Rosa Parks, the successful boycott of public buses in Montgomery, Alabama, led by the relatively unknown Martin Luther King, Jr., and culminating in the gruesome murder of fourteen-year-old Emmitt Till in Mississippi in August 1955 after he supposedly made "improper" advances toward a white woman.[20] For U.S. officials, jazz bands – particularly those led by African Americans – were viewed as a way to both utilize the popular music as a cultural weapon and effectively address the nagging racial issue.

The initial government attempt to introduce the world to American jazz, however, came not via live performances but through the Voice of America radio, most particularly what became the most popular program on VOA, *Music America*, a one-hour show hosted by Willis Conover. The program, estimated to attract upward of thirty million listeners, featured jazz and other contemporary American music. Conover himself attracted quite a fan base and often toured abroad under the auspices of the Department of State. But nothing could replace the real thing, and in 1956 jazz legend Dizzy Gillespie began a tour that eventually took him and his band through Iran, Turkey, Yugoslavia, Greece, Syria, Lebanon, and Pakistan. As a news report on Gillespie's travels noted, "In some places the people had never heard of jazz …, but the music was received with wild enthusiasm and the musicians were treated like heroes."[21] In the years that followed, nearly every important American jazz and swing musician went abroad under the auspices of the U.S. government, including Benny Goodman (who led an integrated band), the New Orleans jazz musician Wilbur de Paris (who took his group to Africa), Dave Brubeck, and Duke Ellington. For nearly a decade, jazz was the biggest cultural gun in the American arsenal.[22]

Another facet of U.S. cultural diplomacy during the Eisenhower years seemed both counterintuitive and a bit old-fashioned. Since the end of the Second World War, the use of culture as a tool of international relations had been seen as a forceful means of countering the misperceptions among friends (and the propaganda spread by the Soviets) that the United States was a cultural wasteland – a nation of gadgets and machines, all used to fulfill the insatiable materialism and militarism that were the foundations of American society. The idea that examples of American consumer goods, or industrial machinery, or technology might also be cultural weapons struck many U.S. cultural diplomats as simply playing directly into the hands of anti-American stereotypes. What was needed was opera, not cars; theater, not kitchen appliances; books, not bombs.

In fact, however, examples of American technical, military, and industrial might had already been used, and used successfully, as parts of the U.S. cultural assault since at least the late 1800s. At world's fairs in Philadelphia and Chicago, and at international expositions such as the one in Bordeaux in 1907, the accomplishments of American factories and laboratories were used to cement the nation's claim to great power status. At Buffalo Bill's Wild West shows European audiences were instructed in how rifles and pistols – as much as grit and determination – helped to "settle" the problems with Native Americans. Even as late as the Second World War, the OWI found that foreign audiences often responded quite positively to examples of U.S. industrial and military prowess. After all, a film about the lowly jeep proved to be one of the most popular films produced by the wartime office. Eisenhower, who saw and appreciated the work of the OWI, and officials within the new USIA quickly concluded that focusing just on the traditional forms of cultural diplomacy – art, music, dance, theater – was shortsighted. Utilizing the nation's greatest strengths – its industrial might and scientific breakthroughs – could be equally effective if showcased in the proper way. Two high-profile examples of this thinking were found in the "Atoms for Peace" and "People's Capitalism" campaigns inaugurated between 1953 and 1956.

On December 8, 1953, President Dwight Eisenhower spoke to the General Assembly of the United Nations and focused on the rising threat of nuclear warfare. In his analysis of Eisenhower's speech Martin J. Medhurst argues that it was "a carefully-crafted piece of cold war rhetoric specifically designed to gain a 'psychological' victory over the Soviet Union." Although it became known as the "Atoms for Peace" speech, the first sections of the talk were straightforward warnings to the Soviets about the "United States' stockpile of atomic weapons, which, of course, increases daily," and that have become, in fact, "conventional status" within the various branches of the U.S. armed forces, all of which were "capable of putting this weapon to military use." Despite having already achieved a "quantitative advantage" in nuclear weapons over the Soviets, the development of new atomic weapons would be "accelerated and expanded." The speech, however, took an abrupt turn when Eisenhower declared, "The United States, heeding the suggestion of the General Assembly of the United Nations, is instantly prepared to meet privately with such other countries as may be 'principally involved,' to see 'an acceptable solution' to the atomic armaments race." It would not be enough to simply "take this weapon out of the hands of the soldiers. It must be put into the hands of those who will know how to strip its military casing and adapt it to the arts of peace." To that end, Eisenhower urged all nations to make contributions from their atomic stockpiles to an "Atomic Energy Agency" to be used to "serve the peaceful pursuits of mankind. Experts would be mobilized to apply atomic energy to the needs of agriculture, medicine, and other peaceful activities. A special purpose would be to provide abundant electrical energy in the power-starved areas of the world."[23]

The newly established USIA acted quickly to make sure that the world was deluged with copies of Eisenhower's sensational speech. Short documentary films were produced that emphasized the possible peaceful uses of atomic power, such as *The Atom and Agriculture* and *The Atom and the Doctor*. Even more audacious were the touring exhibits sent up by the agency to take the message directly to the overseas public. These touring exhibitions were composed of posters, films, lectures, reading materials, and small displays of the peaceful uses to which the power of the atom might be put. These shows were seen by millions: "In 1954, the agency sent touring exhibitions to Italy, Germany, Spain, the Netherlands, and Britain. The exhibit reached India and Pakistan in 1955. In São Paulo, Brazil, 400,000 people visited it during its first six months."[24]

Certainly the most controversial showing of the Atoms for Peace exhibit came in Hiroshima in 1956. Organizing the exhibition in one of the two cities in the world to have suffered through the horrors of atomic warfare struck some in the U.S. government as absurd. When discussions about the possibility of sending the exhibit to Hiroshima began in late 1954 and 1955, "there were compelling reasons against both showing it in 1955 and its inauguration in Hiroshima. We felt that in any case the exhibition might be closely identified with the bomb, thus defeating the real purpose of President Eisenhower's atoms for peace program." Proponents of the idea, however, argued that "the real purpose was of course to disassociate the bomb from nuclear energy," and even some Japanese began to support the exhibit as a way to move beyond the pain of the 1945 bombing toward a more peaceful and prosperous future fueled – quite literally – by atomic power. When the decision was finally reached to open the exhibit in 1956 the USIA went all out to woo visitors and calm the fears of many who thought of atoms as harbingers of death, not peace. One target was women, who were "especially attracted to the guides who were dressed in the latest American fashions." Big, bold colors and massive banners and posters were used to attract the audience and give the exhibit "a festive atmosphere." Once inside, the Japanese saw "a full-scale model of an experimental nuclear reactor, a model illustrating a nuclear fission reaction that used electric lights and panel displays that introduced nuclear physics." Atomic power was sold as something that would lead to "revolutionizing daily life and leisure for the Japanese." There were even interactive displays, such as the "magic hands," which was a mechanical arm designed to handle dangerous radioactive materials but now used to "pick up a brush and write 'heiwa' (peace) and 'genshi ryoku' (nuclear energy)." Despite complaints from some Japanese observers that also being brushed aside were the implicit dangers of nuclear power, the exhibition proved to be immensely popular, attracting over one million visitors.[25]

The Atoms for Peace campaign was successful because it utilized technology as a force for human progress. Selling America's economic success – in other words, selling capitalism – was viewed as more problematic. How could America use its immense production of a vast number of consumer goods as part of its cultural diplomacy without providing unintentional support to communist propaganda about the crass materialism of the United States and/or coming off as an international braggart by literally pushing its industrial products in the face of the foreign audience? The answer came in 1956 with the announcement of the newest USIA effort, People's Capitalism.

As with so many U.S. cultural diplomacy programs, People's Capitalism was the result of cooperation between official and unofficial sources. Theodore Repplier, the president of the Advertising Council, represented the unofficial side. In 1955 he traveled to American diplomatic posts in Africa, Asia, and Europe under the auspices of the Eisenhower administration to review and report on the success of the U.S. information and cultural programs. His conclusions went right to one of the old issues facing those programs: "American information policies had been doomed from the start because they aimed at giving 'a full and fair picture' of the United States, a nation so diverse that to do justice to this aim would naturally lead to contradictions, confusion, incomprehensibility." His solution was simply to apply the lessons of advertising: the "selection of a few key truths that forward the chosen objectives, and the movement of these truths from paper to mind with the force and frequency to make them stick." The slogan he developed was "People's Capitalism," and working with USIA experts on exhibits he helped to bring to life an entire traveling exhibition, "People's Capitalism – A New Way of Living." The People's Capitalism exhibit was given a trial run at Union Station in Washington, DC. Visitors started out viewing a log cabin that "symbolized the nation's origins." Very quickly, however, one learned that from these humble origins had emerged an industrial giant. Right next to a nail-making machine from the late 1700s (which produced a mere sixteen nails per hour) was its modern brother, now churning out over 16,000 nails an hour. The highlight of the tour was a reconstruction of a "typical" modern American home overflowing with furniture and appliances. When some officials noted that the modern house looked almost too good and pristine, "used" furniture and appliances took their place. Neatly typed signs accompanying the exhibits made the message clear: economic rewards in America were "shared with the workers," allowing the United States to become a "middle-income nation" where "everybody became a capitalist." The show started its international run in Colombia in November 1956 where nearly a quarter-million people toured the exhibit. Equally successful showings followed in other nations in Latin America, and the exhibit eventually made its way to Asia before "budgetary and logistical problems forced the Agency to suspend the exhibits for 1957."[26] Nevertheless, the idea of using America's vast consumer and industrial wealth in America's cultural diplomacy campaign had gained an important foothold that would grow even stronger during the last years of the Eisenhower administration.

In dealing with the race issue, the USIA also utilized some new approaches with varying levels of effectiveness. The success of the jazz program prodded U.S. officials to reconsider their earlier qualms about using "notable" African Americans as cultural ambassadors. With the angrier voices of figures such as Robeson, Du Bois, and Baker effectively muzzled or marginalized, the American government now went full speed ahead in utilizing African Americans as both purveyors of culture that might appeal to the foreign audience and as symbols of the U.S. dedication to equality for all. Initially, these efforts were largely confined to the older practice of simply featuring prominent African Americans – such as Louis Armstrong, famous black athletes, and newly appointed Undersecretary of Labor J. Ernest Wilkins in print and radio stories put out by State and the USIA.[27] After the successes scored by black jazz musicians, however, the foreign audience was treated to more and more face-to-face encounters with African Americans.

The Eisenhower administration continued the search for "outstanding" African Americans to serve as official U.S. representatives to "appropriate" nations abroad. And, just as occurred during the Truman years, State Department officials clung to the notion that both the personnel and places were in short supply. African Americans made almost no headway in achieving either an increased number of black Foreign Service officers or an expanded list of available postings overseas. There remained but one African American ambassador, again to an African nation, when Eisenhower left office: John H. Morrow, who was appointed to Guinea in 1959. To try and silence both civil rights activists at home and the Soviets, who continued to hammer away at the United States at the United Nations, Eisenhower and Dulles did approve a number of African Americans as U.S. representatives to the international organization.[28]

As "unofficial" U.S. representatives, however, African Americans found greater opportunities. Journalist Carl Rowan visited India and other nations in South and Southeast Asia with government support. He gave frequent lectures where he was "ALWAYS" asked about race relations in America. In his 1956 book chronicling his trip, Rowan stated that he tried to deal with the matter as directly as possible, but concluded that "the deft fingers of international communism were manipulating my audiences." He went on from his travels to attend the Bandung Conference of 1955 (and became Director of the USIA in 1964).[29] Marian Anderson achieved national and international success in the late 1920s and 1930s with her classically trained voice and in 1955 became the first African American to perform at the Metropolitan Opera. She had often been cited in State and USIA propaganda on the race issue, and in 1957 she accepted an invitation from the American government to do a tour of Asia and sang in such nations as the Philippines, South Vietnam, South Korea, and Pakistan. The long tour proved immensely popular and Anderson was "a highly appealing U.S. cultural ambassador." Her appeal for the U.S. government was not difficult to discern: "Because she performed an art form derived from Europe, she presented African Americans as a vibrant component of American and international life, showcased the exuberance of American culture, and helped redress the American dilemma without the racial stigmas and implications of jazz."[30]

Aside from the jazz performances, however, perhaps the best known of the American cultural weapons utilizing African Americans was the opera *Porgy and Bess*. The show, written in 1934 by George Gershwin, achieved only moderate success in the United States during the 1930s and 1940s; it was not performed in Europe until 1943, ironically in Nazi-occupied Copenhagen with an all-white cast wearing blackface makeup. After a few performances the show was closed when the Nazi Gestapo threatened to blow up the theater. During the early and mid-1950s, however, the opera got a new lease on life as it toured overseas almost nonstop, often supported by the U.S. government. Ellen Noonan, in her extensive study of the history of the show, argues that "the barrage of publicity that accompanied its four-year tour…transformed *Porgy and Bess* from a reasonably well-known opera into a cultural mainstay." It certainly became a mainstay in America's cultural diplomacy, largely because it served so many different purposes. As Noonan explains, even though the opera presented a portrait of African Americans living in poverty and segregation, "it also celebrated the glorious cultural achievement of American citizen George Gershwin." Yet, it could also serve as effective propaganda trumpeting civil rights progress. First, "the offstage identities of the cast embodied American racial progress and opportunity." U.S. officials made sure that the all-black cast had ample opportunities to mingle with the foreign audience before and after shows. Finally, the simple fact that the U.S. government sponsored *Porgy and Bess* with its African American cast was "intended to convince the world that incidents of racial discrimination and violence were exceptional rather than typical." With all of these advantages, it was hardly surprising that the opera was one of the first overseas shows sponsored by the United States in 1954, traveling to Yugoslavia, Egypt, Italy, Greece, Israel, Morocco, and Spain, and again in 1955 when it toured Latin America.[31]

African American sports figures presented another interesting opportunity for America's cultural diplomats in the 1950s. Many could remember the stirring victories scored by Jesse Owens in the 1936 Olympic Games in Hitler's Berlin. Jackie Robinson had just broken the color line in professional baseball in 1947, and he and some of the black players who followed were featured in a 1953 USIA publication, "The American Negro in Baseball." The increasing dominance of African Americans in the sport of boxing was also noted in USIA features on Henry Armstrong (who held the titles in three weight classes at the same time in the late 1930s) and Jersey Joe Walcott, a former heavyweight champion.[32] Yet, reading about these sports heroes was one thing. Seeing African American athletes in action would, it was thought, be even better since not only would the foreign audience be entertained, it would also – as with the other government-sponsored African American cultural diplomats – be a living rebuttal to communist propaganda. In 1956 the Department of State sponsored a goodwill tour of American tennis stars, including the first African American woman to win the French Open, Althea Gibson. U.S. officials also relied on trips abroad by the Harlem Globetrotters. The comedic kings of basketball actually got their start as sports ambassadors when the government sponsored them on a trip to West Berlin just prior to the 1951 Berlin Cultural Festival. Over 75,000 people came out to watch the team and the Department of State took notice, quickly aiding with the global distribution of a film, *The Harlem Globetrotters*, produced by Columbia Pictures and then sponsoring a trip by the team to Latin America in 1952. Throughout the remainder of the 1950s the Globetrotters lived up to their name, traversing the globe – including a visit to the Soviet Union in 1959 – sometimes with direct support from the government, sometimes as a purely business arrangement, but always under the careful eye of U.S. officials eager to use the team as a symbol of American sportsmanship and racial equality.[33]

The touring tennis pros, featuring Althea Gibson, and the world travels of the Globetrotters also served to highlight the fact that sports was becoming another important area of contest in the cultural Cold War. Sending star athletes overseas, however, was a sort of hit-or-miss proposition – sometimes the audiences barely knew who was being introduced or had even seen the individual's sport. The Globetrotters were fine for entertainment but more people came to see the clowning than the competition. Besides, since Russia did not have professional athletes there was little opportunity to demonstrate American superiority in sporting contests. That all changed in the summer of 1952, when the Soviet Union made its first appearance at the Olympics.

Since coming to power in the midst of the First World War the Soviets had studiously ignored the Olympic games. However, by the 1930s many nations – including the Soviet Union and the United States – were increasingly aware that international sporting events were not merely shows of amateur sportsmen engaging in dedication and good sportsmanship. They were, in fact, arenas where contests for national prestige were often played out. Although the "Nazi Olympics" of 1936 are perhaps best remembered by historians today, Barbara Keys explains in her study of sports and diplomacy in the 1930s that the United States fired the first shot by hosting the 1932 games in Los Angeles. According to Keys, "The 1932 Games marked the metamorphosis of the Olympics from a relatively marginal and elitist event into an entertainment extravaganza with wide popular appeal. As such, the staging of the 1932 Games represents the single greatest contribution of the United States to the development of international sport before World War II." And Americans in both the public and private sphere used the games to highlight American culture and gain respect and support for the United States. Hitler's Nazi regime certainly understood this new power, hosting the 1936 games in an effort to both bolster the nation's world reputation and demonstrate the superiority of the Aryan superman. Although the dominating performances by African American Jesse Owens put something of a damper on Nazi enthusiasm, the Berlin Olympics dramatically illustrated the power of sports in international relations. The Soviets stayed away from the Olympics, but as Keys suggests, by the 1930s the communist regime could no longer deny that sports was now an area where athletes, instead of soldiers, could engage in national conflicts. Soviet soccer teams began to travel and play outside of Russia, and soon other sports such as boxing and track and field saw occasional appearances by Russian amateurs.[34]

In 1952 the Soviets went after bigger trophies, announcing that its athletes would participate in the summer games to be held in Helsinki, Finland. These were the second summer Olympics since the end of the Second World War. In the 1948 games in London the United States thoroughly dominated, winning nearly twice as many medals as the second-place team. Now, however, the world waited for the clash of Americans and Soviets in Helsinki. For the Russians, the goal was clear: "The Soviets were intent upon using athletics to display before the world the rapidity of its advancement." Clear, too, was the Soviet success: although the United States won nearly twice as many gold medals, it barely edged out the Russians for the total medal count, seventy-six to seventy-one. Almost immediately, U.S. officials began planning for the 1956 summer games scheduled for Melbourne, Australia. The president of the Amateur Athletic Union of the United States fumed, "We saw a red danger signal at Helsinki and the red was Russia."[35]

For the American government, the real battle for Melbourne would be fought on the cultural and propaganda level. Even before the games took place the USIA was busy emphasizing that the Soviet athletes were "amateur" in name only – they received significant amounts of state funding – and that the athletes themselves were on a short leash held by their communist masters. Through an avalanche of posters, pamphlets, news stories, photographs, and short films, the USIA sought to portray the athletic events in Melbourne as part of a larger battle between freedom and totalitarianism. The materials sought to emphasize the role of the United States "in upholding Olympic principles of peace and fellowship, as opposed to pursuing a political agenda." In his study of the Olympics and the Cold War, Toby Rider found that much of the USIA output tended to focus on individual athletes. Women, for example, were highlighted for their achievements and status within American society, in contrast to Soviet propaganda that portrayed them as frivolous party girls or unhappy homemakers trapped by their bourgeois surroundings. The race issue was also covered through publications that "attempted to present an image of U.S. racial and ethnic diversity through portraits of U.S. Olympians."[36]

Once the Games began, however, it was the Soviets who dominated. Not only did the Russians win more gold medals than the United States, they crushed the United States in the total count, outdistancing the Americans by twenty-four medals. One of the few consolations for the defeated U.S. team was heavyweight boxer Pete Rademacher's first-round knockout of his Russian opponent to take the gold medal.[37] The United States also managed to score some important propaganda points in Melbourne. Coming just months after Soviet troops smashed the Hungarian Revolution, American newspapers gleefully reported the clash of the water polo teams from Russia and Hungary that soon devolved into a brawl that left the swimming pool water crimson with blood. Even more grist for the American propaganda mill was provided by the defection of nearly forty athletes from Eastern European nations after the games concluded.[38]

The 1956 Summer Olympics also saw the art program seemingly rise from the ashes of *Advancing American Art*. In fact, the art program never entirely disappeared. During the late 1940s and early 1950s the Department of State worked – quietly, to be sure – with private groups such as the American Federation of Arts, the Museum of Modern Art (MOMA), and the Smithsonian Institution to send American art into West Germany and elsewhere in Europe. MOMA handled most of the U.S. shows at the prestigious Venice Biennale. By 1955–1956, the USIA was ready to try again and directly sponsor some important American art exhibits – often featuring modern art. In 1955–1956, the agency announced that it was working with the AFA for the preparation of three major exhibits for shows overseas: *Universities Collect, American Painting, 1900–1950*, and the jewel in the cultural diplomacy crown, *Sport in Art*.[39]

Sport in Art seemed the perfect answer to all of the past critics who suggested that the art shows sent overseas did not truly represent America. What was more American than sports? The resulting collection was the result of collaboration between the USIA, AFA, and America's leading sports magazine, *Sports Illustrated*. It encompassed over 100 works of art including paintings and watercolors, sketches and drawings, and even sculpture all centered on the theme of sports. Although some of the art was modern in nature, the exhibit also featured some of the best works of premodern American artists, including George Bellows. *Sport in Art* was a truly awe-inspiring collection – as it was intended to be. After a few showings in the United States the exhibit was scheduled for a lengthy stay in Melbourne coinciding with the 1956 Summer Olympics. The United States would show that it could be both virile and cultured.[40]

From 1954 into 1957 the U.S. government threw everything it could at the world in order to win the cultural Cold War. From the "high" art of opera and classical music, to the more popular forms such as jazz and boxing, the Department of State and the USIA, working closely with private individuals, artists, and organizations, sent pieces of America to nearly every corner of the planet. Even the redheaded stepchild of the nation's cultural diplomacy – art – seemed to be welcomed back to the fold. But it was more than simply the quantity of cultural products shipped overseas; it was also a matter of quality. Audiences, particularly in Europe, clamored for as much jazz as America could provide. Tickets for *Porgy and Bess* shows were often found being scalped to waiting hordes of buyers. American sports figures were both entertaining and successful. An added bonus was that so much of what was so successful in terms of bringing American culture to the foreign audience was also effective in blunting criticism of the U.S. civil rights problem. From the stirring voice of Marian Anderson, to the comedic athleticism of the Harlem Globetrotters, to the jazz renderings of Dizzy Gillespie, American officials were confident that the tale being told to the world was one of equal rights for African Americans. Perhaps the problems that haunted, and nearly derailed, the cultural diplomacy of the Truman years had finally been put to rest.

Perhaps. But behind the newspaper and magazine reports in the United States about how America was battering and besting the Soviets at the cultural game, and the steady stream of messages from U.S. posts around the world about the success of this or that program, lay the undeniable fact that America's cultural diplomacy was still riven with problems, contradictions, and controversies. Some of these were issues that extended all the way back to the unofficial efforts of the nineteenth century. Others were of more recent vintage, reflecting the difficulties that the post–Second World War program of cultural diplomacy experienced in getting off the ground. And finally, some of the issues were brand new – and often completely unexpected.

One new, and unexpected, problem came from the sheer magnitude of the U.S. cultural events sent abroad combined with a much wider geographic distribution of those efforts. So many of the earlier attempts at cultural diplomacy centered on western Europe, and then Latin America, and generally focused on more "traditional" cultural forms of music, dance, and theater. Now, however, foreign audiences throughout Europe, Latin America, Africa, and Asia were being introduced to jazz, modern art and dance, and a dizzying array of other attempts to introduce them to American culture. It did not always translate into popular appeal – or even work at all. Fosler-Lussier recounts the frustrations of the American embassy in Cambodia in trying to please the foreign audience:

> Half the audience for the harmonica player John Sebastian left the hall within the first few minutes of the concert, although the rest applauded enthusiastically. The same was true of the Westminster Choir. The piano provided for Marian Anderson's performance was terribly out of tune, and although the audience appreciated 'the force of her personality,' they disliked her operatic repertoire. When the Benny Goodman jazz band

visited, the Cambodian sponsor made no arrangements for a piano or a sound system, leaving the band without essential equipment. A local newspaper called Goodman's music "the gobbling of turkeys." Kellogg had cancelled the scheduled performances of the Golden Gate Quartet, a singing group specializing in popular songs and gospel numbers, because when he played a recording of the quartet for the Cambodian minister of public instruction, the minister asked, "Do you have anybody who can sing in Cambodian?"[41]

For the audiences overseas, the overwhelming onslaught of so many different arts and artists could sometimes seem less like a polished and pleasing symphony than a bewildering cacophony.

One problem that continued to plague America's cultural diplomats was congressional criticism, interference, and lack of funding. Congress had already shown the damage it could cause during its assaults on *Advancing American Art*. Despite Eisenhower's very public support of cultural and information programs (and the fact that the chief congressional troublemaker Joseph McCarthy had been rendered politically irrelevant after the televised hearings of his investigation into the U.S. Army in 1954), Congress continued to view the programs with skepticism and often outright hostility. The art program, even in its somewhat truncated form in the early-Eisenhower years, still served as a lightening rod. The unchallenged leader of the congressional attacks was George Dondero. Before leaving Congress in 1957 Dondero left behind him a string of incredible accusations and an art program he managed to whittle down to its bare essentials. He did not bother himself with issues of style (and he often mangled the artists' names); he went right for the jugular, claiming that modern art was "shackled to communism."[42] Other congressmen concentrated on the cost of the program. During 1955 hearings into the expenses for a dance company and a production of *Porgy and Bess* recently sent overseas, it became clear that many congressmen still had trouble spending money for culture activities. One charged that "It certainly appears to me that you have a mighty loose way of handling the taxpayer's dollars." Another argued that the matter went beyond dollars and cents:

I wonder where in the Constitution you can find anything that gives me the right to spend the taxpayers' money for projects of this sort?...Just how responsible are we as representatives of the people when we vote to continue this madness until the crash takes us over? I just simply cannot find the justification to take it away from the people. I am out of sympathy with it.

With that sort of thinking it is hardly surprising to discover that the U.S. cultural programs perpetually operated with little more than shoestring budgets and constant uncertainty about future allocations from Congress.[43]

The congressional attacks by individuals such as Dondero also revealed the continuing issue of censorship. Many members of the American cultural and intellectual community were still reeling from the Eisenhower administration's acquiescence to McCarthy's rampage against the American libraries in Europe, but at least in that case it was Congress that was the recipient of much of the rage. As the 1950s went on, however, it became clear that while individuals such as McCarthy and Dondero might sound the initial tocsin, the Department of State and the USIA were not simply responding to the accusations but actively participating in censoring what went overseas. The first sign of what was to come appeared in 1956. The Symphony of the Air had just completed its fabulously successful tour of Asia under U.S. government sponsorship. Desirous of building on the Symphony's triumph, the Department of State announced that it would now be sent to another trouble spot for America, the Middle East. Yet, almost as soon as the new tour was being advertised, it was summarily canceled without explanation. According to Donald Meyer, the reason for this unexpected action by the U.S. government soon emerged. Congressman John Rooney contacted the Department of State to inquire into rumors that at least ten of the Symphony's members had connections to communism. The FBI now entered the fray and confirmed Rooney's fears; he thereupon held a hearing at which he grilled government officials about why checks on the political affiliations of the Symphony members were not held before being sent overseas. With little fanfare, State canceled the Middle East tour. Meyer concludes that both the "evidence" for the accusations and the FBI's report were "flimsy at best." The impact, however, was quite real: the Symphony "never recovered from this altercation....The orchestra never regained its stride and never left the country."[44]

At almost the exact same time, a similar controversy was brewing over the *Sport in Art* exhibit. After successful showings in Boston and Washington, DC, the collection was scheduled to visit Dallas before leaving on the long trip to Melbourne, Australia, in time for the 1956 Summer Olympics. Before one person in Dallas could even see the show, an organization named the Dallas County Patriotic Council lashed out, claiming that at least four of the artists whose works were represented in *Sport in Art* were members of "communist front" organizations. The Dallas Museum of Fine Arts dismissed the criticisms and went on with the exhibition. Any notion that the works of art would be used in America's cultural diplomacy was, however, dead in the water. Even as the Dallas museum was facing down the critics, the USIA met to consider its options. Officials quickly decided that two things had to immediately take place. First, the offending artists would be removed before shipping *Sport in Art* to Australia. Second, in the wake of the problems with the art show and the nearly simultaneous episode with the Symphony of the Air, henceforth "a national Agency name check should be instituted on all artists who are to be used in future exhibitions sponsored by the Agency." The USIA recognized the dilemma – censoring the artists would "jeopardize our cultural status in the world." With this in mind, the agency simply announced that the Australian leg of the tour was being canceled due to "budgetary considerations." Very quickly, however, news stories appeared laying out the truth: *Sport in Art* had been sacked due to charges regarding certain artists' political affiliations. In addition, the two other large AFA-organized exhibits – *Universities Collect* and *American Painting, 1900–1950* – were also under pressure to remove specific artists' works (including a Picasso from the former). USIA officials hemmed and hawed, but eventually admitted to Congress that it now had a "policy against use of paintings by politically suspect artists in its touring art shows."[45]

Instead of fending off congressional censorship, the USIA now took it upon itself to do the censoring in-house. The process it devised was simplicity itself. Any artist who died before 1917 "shall be ipso facto considered cleared." Others who were "avowed Communists" or "Fifth Amendment Refugees" would be excluded without further consideration. Anyone who fell in the gray area between dead and communist would go through a more laborious name check system. This system, in use until at least the early 1960s, subjected lists of artists proposed for inclusion in overseas shows to strenuous investigation, often relying on the guidelines put forward in 1953 after the controversy with McCarthy and the books in the nation's overseas libraries. The ridiculous depth to which this process was willing to go is revealed in a 1961 security report on the realist artist Ben Shahn. Although concluding that Shahn's "security rating" placed him in a "dubious category," the agency relented and allowed his print entitled *Wheat Field* to be shown. After all, officials decided, "the subject matter of the print is completely innocuous."[46]

The discovery of the USIA's censorship policy was merely one example of a problem that had long plagued U.S. cultural diplomacy – the relationship between the government (that provided the funding and international contacts) and the private sector (that provided the talent and expertise). The cancellation of the art exhibits in 1956 left the AFA angry and bewildered. The organization's president warned about the results of the USIA's actions: "Public notice will be served to the world that freedom of expression (of which freedom of the arts is an inseparable part) is subject to official and serious infringement." Margaret Cogswell, who worked in the foreign exhibits division of the AFA, was crestfallen. In the AFA, there was general "disbelief that it was happening," especially since "within the whole art world there wasn't one soul who thought we should cancel."[47]

Beyond censoring some artists and art, the U.S. government also found itself embroiled in difficulties convincing its cultural diplomats to send the proper message – or even participate. Many of the artists saw themselves as just that – artists who happened to be performing overseas with assistance from the U.S. government. Certainly one of the most embarrassing situations occurred when jazz great Louis Armstrong abruptly cancelled his tour to the Soviet Union in the wake of racial violence in Little Rock. "Satchmo" had long been considered an ideal participant in the cultural program – he was personable, talented, and had already acquired a worldwide reputation. But when whites in Little Rock barred black schoolchildren from attempting to integrate a local high school, and the Eisenhower administration seemed reluctant to act, Armstrong unloaded, declaring that "the way they treat my people in the South, the government can go to hell," before concluding that "it's getting so bad a colored man hasn't got any country."[48]

Armstrong's criticisms also served to highlight one critical and continuing issue for U.S. cultural diplomacy – the inability to effectively deal with the race issue. Marian Anderson, Dizzy Gillespie, and the various African American athletes might find audiences abroad who delighted in their talents, but even their most brilliant performances could not obscure the ugly racial incidents that appeared in American newspapers nearly every day. The U.S. government could trumpet the progress being made and point with pride to the 1954 *Brown* Supreme Court decision as concrete evidence of the nation's commitment to equal rights for all Americans. Nevertheless, the violence persisted and white resistance increased, all climaxing in the conflict in Little Rock, Arkansas, in 1957 over the issue of public school desegregation.

All in all, 1957 was a bad year for America's image abroad. The Soviets shattered the aura of America's technological superiority by firing *Sputnik* into orbit around the earth. The toxic racism on display in Little Rock, accompanied by pictures of terrified African American schoolchildren cowering beneath a withering fire of insults, spit, and thrown objects, was splashed all over the front pages of American newspapers – and the foreign media. Although Eisenhower was eventually applauded for sending in U.S. troops to protect the children, much of the world was left to wonder exactly what kind of "leader of the free world" needed its armed forces simply to ensure that young African Americans could attend schools with whites? Not surprisingly, the Soviets had an absolute field day with the events in Little Rock since, once again, they did not have to resort to exaggeration or lies to prove their point – all they had to do was reprint the pictures and stories from American newspapers and magazines.[49] The initial U.S. response to the negative foreign reaction was not terribly impressive. The Eisenhower administration argued the events at Little Rock had been "widely misunderstood and misinterpreted." What was needed in this moment of crisis was the "sending to Black Africa of American negro athletes and athletic teams (such as the Globe Trotters, and Althea Gibson).... Good negro jazz musicians or jazz orchestras would also make a very favorable impact." As a Filipino journalist pointed out, "the official glorification of a Marian Anderson or a Richard Wright hardly proves anything....What must be shown is what is being done to save the millions of Jacks and Janes from the score or so of Governor Faubuses [Faubus was the governor of Arkansas]."[50] Fortunately for U.S. cultural diplomats, an opportunity to do just that was right around the corner.

The 1958 World's Fair in Brussels, Belgium, provided a unique and significant setting for using American culture as a tool of international relations. Instead of sending parts of the nation around the world, the world would now come to see America presented in a single, coherent exhibit. Organizers of the American exhibition hall pulled out all of the stops in an effort to awe and impress the foreign visitors. In the face of the *Sputnik* surprise, the American public now argued that cost was no matter – the United States had to make a big cultural splash in Brussels. When some congressmen protested, newspaper editorials called them out arguing that "We're Set to Be Shamed at Brussels" because of the usual penny-pinching. American officials reached back to an old and trusted collaborator, Walt Disney, whose company came up with the extremely popular *USA in Circarama*. According to Sarah Nilsen's study of American film at Brussels, Circarama "was the smash hit of the fair. Surveys of top attractions at the American pavilion consistently placed the Circarama as number one," and at least twenty people actually passed out from the heat waiting in the very long lines to get into the theater. Those patrons who remained conscious were treated to what was literally a whirlwind tour of the United States as images filmed by nearly a dozen cameras flowed around the circular theater. Visitors also got a chance to "experience" American democracy by using voting machines to select their favorite U.S. politicians, actors, and musicians. To counter *Sputnik* (which was heavily featured at the Soviet pavilion, set directly across from the American building), there was also a Nuclear Energy Exhibit, where people could work a pair of electromagnetic hands. To tell more about who Americans were, the pavilion also contained an "American Streetscape," a bookstore, an all-American restaurant, and a theater for music, dance, movie, and theater performances.[51] America's cultural diplomats believed that more could be done at Brussels, particularly in addressing one of the most troubling contradictions of the cultural program and forthrightly facing up to one of the nation's thorniest issues. To that end, the American pavilion also included a display of mostly abstract expressionist art and, in a separate building, an exhibit that spoke to the U.S. civil rights problem.

The nasty publicity surrounding the cancellation of the *Sport in Art* trip to the 1956 Olympics and other art shows destined for overseas exhibition gave America's cultural diplomacy a black eye. The USIA's admission that it had instituted a "security check" for all artists proposed for inclusion in foreign shows directly contradicted one of the main messages U.S. officials hoped to convey – that America was a land of free expression and, in particular, freedom of the arts. Once again, art would be used to answer the widespread view of "America as the land of gadgets and gimmicks – and little else." To try and please the art-savvy European audience that would likely dominate at the 1958 fair, the USIA insisted that only "contemporary" paintings would make up the exhibit in the American pavilion. And, in an effort to try and avoid the anti communist controversies that surrounded earlier exhibits, it was decided that the artists themselves would need to be 40 years of age or younger (this was later raised to 45). This meant that "many of the 'subversive' artists who came to maturity during the 1930s and early 1940s would automatically be eliminated." Eventually, seventeen artists were chosen for the exhibit, including some well-known figures such as William Baziotes and Robert Motherwell as well as many young painters virtually unheard of outside of the art world. To provide a human touch to the exhibit, their paintings were shown next to displays containing pictures and brief biographies of the artists, as well as personal statements from the painters.[52]

The most surprising – and certainly controversial – showing put on by the Americans at the 1958 fair was what came to be known as the "Unfinished Business" exhibit. The controversy erupted from the section of the exhibit dedicated to the "Unfinished Business" of civil rights in America. The basic idea behind the exhibit was both simple and direct. Since the entire world already knew how bad the race situation was in the United States, why not simply own up to the problem and discuss how the nation was going to deal with it? There were actually three problem areas on display in the exhibit (which was set up in three smaller buildings connected by a catwalk on the grounds of the U.S. pavilion): the housing problem in America's inner cities, soil erosion and the impact on crops, and civil rights. The first small building contained newspaper clippings forthrightly laying out the problem areas; the second contained photos and information detailing what the United States was doing to address the problems; and, in the last room, there were displays illustrating the ultimate goals. For the civil rights problems, this translated into news and magazine stories with pictures and headlines detailing racial violence and discrimination; statistics on the progress being made in education, jobs, and equality for African Americans; and a massive picture of black and white children playing ring around the rosy together – a symbol of a truly integrated society. Visitors would be escorted through the displays by young American guides, some of them African American.[53]

Although the U.S. pavilion worked hard to tell foreign visitors the truth about America, the modern art and "Unfinished Business" proved to be harder sells to the audience back home. As usual, conservative art critics and groups in the United States savaged the paintings, particularly the abstract expressionist works. Congressman Albert Morano expressed exasperation at the fact that "the great names of American painting have been deliberately omitted from our display. I see ... no Trumbull, no Peale, no Remington or Sargent, nor even Grandma Moses." American officials and members of the AFA expected as much. One remarked before the show debuted that "It is fair to say that the exhibit will have a certain shock value and may not completely satisfy those among us to whom Norman Rockwell represents the height of American art." However, the plan to use younger artists did have the desired impact. Although some critics and congressmen complained about the "'long-hair' influence" that went into the selection of such modern art, there were few of the red-baiting comments associated with the art and artists from earlier shows. Like Truman before him, Eisenhower did enter the fray, but only to wonder whether "the fair was the place to try to teach sophistication to the public or to American tourists." Despite this caveat, the president concluded that he would not "set myself up as a critic of any artistic exhibition."[54] To all appearances the art program had finally come of age – as long as that age was less than 45.

The reaction to the civil rights section of "Unfinished Business" was much more powerful and, eventually, destructive. The attacks began even before the fair opened. As soon as word leaked out in the American press that America's race problem would be on display in Brussels, Southern congressmen lashed out. Senator Herman Talmadge from Georgia was incredulous that an official U.S. exhibit would "apologize for racial segregation in the United States." If the government insisted on keeping the exhibit, Talmadge demanded that the Southern side of the story also be included. L. Mendel Rivers and Strom Thurmond, both from South Carolina, and Prince Preston from Georgia all complained long and loud about what they viewed as an "insult" to Southern Americans. They were furious over the notion that "segregation was a problem the United States must solve," particularly when other national problems – such as "crime and the influx of Puerto Ricans" – could have been featured. Others insisted that the focus on the race problem was "an invitation to communist propaganda." The most damaging assessment, however, came from Eisenhower, who, despite his recent actions in Little Rock, would never be mistaken for a staunch supporter of civil rights. In the midst of the congressional backlash the president wrote to the officials in charge of the U.S. pavilion to express his misgivings:

> When we send our children up to receive their diplomas in high school, we have them put on their best clothes and do not show them in their jeans and sneakers. There is no reason in [my] judgment why we should not put our best foot forward at an exhibit such as this....Also, [I object] very strongly to the "finger pointing" implicit in the setting up by a New Englander of an exhibit critical of the South on the racial problem.

In short order, the civil rights section of "Unfinished Business" underwent severe revisions. The newspaper headlines were crumpled up and overlapped, making some of them nearly unreadable. A picture of a young African American male dancing with a white woman was unceremoniously ripped from the wall and the large picture of the black and white children playing shrunk down considerably. All of this was to no avail. The heated attacks continued and, despite the fact that reports from Brussels indicated that the exhibit was having a positive impact on the Europeans who visited,

"Unfinished Business" was quickly and quietly closed, later to reopen with a focus on the always-controversial issue of public health. A number of African Americans protested the move, but their voices were drowned out by the chorus of their fellow citizens who saw segregation not as a problem, but a completely acceptable way of American life. Even the necessity of blunting the most effective line of communist propaganda could not overcome the real truth about America: most African Americans still lived in second-class citizenship.[55]

In 1959, U.S. cultural diplomacy invaded Russia. The American National Exhibition in Moscow was one of the results of a 1958 cultural exchange agreement signed by the United States and the Soviet Union as part of the campaign of "mutual coexistence" that was, at least publicly, embraced by the two competing superpowers. A Soviet national exhibition opened in New York earlier in 1959 and, despite the unending highlights of the successful *Sputnik* launching two years before, ended up being more a novelty than a revelation for the Americans who visited. The massive U.S. exhibit in Moscow was, in many ways, a decided change from the cultural diplomacy efforts seen during the earlier years of the 1950s. Instead of focusing on the idea of "humanism" as it did at the Brussels fair the year before, the Americans now simply tried to bury the Soviet citizens under an avalanche of consumer goods. As Walter Hixson explains,

> Moscow embassy diplomats familiar with Soviet life agreed...that an emphasis on consumerism would prove most effective. The Soviet public would display intense interest in items such as American shoes, clothing, reading material, and records, all of which sold for high prices on the black market. Also effective would be a food display that would "dramatically present American food purchasing methods and packaging, variety of prepared and ready to eat products (not dreamed of here), and attention to consumer wants." Washington would supply "as many Sears Roebuck, Montgomery Ward, and other catalogs as possible."[56]

Huge crowds of Russians poured into the exhibition grounds to gaze at American automobiles, television sets, kitchen appliances, and clothing. Visitors who worked up a thirst could indulge in free Pepsi-Cola. A massive computer from IBM was on display. The centerpiece, however, was a fully equipped "modern" American home. This was where, on the opening day, Soviet premier Nikita Khrushchev and Vice President Richard Nixon engaged in what would become known worldwide as the "kitchen debate." Surrounded by news cameras and reporters, the two men stood among the gleaming kitchen appliances and exchanged barbs. The Russian declared that "all our new houses" had the exact same kind of kitchen, while Nixon flippantly remarked that Khrushchev reminded him of a congressman carrying on a filibuster. Cooler heads finally prevailed, as Nixon apologized for not being a "good host" and the Soviet leader thanked the U.S. guides for "letting us use [your] kitchen for our argument." With that, one of the most famous episodes in the Cold War was over.[57]

Little noted at the time, however, was Khrushchev's tour through the exhibit of modern painting and sculpture. Unaccompanied by Nixon, the Russian leader was quite free to express his distaste with the artwork. Stopping in front of a work by John Marin (whose work survived not only the *Advancing American Art* disaster but also the USIA security checks), Khrushchev sneered that "It reminds me of a little boy making a puddle on the floor!" The people who painted such works were "obviously crazy," and the people who liked it were "crazier still." In the sculpture display, Khrushchev observed a modern piece depicting a woman. He simply shook his head and declared that "only a homosexual could have done such a statue since he obviously didn't think much of womanhood."[58]

Khrushchev was not the only person taken aback by the mostly modern art shown in Moscow. Perhaps because the Moscow show received such massive press coverage, congressmen smelled blood in the water and went in for the attack. Francis Walter of Pennsylvania picked up the banner carried in previous years by McCarthy and Dondero and lacerated the selection process as "repulsive." Why, he asked, should the United States "glorify so-called artists who stand for nothing that this country represents and for everything it is opposed to"? During an appearance on national television Walter was challenged by an interviewer who asked whether such efforts to censor the American art at Moscow were like what the Soviets had recently done in banning the book *Dr. Zhivago*. The congressman's response was certainly direct: "Not at all. The basic difference is that *Dr. Zhivago* is a very good story. This is very bad art." Eisenhower himself was uneasy, not just about the modern art but also some works that seemed to satirize American society. Sensing, however, that censoring an American art show in the middle of Moscow might look particularly suspect, U.S. officials compromised and sent twenty-six other paintings – all from the nineteenth and early twentieth centuries – to supplement the collection on display.[59]

The art exhibit in Moscow was also one of the very few U.S. cultural exhibits overseas that left a clear and interesting record of the immediate responses of the audience. A "guest book" sat inside the exhibit and Russian visitors were encouraged to enter their reactions to the paintings. Not surprisingly, many of the comments expressed bewilderment and/or anger. One Russian wrote that the U.S. should "keep it at home and use it on ranches to scare off crows"; another complained that "daubing by dumb animals cannot be called art." Yet, among the slings and arrows were numerous comments that American supporters of the art exhibit pointed to with pride: "We like your exhibition and the abstract art"; "The search for something new!"; "Each type of art has a right to existence. Every person has his own taste. Art is free and everyone has a right to create." The

American guides reported that as the show went on more and more Russians defended the exhibit against the attacks of their fellow countrymen.[60] Cultural diplomacy worked on both levels: as a demonstration of America's creativity and its dedication to freedom of thought and expression.

Lost in all of the loud and passionate discussions about the art exhibit was a deep irony. For many, many years Americans, both in and outside of government, who supported the idea of using the nation's culture as part of its diplomacy agreed on at least one important point. From the time of the nation's birth, the United States had been looked upon as uncultured, boorish, and materialistic. In the post–Second World War period, a primary goal of the nation's cultural diplomacy would be to counter the notion that America was simply a nation of "things" – machines, cars, and consumer items slavishly devoured by its consumer mentality. With art, with music, with theater, sport, and literature, our cultural diplomats would demonstrate that the United States also had taste, cultivation, and a soul that embraced freedom and creativity. After struggling for so many years to reveal this truth about America, they had finally succeeded in Moscow – with an art exhibit surrounded by cars, refrigerators, color televisions, stereos, and fashion models.

The Eisenhower years certainly lived up to their reputation as the golden age of America's cultural diplomacy. Not only did the establishment of the USIA provide such undertakings with a stable and (somewhat) independent platform, the variety and depth of U.S. cultural undertakings abroad was nothing less than stunning. During the Truman years cultural diplomacy always seemed to be skating on thin ice. From 1953 to 1961, however, it seemed as though every possible avenue for cultural outreach came into play. The fine arts – orchestras, operas, dance, and painting and sculpture – circled the globe. So-called "popular culture" also came into its own through the increasing importance of jazz and sports as part of the nation's cultural arsenal. Technology, science, industry, and consumer goods – once considered to represent some of the very things about America that the fine arts and popular culture were supposed to dispel or mask – also found their way into popular and important exhibits around the world. At Brussels in 1958 and, more importantly, in Moscow in 1959, the total power of America's cultural offensive was brought to bear to impress U.S. friends and counter Soviet efforts.

Only in the area of race did America seem to fall short. Despite the increased utilization of "outstanding" African Americans as both official and unofficial cultural diplomats in the fields of jazz, sports, and theater, and the originality of the "Unfinished Business" exhibit at Brussels, it was clear by the end of Eisenhower's second term that the nation had been mostly a failure in conveying to the world a message about race relations in America that emphasized the progress of African Americans and civil rights as a national goal. By 1961, race remained America's "Achilles heel."

Nevertheless, America's cultural diplomats were mostly optimistic as they prepared for a new president. The USIA seemed to be on solid footing. The realm of cultural diplomacy now included so many aspects of American life that it seemed impossible that the world would not see and understand the nation and its people. The 1960s, so they believed, would witness the ultimate fulfillment of the goal that had long eluded them – to tell the truth about America.

CHAPTER FIVE

The Slow Death of American Cultural Diplomacy, 1961–1999

It all started off so promisingly. With the election of John F. Kennedy in 1960 many people in State, the USIA, and the private sector who spent the past decade and a half trying to convince their associates, Congress, and a skeptical American public that culture could play an important role in the nation's foreign relations felt that the man who would soon turn the White House into Camelot would also manage to breathe new life and energy into their cultural programs. All that was needed, they felt, was the right man to lead the charge.

Edward R. Murrow was probably better known to most Americans than their own congressmen or city council members. He stood as a giant in the world of journalism, and the mushrooming medium of television brought him into millions of homes. Already famous for his Second World War radio broadcasts from Great Britain, Murrow turned to television in 1951 with his show *See It Now*. Over the next nine years he became a familiar face and voice as Americans tuned in to see some of his most famous broadcasts, such as the 1954 show that skewered Joseph McCarthy and 1960s *Harvest of Shame* that exposed the exploitation of America's migrant farm workers. When Kennedy requested that he take over as director of the USIA, he felt it was his duty but he also saw it as an opportunity to tell the truth about America to a worldwide audience.[1] No one could have realized at the time that both Murrow and the early optimism about America's cultural diplomacy program would be gone by the end of 1965.

The American exhibits in Brussels in 1958 and Moscow in 1959, in many ways, marked the high point for government support of a vibrant program of cultural diplomacy. This is not to suggest that after 1960 the cultural programs from State and the USIA immediately withered and died.

Indeed, for a few years in the 1960s it appeared to some of the stalwart supporters of the use of culture in the nation's diplomacy that the best was yet to come. By the mid-1960s, however, the unresolved contradictions and problems that frustrated America's attempts to use culture to tell the world the truth about the United States, together with new and unforeseen issues, worked to slowly crush the life and spirit out of both the programs and the people who supported them. By the end of the 1960s, cultural diplomacy had begun a steady downward spiral. Thirty years later, the USIA was gone and, with it, much of the last remaining interest in the possibilities for culture as a tool in America's international relations.

In 1961, however, the outlook for America's cultural diplomacy programs looked brighter than ever. The charismatic Kennedy was in the White House, and it was soon apparent that his administration had an intense interest in the arts. Figures such as the playwright Arthur Miller, novelist John Steinbeck, and abstract expressionist painters Mark Rothko and Franz Kline were part of the inaugural gatherings in Washington. The world-famous cellist Pablo Casals played in the White House in late 1961. Kennedy's wife, Jacqueline, was the more culturally sophisticated of the two, and she also helped to make culture and the arts an important part of the national heritage. And, of course, the naming of Murrow to the directorship of the USIA suggested that bringing American culture to the world would be of continuing importance.

At least initially much of this early optimism seemed to be warranted. Ironically, it was the much-maligned arts program that led the way. The fact that large art shows, including many modern and abstract expressionist pieces, were part of the exhibits in Brussels and Moscow encouraged the supporters of the art program to broaden their horizons. In the early 1960s, government-sponsored art shows (often in collaboration with private organizations, museums, and even businesses) quite literally circled the globe. Europe had always been a main focus for the art program, but exhibits now popped up all through Asia, Latin America, the Middle East, and Africa. This was hardly surprising. The late 1950s and early 1960s were years of turmoil, anti colonialism, and revolution in much of what was then referred to as the "Third World." With dozens of new countries entering the United Nations each year the USIA discovered a new and large audience to which to tell the many truths about America.[2]

After the success of riling up the Russian audience in Moscow in 1959, the art program also continued to ply its trade in the Soviet Union. Indeed, the entire purpose now seemed to be to elicit vehement attacks on the modern art exhibits by the Soviet government and press. The more heated the denunciations (and the more the communist government cracked down on displays of modern art by contemporary Russian painters), the more the USIA felt it was hitting the enemy where it hurt. After the Russians raked one U.S.-sponsored exhibit over the coals, a USIA official gleefully observed, "We've really drawn blood this time." In testimony before Congress, another

USIA spokesperson explained how the agency evaluated the impact of its art exhibits in Russia: "the more frequent the criticism the more impact it is having on Soviet audiences." The rationale was the same as that used to defend the earlier Moscow show: while many – perhaps most – Russians hated the modern art, it succeeded in reaching a smaller, but influential, sector of Soviet society. Thus, the USIA tended to shrug off the dozens of criticisms of any particular show and focus instead on the scattered positive remarks that suggested that the message of artistic (and, hence, political) freedom implicit in the modern art shows was received.[3]

Now, however, it was time to go for bigger game – on the biggest art stage in the world. Prior to 1964 the United States, alone among most of the great powers, never officially sponsored an American pavilion at the Venice Biennale. In fact, most of the European nations, including Great Britain and France, established national pavilions at Venice prior to the First World War. It was not until 1930 that the United States had its own building, but it was not built by the government – private donations solicited by the Grand Central Art Galleries of New York paid for the small building that finally provided a separate space for the exhibition of American art at the Venice Biennale. The expense of keeping up the building prompted the Galleries to offer the building for sale to the U.S. government in 1948. Coming hard on the heels of the *Advancing American Art* disaster, it was hardly propitious timing and the American government politely but firmly declined. Nevertheless, embarrassed by the lack of an official U.S. presence in Venice the Department of State gave its tepid support to the 1952 American show, although the Museum of Modern Art really handled the day-to-day operations from 1950 to 1962.[4]

Following the 1962 show in Venice, MOMA informed the U.S. government that it no longer had the resources to handle the American presence at the Biennale (or the other large international art show, the São Paulo Bienal). Shortly thereafter, the USIA agreed that it would handle the American exhibitions at both big shows. Working with private American museums and the AFA, the USIA now jumped directly into the big time as far as the art world was concerned. The success of individual exhibits of American art around the world was one thing; a good showing at São Paulo and Venice would announce to the world that American art had finally arrived. Alternatively, a poor showing would be disastrous. Ever since the late 1940s, the United States had attempted to use its modern art to demonstrate both its position at the vanguard of the fine arts and to send a powerful message about artistic freedom. Now, however, American art would be displayed not in carefully controlled and selected venues – it would be viewed side by side with the art from around the world. The successes would catch even the USIA temporarily off-guard: Americans won the grand prize for painting at São Paulo in 1963 and Venice in 1964.[5] From hiding in the shadows of cultural fairs in West Berlin in the early 1950s, America's modern art had now taken the world by storm and the role of the arts program in U.S. cultural diplomacy seemed to be – finally – on solid footing.

American cultural diplomacy dealing with the nation's race problem, despite some initial refocusing, also appeared primed for success. With a president in the White House who made civil rights an important part of his campaign, State and the USIA were ready to spread the word that America was not only cognizant of its race problem but was now ready to take positive action as well. Yet, much had changed since the ugly Little Rock crisis of 1957 and the embarrassing failure of the "Unfinished Business" exhibit at the 1958 world's fair. A more active and vocal civil rights movement pressured the U.S. government to adopt a different tone in the messages it sent abroad about the nation's racial issues.

Between 1961 and 1966 it appeared that the walls around the "lily-white club" of the Department of State were truly coming down. Clifton Wharton, Sr., was named the first African American ambassador to a European nation when he was sent to Norway in 1961. Three black ambassadors came from the world of academia: Mercer Cook to Niger in 1961, Elliott P. Skinner to Upper Volta in 1966, and Hugh Smythe, the first African American ambassador to the Middle East, went to Syria in 1965. Patricia Roberts Harris broke another barrier when she became the first African American woman to serve as an ambassador, going to Luxembourg in 1965. A number of other African Americans were named to various posts in the Department of State and the United Nations during those years.[6]

Of particular interest both in the United States and abroad was the meteoric career of Carl Rowan. The journalist went on a government-sponsored trip to India and South Asia in the mid-1950s, but in 1961 he took his first official position when he was named as deputy assistant secretary of state for public affairs by the incoming Kennedy administration. Two years later Rowan was appointed as the U.S. ambassador to Finland. His stay in Finland was brief. Decades of incessant cigarette smoking finally caught up with Ed Murrow, whose battle with lung cancer forced him to step down as USIA director in early 1964. President Lyndon Johnson almost immediately selected Rowan as Murrow's successor. His rapid rise in the U.S. foreign policy making bureaucracy did not go unnoticed by the African American press that crowned him the "new chief salesman for Uncle Sam and for millions of global inhabitants." The primary focus of Rowan's salesmanship was never in doubt – America's civil rights problem. As early as his first appointment in 1961, Rowan made it clear that the race problem would no longer be portrayed as it had been at the "Unfinished Business" exhibit that started with pictures and stories about racial violence and segregation. Speaking before an audience in Washington, DC, Rowan argued that "had I come to speak before your members eight years ago, I would have spoken only of the injustices and humiliations meted out to Negroes, but the day is long since past when I, or any other American, could afford to think of the social problems that beset us in any such narrow terms." The main problem that now existed concerning America's race problem was to "put it in perspective. We must show that the picture is not one of whites vs. Negroes, as our enemies would depict it, but of the vast majority of whites and Negroes striving together for progress."[7]

One relatively new way in which the USIA spoke to the race problem was the use of films. Both State and the USIA were involved with film long before 1961, sometimes working with Hollywood, sometimes producing their own short films on a variety of topics. But when Murrow took charge, the cultural medium began to take center stage. Nicholas Cull writes that "In the course of 1962 the USIA produced thirty-six films within the U.S.A., a further 147 overseas, and issued 197 newsreels. They had 50,000 film prints in circulation in 106 countries, reaching an estimated audience of 600 million people." Some of these films were enormously popular, none more so than the 1964 production, *John F. Kennedy: Years of Lightning, Day of Drums*, that celebrated the life and accomplishments of the recently assassinated president. Many of the most notable successes, however, occurred when the topic was the civil rights issue in America. The 1964 film, *The March*, was a dramatic presentation of the civil rights march on Washington, DC, made most famous by Martin Luther King's "I Have a Dream" speech. Even more successful was *Nine from Little Rock*, a film focusing on the young African American students who braved the anger and resentment of many whites by integrating Central High School in Little Rock, Arkansas, in 1957. In 1965, it received an Oscar for the year's best documentary short.[8]

By 1965, in fact, the USIA felt the battle had been won. With the passage of the landmark civil rights legislation of 1964–1965, the U.S. government steadily lost interest in trying to tell the world the truth about America's racial problems since, in its eyes, the truth was now self-apparent. USIA director Rowan explained the change: "The impact of racial happenings in the U.S. over the past year has been negative. However, now as before, generally adverse reactions to U.S. race relations are outweighed by other impressions of America which in the net produce a highly favorable overall opinion." Another official noted that even in Africa, long interested in the civil rights struggle in America, "widespread criticism of us on this issue has waned in recent months as a result of the measures we have taken to resolve this problem." A USIA report in the wake of the 1964 and 1965 civil rights legislation dismissed the idea of continuing to focus on racial issues: "*Does the racial issue as a propaganda problem preoccupy us more than the facts warrant?* The answer seems to be, probably *Yes*." In fact, continuing to deal with the issue was counterproductive since doing so meant that the United States was always putting "our worst foot forward, that we confused a kind of crusading masochism with freedom from hypocrisy, or that we were unfairly presenting a section of the US."[9] Translation: There would be no further "Unfinished Business" exhibits. As far as the USIA was concerned, the business was satisfactorily finished.

This did not preclude the continuing use of jazz as a tool of America's cultural diplomacy. As Lisa Davenport explains, several factors combined to create a change in the way the United States employed its "jazz diplomacy." While jazz groups and artists still traveled to Africa and elsewhere around the world, the focus began to shift to sending more of the music into the Soviet Union and Eastern Europe. Partially, this was due to what Davenport describes as the "elitism" of the music advisors in the Department of State, many of whom felt that Africans were too "unsophisticated" to truly appreciate the intricacies of jazz. More important, however, was the fact that jazz was increasingly seen as a potent anti communist weapon: "American and Soviet officials recognized the unyielding appeal of jazz among [the] Soviet people as audiences markedly grew." The fact that the Soviet government often criticized the "decadence" of jazz music only increased the U.S. desire to use jazz in Russia as a form of "cultural containment" that "targeted those countries that had grown increasingly independent from Moscow." Well-known jazz acts such as Benny Goodman and Gerry Mulligan visited the Soviet Union, and Willis Conover, famous for his VOA shows that featured jazz music, toured Estonia and Romania. The growing popularity of jazz even drove one Soviet fan to argue that the music had not originated among the African American population of the United States, but in the Russian city of Odessa.[10]

In 1962 another milestone in the culture war with the Soviet Union was reached when the acclaimed New York City Ballet toured Russia. Ballet had always been a particularly potent weapon in the Soviet cultural offensive, with the Bolshoi Ballet leading the charge. By 1962, both the Bolshoi and the Kirov Ballet had toured the United States. It was time to answer back. A short trip through Russia in 1960 by the American Ballet Theater had been a start, but now it was time for the more prestigious New York City Ballet, led by George Balanchine, to invade. The tour through five Soviet cities, including Moscow and Leningrad, was greeted with generally enthusiastic responses from the Russian audiences. As it turned out, the company was in the Soviet Union during the height of the Cuban missile crisis, but that did not dampen the reception. As one member of the troupe recalled, "the danger of our situation hardly percolated down to the dancers, who night after night within the Kremlin's walls heard six thousand voices yell for fifteen minutes after every performance: 'Bal-an-chin, Bal-an-chin!'"[11]

American cultural diplomacy seemed at its high point by the mid-1960s. Its modern art had taken the world by storm, winning the most prestigious international awards. Jazz continued to provide a sonic weapon and, along with the best-known American ballet troupe, had now invaded the Soviet Union. USIA-produced films not only were viewed by appreciative overseas audiences but also gained critical and artistic acceptance in the United States by winning an Academy Award. Progress in utilizing African Americans as cultural diplomats seemed successful on every level, from the government appointments of blacks to very visible positions in the Department of State and the USIA, to the continuing emphasis on "notable" African Americans in cultural presentations such as jazz. Yet, in just a few years America's cultural programs overseas would be in tatters and by the 1990s would be almost extinct.

At first glance, it appears bizarre that at the very time that U.S. cultural diplomacy seemed to be at its zenith the very agencies responsible for handling the cultural programs would make significant bureaucratic changes. Such changes, however, were merely the latest evidence of the continuing battle between those who saw cultural diplomacy as a propaganda weapon and those who viewed it more in terms of its value to a wider humanity. In 1963, the Department of State made the decision to cancel its long-standing contract with ANTA, the group that handled much of the nuts and bolts work related to cultural performances abroad. An article in *Billboard* announced a "complete shake-up of the U.S. Cultural Exchange program" which would result in "eliminating the role of the American National Theater & Academy." It quoted Lucius Battle, assistant secretary of state for educational and cultural affairs, as characterizing the long relationship between State and ANTA as a "combination of 'inspiring achievement' and 'troublesome obstacles'." Instead, State would now operate under a new direction that would "give the State Department full responsibility for management of overseas tours" and "make long-range plans on a continuing basis for world-wide presentations." According to State, the main issue had been vaguely defined "organizational inadequacies."[12]

Battle was equally vague during a three-hour meeting with ANTA officials just two weeks after the article appeared. He summarized a Department of State study commissioned in late 1962 that concluded that "ANTA should no longer help administer the exchange programs." Even years later during an interview Battle continued to be relatively mysterious: "I terminated the overseas performing arts that they [ANTA] were sending abroad. I took the termination action because the contract had become a disaster; everything in the world had gone wrong with it. There were some real scandals just under the surface and I found out about them. So I decided to start over."[13]

The real reason, however, was more complicated than mere "organizational" difficulties. Partly, the decision to split with ANTA was due to the fact that State simply felt that it was better off handling the cultural programs on its own. This, of course, was a far cry from the 1950s when the department was more than happy to use ANTA as a shield against criticisms concerning both government interference with the arts and the quality of the art (and artists) sent abroad. Things had changed since then, and ANTA's utility as a buffer from attacks no longer applied as it once had. Perhaps it was because of the successes at Brussels in 1958 and, even more significantly, in Moscow in 1959. Critics of the cultural programs still existed, of course, but they were becoming less and less significant as it became clear that culture could be an effective weapon in the Cold War. It was also clear that State was now ready to take the lead. In the report cited by Battle, there was "concern that neither ANTA nor the panels, because of their isolation from foreign policy issues, could adequately do long-range planning. The State Department, they felt, was in a better position to decide where and when to send artists."[14]

In something of an irony, the jazz program served as a microcosm of the growing rift between State and ANTA. Lisa Davenport argues that by 1962–1963, a growing number of State officials – both in Washington and abroad – felt that the jazz program had served its purpose and should be retooled. Public affairs officers in U.S. missions overseas complained about both the quality of the music and the run-ins they had with various artists over a number of issues. Continuing racial clashes in the United States belied the message of racial progress and equality that the jazz tours were intended to impart. In addition, State felt that targeting Africa was now an obsolete idea: "American officials surmised that jazz diplomacy could no longer engender the support of educated leaders and intellectuals." Communist governments, as well as America's European allies, were sending in "stupendous cultural products" and "'sophisticated' performing arts troupes." State now advocated "sending 'sophisticated' examples of American 'high culture' to Africa, including an orchestra or a chamber group." Africa had been "saturated" with American jazz; it was time to defy the "notion that jazz was all the United States had to offer." This met with howls of protest from ANTA. The group argued that officials in State did "not understand the role of jazz or black artists in cultural affairs and that their elitism undermined cultural efforts." All of this had little impact on Battle, and from early 1963 onward the Department of State would handle the performing arts.[15]

Shortly thereafter, the USIA dropped another bombshell when it announced that it was ridding itself of the art program and shipping it off to the Smithsonian. In early 1965, the agency announced that it would no longer sponsor the U.S. exhibits at the Venice and São Paulo shows. Despite the recent successes scored by American artists at those prestigious art exhibitions, old problems led to the sad decision: as one reporter concluded, "an old hot potato has once again been dropped with a thud." Grand prizes were nice, of course, but the USIA still felt heated criticisms from the usual suspects. Conservative art groups complained about the abundance of modern art in the shows. Congress was still wary of anything having to do with the arts, and Representative Francis Walter still patrolled the waters of American culture for any signs of un-American behavior. Some U.S. art critics even criticized the success at Venice in 1964, complaining that the emphasis on pop art was "showmanship for its own sake." Worse yet had been some unnerving comments from the European audience, particularly after Robert Rauschenberg won the top prize. Various articles branded the art as "dehumanized," "despiritualized," and "devoid of all human values." The USIA, with so many other informational tasks to accomplish, simply had enough.[16]

In November 1965, the USIA signed an agreement with the Smithsonian Institution, giving the latter control of the international art program. The USIA would continue to provide some funds, but the Smithsonian would now pick up the "hot potato." It was hoped that such an arrangement would allow the art program to continue, but without "official" USIA participation. The Institution, regarded by many as the repository of American knowledge and culture, would not have to face the same kinds of criticisms previously leveled at State and the USIA; the USIA, for its part, could portray itself as having recognized that art was properly the bailiwick of "private" hands. That, at least, was what the public heard. What it was not privy to were the battles that erupted almost immediately as the USIA continued to insist on "policy guidance" for the art shows put together and run by the Smithsonian. In an early memorandum to the Institution, USIA officials suggested that there be two types of art exhibits: one, aimed at the "artistic elite in Western Europe," would feature the "most advanced and talked-about work from our contemporary production"; the other would be geared toward the "broader cultivated public which, while less sophisticated in its taste for art, forms its judgment of peoples in part at least from what it knows or thinks it knows of their cultural achievements." For this audience, the exhibits should be "good shows, not inferior in quality, but less 'avant garde' and more comprehensible to the non-professional audience. These shows should be retrospective in nature." Officials at the Smithsonian were taken aback by these "recommendations." They saw the art program's goal in a very different light: "to show current activity in the visual arts, in vivid and informative installations, geared to sophisticated European audiences." From the beginning, therefore, the Smithsonian–USIA partnership was shaky, to say the least.[17]

As it soon became clear, the entire cultural diplomacy enterprise of the United States was on shaky grounds. Many U.S. officials seemed confident that the cultural war with the communists had been won: American art was winning international recognition; the new civil rights acts meant that this particular sore spot could now be put to rest; and the successes at Brussels and Moscow in the late 1950s suggested that the "American way of life," including art, science, technology, and mass consumerism, was now embraced by friend and, possibly, foe alike. In part, this hubris facilitated the recent administrative changes. State now believed it could dispense with much help from the private sector – it had sufficiently mastered cultural diplomacy and knew how to use it. The USIA felt comfortable in jettisoning the troublesome art program; after all, the art war was over and the United States was the winner. However, an unpopular and brutal war in Vietnam, the resurgence of even more destructive race problems, and a resulting wave of anti-Americanism around the world soon challenged those optimistic assessments. By the mid-1960s the cracks – some new, others that had simply been spackled over for the past twenty years – in America's program to use culture as part of its international relations emerged full force. Before the 1960s were over, the once bright hopes of 1961 seemed all but extinguished.

As it turned out, the USIA dumped the art hot potato at just the right time. The U.S. involvement in Vietnam had a devastating impact: as much as the supporters of the art program might want the American paintings, drawings, and sculptures to speak an international language of understanding, for increasing numbers of people any examples of American culture were simply manifestations of an imperialistic and militaristic power. At the 1968 Venice Biennale, student protests threatened to close down the entire exhibition. Claiming that the show and the art were "fascist" and "capitalist," the young protesters particularly targeted the U.S. pavilion shouting slogans such as the tried and true, "Yankee Go Home," and the Vietnam War-inspired, "Ho Chi Minh." Margaret Cogswell, who was working with the Smithsonian's art program, recalled that,

> There were a lot of demonstrations – Carlos the Jackal was said to have been there, stirring things up. We found it exciting, but rather alarming, especially from the point of view of the safety of the works borrowed for the exhibition. I recall a demonstration in front of the US Pavilion, and worries by Norman Geske, US Commissioner, that something terrible might happen.

Nothing happened to the U.S. art on display, but the damage to the American art program was just beginning. A year later, American artists took matters into their own hands by withdrawing from participation at the 1969 São Paulo Bienal in protest against both Brazil's repressive dictatorship and the U.S. support of that regime. As Claire Bower explains in her insightful piece on American art diplomacy, a number of American artists and art groups became increasingly radicalized during the late 1960s and early 1970s, and their protests against American foreign policy, particularly the war in Vietnam, became an additional and unforeseen problem for both USIA and Smithsonian officials.[18]

Matters came to a head at the 1970 Venice Biennale. In an effort to forestall protests from both the Italian students and American artists, the Smithsonian organizers hit upon the idea of turning the U.S. pavilion into a "workshop" focused on the production and display of graphic arts. American artists would serve as instructors and mentors; students would include "outstanding American and Italian art students" who would "carry back to their universities a heightened sense of empathy for the international community of artists." The Smithsonian stressed the international focus of the workshop rather than the typical national art exhibit. This, it hoped, would "depoliticize" the entire affair. It soon became apparent, however, that after years of trying to infuse American art shows with distinct political messages it would prove difficult to divorce the two in 1970. Just as planning for the workshop was under way, the Vietnam War took another ugly turn when President Richard Nixon announced the U.S. invasion of Cambodia which led to angry protests on American college campuses and the killings of students at Kent State University and Jackson State University. In response, a group of artists formed the Emergency Cultural Government (ECG) that included such luminaries as Andy Warhol, Roy Lichtenstein, and former grand prizewinner Robert Rauschenberg, to protest the U.S. exhibit in Venice. Once again, many American artists declined to participate and there was some thought given to simply abandoning any pretense of a U.S. show. The result was a poorly attended workshop that drew barbs from many American art critics. Perhaps the highlight of the entire episode was the production of one particular poster by artist William Weege, who characterized himself as an "All-American Artist." The poster in question was emblazoned with the words "Impeach Nixon" and Weege began distributing copies to interested visitors. A Smithsonian official was furious and demanded that he stop production of the poster. The reasoning dripped with irony: "once an American artist goes abroad, especially if he is on an official government project, he is an American first and always." So much, apparently, for the emphasis on internationalism. Weege stormed out of the workshop for a short time before returning – without the offending poster.[19]

U.S. officials also struggled with the civil rights component of its cultural programing by the mid- to late-1960s. One notable cultural diplomacy casualty was the opera *Porgy and Bess*. During the 1950s the American government sponsored a number of tours of the show around the world in an effort to both demonstrate U.S. cultural achievements and to highlight the African American actors and actresses as exemplars of racial progress. By the early 1960s, however, many African Americans wanted nothing to do with the opera or its messages. Jazz legend Duke Ellington fumed in 1964, "Porgy and Bess, those people in alleys, waking up, dusting those carpets out of the windows and beating their brooms in time and all that bullshit. You want to know about America, we're going to make a cultural exchange, we send you Porgy and Bess, this is the complete image of our Negro." African American newspapers also spoke out against government sponsorship of the show abroad, claiming that it gave the foreign audience a stereotyped and demeaning portrayal of black society and culture. The State Department heeded the warnings – the opera continued to tour many foreign nations, but now it would do so without government support.[20]

The reliance on "notable" African Americans to serve as cultural ambassadors also proved more and more problematic. As in the 1950s, some of the most famous African Americans were also those most critical of the U.S. government. Malcolm X, Eldridge Cleaver, and the Black Panthers were most certainly notable and garnered wide press coverage in America and abroad, but they were hardly the messengers American officials were looking for. And, unlike the 1950s, the power of the civil rights movement made it difficult for the U.S. government to silence or marginalize such figures and groups. Even in the area of sports, where American officials had long looked in order to find popular African American figures to publicize in publications and films or send abroad, the tide had turned. Cassius Clay was now Muhammad Ali, a member of the Nation of Islam and in the early stages of a very public court battle with the U.S. government over his refusal to be drafted to fight in Vietnam. Matters escalated at the 1968 Olympic Games when two black athletes, Tommie Smith and John Carlos, mounted the dais to accept the gold and bronze medals in the 200-meter dash. As the American national anthem played, the two athletes raised their hands, both in black gloves, in a black power salute and bowed their heads.[21]

All of this was evidence of something that U.S. officials had great difficulty in understanding. Many of them believed that with the passage of the 1964 and 1965 civil rights legislation the "race problem" had come to a successful conclusion. Despite their hopes, however, the problem simply refused to go away, and the surge of racial violence after the laws were on the books befuddled and frustrated the American government's attempts to tell the world about how the United States solved its most controversial problem. When race riots broke out in Harlem in 1964 and, even more destructively, in Watts in 1965, U.S. officials struggled to explain what was happening to the world audience. Soviet and Chinese propagandists had little trouble in pinpointing the reasons for the racial violence – the continued oppression of black Americans. More disturbing to officials at State and the USIA, the communists began to very clearly draw lines of connection to the "brutal war of imperialism" against the Vietnamese people. The American responses during the remainder of the Johnson years and well into the Nixon presidency ranged from the traditional, to the truly bizarre, and finally to attempts to simply "whiten" the entire story.

One of the trusted traditional methods, still regarded as valuable even after the violence of 1964 and 1965, was to put forward notable – and more "moderate" – African Americans as alternatives to the headline-grabbing radicals. Some of the names bandied about for possible USIA features were political figures such as Cleveland mayor Carl Stokes and Senator Edward Brooke, civil rights leader Whitney Young, and singer James Brown. Yet, the use of famous African Americans as answers to criticisms about America's continuing civil rights problem now underwent a subtle shift. Focusing entirely on black Americans might imply that "U.S. civil rights protests are being made only by Negros or that the progress thus far has been made only by Negros." As one USIA report put it, the danger in this was that it would "suggest that what has occurred or is occurring in the US is a successful War of People's Liberation. Emphasis should be on change, evolution, *not* dramatic revolution in our conscience, folkways, or political life." Instead, USIA products should keep the "emphasis on the response of the white community, not the fate of the Negro. We should avoid, in short, the black-and-white treatment, prefer[ring] the low key, mulatto, as it were coverage." In short, the focus would be on helpful whites (particularly those in the federal government), not angry African Americans. The results were mixed, to say the least. In trying to put the destructive Watts riots into the proper "perspective," USIA underwrote a film that would try to explain the violence. When the project was completed, USIA officials were not pleased. It demanded that scenes showing "'neglect, discrimination, hopelessness, frustration, etc.,' will be eliminated." New scenes "will be integrated and show caucasian assistance, not caucasian dis-interest." The entire work was eventually torpedoed, replaced by a film purchased from a company that recently opened a new business in Watts that produced tents for the military. (By 1968, the company had reduced its workforce by one-third and was nearly financially insolvent.[22])

These tepid responses did little to address the fact that civil rights in America continued to be an important and controversial issue among the foreign audience as well as an exceedingly tempting target for communist propaganda. The violence of the "long, hot summers" that continued throughout the 1960s, the media attention given to black radicals, and the assassination of the leading spokesman for passive resistance, Dr. Martin Luther King, all made it impossible to ignore the issue in USIA's output. By the time the Nixon administration came into office in 1969, another change had taken place in the tone of the civil rights message for the international audience. Instead of ignoring the violence, USIA took a two-track approach. First, the racial violence needed to be put into the larger perspective of protest (particularly by the young) that characterized the 1960s not only in the United States but also around the world. The protests were simply examples of democracy at work; instead of being evidence of the failure of America's civil rights legislation, the protests were merely signs of the rising expectations among African Americans. Second, although acknowledging the violence, the USIA would stress that most African Americans (and their white supporters) favored nonviolence. The foremost example of this approach was the 1970 documentary *I Am a Man*. It focused on three African Americans – Stokes, Ernest Green (one of the Little Rock students from 1957), and Jesse Jackson. The film would emphasize that "less visible, less often reported, civil rights activity goes on steadily, and is more fundamental to civil rights progress than the outbreaks of violence that make headlines." However, even the "militant activity when it comes must be recognized as part of the pattern of real change, a necessary part." As the narrator explains, "Black Americans awake to a new time. The struggle has often been militant. The struggle has sometimes been violent. But rioting and destruction have not brought solutions. More thoughtful and practical solutions, most Negroes feel, are the only answers. Sometimes their frustrations explode in violent acts and violent talk. They rage at what has not been done."[23]

The USIA also continued to use famous African Americans to send its message. One short film focused on the former boxing champion Archie Moore, who "offers an alternative to rioting, looting, and burn-baby-burn. It's studying, working, and learn-baby-learn." And in what can only be characterized as one of the most perplexing USIA projects dealing with civil rights, the agency funded a TV series starring the well-known comedian Nipsey Russell. Featuring black and white guests, at least two episodes were produced for French TV and were shown in various African nations. The hope was that the funny and charismatic Russell would be a spokesman for "the progress of civil rights in the U.S." Whether that message got through or not is uncertain. What is clear, however, is that other parts of the show – particularly those sections featuring scantily clad dancing women – caused consternation. In Ethiopia, one critic worried that the "suggestive dancing" might lead to "wild, frenzied dancing" among Ethiopian young people that would lead to physical and moral harm. An American official observed that "There is a girl trio...and they do put on a very healthy display of grinds. I'm not sure how this will be received." Whatever the reception, it was clear that the USIA was seriously adrift on the issue of civil rights. By the early 1970s, the basic message was distilled down to a simple statement: "our minorities are making significant strides in attaining equal opportunities." The wording was important. Equal rights had been replaced by equal opportunities, reflecting the Nixon administration's desire to "close the economic gap between the races by 'getting more Black people to behave like whites,' that is, 'get into business, go to school, become homeowners.' At stake for Nixon was social stability: 'People who own their own homes don't burn down their neighborhoods'."[24]

Along with the struggles concerning older issues such as the government–private relationship in cultural diplomacy, the always-controversial arts program, and dealing with the civil rights problem, the late 1960s also witnessed another blow that seriously undermined America's cultural efforts abroad. In 1966 the *New York Times* ran a series of articles detailing the CIA's multifaceted activities, including its involvement with "private" cultural and intellectual organizations such as the Congress for Cultural Freedom (CCF), often by funneling money through the Department of State and the USIA. This was followed in March 1967 by a piece in the magazine *Ramparts* exposing the Central Intelligence Agency's involvement with the United States National Student Association and its recruiting of foreign students visiting the United States and "turning them into spies against their own homeland." It further expanded upon the earlier revelations from the *New York Times* by outlining how the CIA ended up funding "private" groups and individuals involved in cultural activities.[25]

The revelations about the CCF were particularly unnerving for America's cultural diplomats. Established in 1950, and secretly funded by the CIA, the organization "engaged in an extraordinary array of activities, including festivals, seminars, and concerts, all designed to demonstrate to intellectuals the cultural advantages of political freedom." It soon established a presence throughout Europe. According to Hugh Wilford, the "most successful venture in Britain was undoubtedly its magazine *Encounter*" that "rapidly established a reputation as the foremost journal of 'serious' political opinion and cultural expression in the English language." Like the CCF, the magazine "remained financially dependent on secret subsidies from the CIA." The CCF also funded publication of the magazine *Quadrant* in Australia, "one of twenty magazines the Congress of Cultural Freedom published in Europe, Africa, Asia, and Australia." The impact of these stories on America's cultural diplomacy abroad was quick and devastating. Paul McGarr notes that in India exposure of the fact that

> the Indian Committee for Cultural Freedom, a local offshoot of the CCF, had accepted money from the CIA provoked an outpouring of public indignation. Chester Bowles, American ambassador in New Dehli at the time, lamented that fallout from the *Ramparts* furor was likely to prove particularly damaging to United States' standing in India, "where we [the US] had developed especially close and extensive relationships with Indian universities and with individual scholars, none of which were in any way connected with intelligence operations."[26]

After a promising start in 1961, by the 1970s, America's cultural diplomacy program was in tatters. The Department of State had taken over cultural programing from ANTA, but then seemed little inclined to follow through with anything approaching the vibrant music, theater, and dance programs of the 1950s and early 1960s. The arts program had completely exploded, with the American artists themselves boycotting U.S. presentations abroad. Dealing with the race problem had become a muddled (and sometimes baffling) series of stops and starts with no clear or consistent message to give the international audience, particularly in the wake of the post–civil rights legislation violence. African American athletes had seemingly turned against their own country. Even the early optimism about African Americans being appointed to high visibility positions in the foreign policy bureaucracy turned sour. A 1969 article by political scientist John A. Davis (who had been hammering away for more opportunities for African Americans in the Department of State since the 1940s) concluded that little had changed:

> three Negro ambassadors, two in Africa; two Deputy Assistant Secretaries of State, none in African areas; nineteen Foreign Service Officers; eleven Junior Foreign Service Reserve Officers; and twenty-four Foreign Service Reserve Officers – a drop of twenty-seven since 1967. This picture is a disgrace, a monument to bureaucratic rigidity and an embarrassment to the United States everywhere in the world, especially in Africa and Asia.[27]

All of this topped off by another very public embarrassment for the United States in the form of media revelations about the CIA's secret funding of "private" intellectual and cultural groups, meetings, magazines, and festivals around the world. In such an environment, it was not only tougher and tougher to tell the world the truth about America – it was getting harder and harder to get the world to listen.

Perhaps the most difficult hurdle to overcome was a lack of interest by the Nixon White House. As Nicholas Cull observes, "Nixon and Kissinger had little tolerance for any role of public diplomacy in the foreign policy process. Kissinger sidelined the USIA director to an obscure NSC subcommittee."[28] This is not to suggest that cultural diplomacy simply disappeared. It continued to spring up at unexpected moments, but had lost much of its focus, drive, and – most significantly – place as a recognized and important component of U.S. foreign policy. As Cull notes in his thorough study of the USIA, the agency continued to turn out interesting pieces of work. Two films – *Czechoslovakia, 1968* and *An Impression of John Steinbeck: Writer* – were nominated for Academy Awards in 1970 for best documentary short film; *Czechoslovakia, 1968* won. American libraries overseas began stocking "liberal books" which "marked the end of the McCarthy-era library book black list." Even sports made a bit of a comeback, highlighted by the so-called "ping-pong diplomacy" episode of 1971 when the U.S. ping-pong team visited China and was hailed as a diplomatic breakthrough leading to Nixon's visit to China a year later. Jazz diplomacy also continued to serve as a cultural entry point into the Soviet Union. The New York Jazz Repertory group toured Russia in 1975, playing to sell-out crowds.[29]

The U.S. pavilion at the World's Fair in Osaka, Japan, in 1970 highlighted both the once bright promise of American cultural diplomacy and the continuing problem related to telling the world the truth about America. As one U.S. official noted, such fairs continued to be a battleground in the Cold War. Osaka "mattered because the cultural arena was claimed equally by both sides, and at various levels. There was an almost implicit agreement that winning militarily, winning economically, and winning politically were all important goals, but that winning culturally would also be a major victory." Confusion, however, abounded almost from the very beginning of the fair due to the fact that there was not just one U.S. pavilion, but numerous "American" pavilions around the fairgrounds. The USIA sponsored the "official" pavilion, but various American businesses set up separate exhibits, as did many U.S. states and cities. This was "not only confusing to the average fairgoer but in some cases, downright irritating." As at the 1958 show in Brussels, American art also proved irritating. One of the largest exhibits in the U.S. pavilion was a collection of pictures by some of America's best-known photographers. And, like the controversial "Unfinished Business" exhibit more than a decade before, the pictures often showed the rougher edges of American society. Censorship, however, meant that one particularly rough edge would not be shown: the war in Vietnam. A photo by Diane Arbus showed a young American man wearing buttons that said things such as "Bomb Hanoi" and "Vietnam: Support Our Boys." U.S. officials quickly informed the exhibit organizers that anything having to do with Vietnam was off limits and, after much discussion, the offending image was removed. The pictures of tenements and other unsavory aspects of the United States were often criticized by American visitors, but the Japanese press loved the "truthful" presentation of the United States. One U.S. official summed up the irony of the situation: "We may not have made it with the Americans, but we certainly made it with the Japanese." Andrew James Wulf concludes in his study of U.S. international exhibitions during the Cold War, "the gritty realism of *Ten Photographers* revealed the colliding values of both a conservative and liberal America." As was the case with so much of America's cultural diplomacy, the truth(s) was in the eye of the beholder.[30]

From the photographs, visitors were treated to a whirlwind tour of America, from a retrospective exhibit of American painting ("It was a bore."), to Babe Ruth's baseball uniform, American race cars, architecture exhibits, a display of Native American folk art, a room dedicated to Shaker arts and crafts, and a pop art display featuring a giant ice bag sculpted by Claes Oldenburg. The undeniable hit of the pavilion, however, was the exhibit on space, featuring space suits, the *Apollo 12* capsule, and what became the single most popular item on display, a rock from the moon. There was no denying that the American pavilion was popular with the crowds who waited for hours to go through the exhibits. (The wait was apparently too much for one visitor who went to the bathroom on a cardboard art piece. As an exhibit organizer put it, "But anyway, that was life in the U.S. pavilion at Osaka.") Yet, what did the American show in Osaka really mean to those who saw it? As Wulf argues, "The U.S. pavilion at Expo 70 should be remembered as the uneasy and altogether awkward mingling of American scientific ingenuity, pop culture, and avant-garde art forms, all housed in the radically designed 'Band-Aid' [the derisive term used to describe the flat, oblong shaped pavilion]."[31]

The cultural diplomacy program proceeded by fits and starts throughout the remainder of the 1970s, 1980s, and into the 1990s. The period was characterized by a nearly constant state of flux, with the reorganization under the administration of Jimmy Carter (in which cultural and educational matters were taken out of State and put into the USIA which was now renamed the United States International Communications Agency), followed by another reorganization in 1983 in which the USIA name was restored, and, in 1999, the final reorganization scheme in which the USIA was dissolved and its duties moved back into the Department of State. Throughout this dizzying and baffling series of changes, America's cultural diplomacy suffered a fairly steady decline. Nicholas Cull explains that,

> Of all the elements of public diplomacy, cultural diplomacy fared least well during the period. The USIA lost most of its magazines, its Arts Ambassador projects, and most of its cultural centers and libraries too. Despite some well-considered programs, and the creativity of officers in the field in raising private money and piggybacking on other events, cultural diplomacy suffered a lingering death by a thousand cuts.

Some of this, as retired Foreign Service officer Juliet Antunes Sablosky argues, was due to the "ideological bent of senior political appointees in the Educational and Cultural Affairs Bureau." During the Reagan years,

> it was charged that senior management officials were reviewing selections for the American Participants program, USIA's overseas speakers program, in an effort to discourage the use of people whose views were considered incompatible with those of the administration. The existence of a "black list" was denied by the agency. However, the American Participants program was hurt by the negative publicity.

Just as serious were the budget cuts that plagued the cultural programs. By 1998, USIA's budget was one-third smaller than it had been just five years earlier, and the agency's personnel were reduced by a like number. In 1997, the Arts America program was eliminated: "It had administered overseas performing arts programs, fine arts exhibitions, and speakers/specialists in the arts." The embarrassment came to a climax in 1992 when the United States nearly withdrew from the Seville World's Fair. As Cull notes, "many in Congress failed to see its relevance to the United States," and when it finally did take action it approved a paltry $13 million. An American pavilion was hastily constructed, but "the U.S. site remained derelict" and the U.S. building "looked incongruously small on the large site that the Spanish had provided for their 'guest of honor'." Meanwhile, Canada spent $28 million for its pavilion.[32] It almost reminded one of Teddy Roosevelt's battle to secure funding for the Bordeaux exposition over eighty years before.

Even one of the most reliable forms of cultural diplomacy, sports, went into decline. Ever since the Soviets announced their intention to participate in the Olympics beginning in 1952 the games became a cultural battlefield between the Russians and the Americans. At the Summer Olympics (where the United States traditionally dominated), boxing, basketball, gymnastics, and other sports were turned into tests of will and national pride; during the winter games, hockey and figure skating played the same role. Who won the most medals (and, almost as important, who won the most gold medals) became an issue of international importance. As Allen Guttmann observed in his study of the Cold War Olympics, "As the games have become increasingly important in the political sphere, the success or failure of the Olympic team, as measured in the unofficial medal counts, has often overshadowed the performances of the men and women who actually ran, jumped, threw, wrestled, rode, and otherwise displayed their physical skills."[33] Nevertheless, controversies over those performances became commonplace. The Soviets attacked the U.S. athletes as amateurs in name only, arguing that the corporate sponsorships of the American team meant they were simply tools of capitalist imperialism. The United States responded by arguing that not only were the Russian (and other Eastern Bloc) athletes complete puppets of the state, but it also suggested that steroid and other illegal performance-enhancing drug use – particularly in regard to East German athletes – was commonplace. Scoring also became a source of conflict. In sports such as figure skating and boxing, where the outcome depended not on the clock or a final score but on "objective" judging, there were few times where an American won over a communist opponent, or vice versa, when charges of favoritism were not leveled. To be sure, the scoring in some contests did seem to vary wildly depending on the national origins of the judges.[34] It was in the sport of basketball, however, that one of the most controversial episodes in the U.S.-Soviet rivalry took place at the 1972 games. The United States had long dominated basketball at the Olympics, but a goodwill tour of America by the Soviet team in 1971 served notice that the Russians were ready to challenge that supremacy. Despite the Americans' best efforts – including putting some teams on the floor that featured professional players – the Soviets won the first eight games of the tour before finally losing by three points in the last contest. "The whippings of that 1971 tour served as a wake-up call for the Americans and proved that the Soviet team could no longer be readily beaten by just an average American amateur team." No one, however, could have expected what was to come. At the Munich Olympics in 1972, already reeling from the terrorist attacks that killed nearly a dozen members of the Israeli team, the Soviets and the United States met in the finals for basketball. It was a close game throughout, but it looked as though the Americans would pull it out when they went ahead by one point with just three seconds left. Then, in one of the wildest and certainly the most heatedly debated finishes in the history of Olympic sports, the Soviets won – after three replays of making their in-bounds throw, referees and timekeepers screaming and being screamed at, and a disbelieving U.S. team left frothing with accusations about cheating and biased officiating. The U.S. team's anger was so great that it did not even accept the second-place silver medals, arguing that it deserved the gold.[35]

From there, things went steadily downhill as international politics threatened to completely overwhelm the games. Following the Soviet invasion of Afghanistan in November 1979, President Jimmy Carter announced that the United States would be boycotting the summer 1980 games that were to be held in Moscow. (The winter games, held in Lake Placid, New York, in February 1980, went on as planned. The United States got some revenge for its basketball loss in 1972, as the American hockey team pulled off the "Miracle on Ice" by defeating the heavily favored Russians.) For U.S. athletes, it was a bitter pill to swallow. Some supported the decision, but others expressed anger over the intrusion of foreign policy into the amateur games. As one put it, "I must accept the inescapable conclusion: I am a pawn." The Carter administration blithely assumed that its allies, and many other nations, would join in the boycott and actively campaigned to have them do so. Over sixty countries did, such as the People's Republic of China, but most of Western Europe – including France and Great Britain – ignored the pleas from the United States. They joined eighty-one nations in

Moscow. Naturally enough, the Soviets retaliated by boycotting the 1984 games scheduled for Los Angeles and convinced sixteen of their allies to follow suit. With the Russians (and the very strong Cuban boxing team) out of the competition, the United States racked up nearly 175 medals, winning four times the number of gold medals as any other nation in Los Angeles.[36] But nothing really came out of the political machinations surrounding the Olympics untarnished, and with the end of the Cold War the rivalry was over.

The death of much of the cultural programing from the United States came as a result of a changing world environment and a budget-cutting Congress that zeroed in on the always-vulnerable cultural side of American diplomacy. Cultural diplomacy's supporters initially claimed that the collapse of the Soviet empire during the late 1980s and early 1990s was evidence of how powerful a tool culture could be in America's foreign policy. It quickly became clear that many others saw a different meaning:

> Despite USIA's downsizing and reinventing, some felt it had outlived its usefulness. The post-cold war reaction was similar to that which had followed the two world wars. It was fine to have information activities and even cultural exchanges during times of crisis; however, once the crisis was past, Congress seemed eager to dismantle the organizations involved and return to the status quo antebellum.

And Congress was certainly in a budget-cutting mood during the 1990s. As one new member of the House of Representatives put it, the cultural programs were, "Wonderful programs; the U.S. government can't afford them. It will burden my children with national debt."[37]

The acknowledged leader of the Congressional assault, however, was Senator Jesse Helms. A long-standing antipathy toward both governmental involvement with the arts and much of the foreign policy making bureaucracy led Helms to target the USIA, particularly its cultural diplomacy activities. He was assisted in the effort by the controversial figure of Steven K. Berry, a former member of State who was fired for his part in using his office to locate materials that would discredit President Bill Clinton. Berry had an ax to grind and now found the perfect way to do so: "Privately, Berry hoped that the consolidation of the USIA into State might change the culture at Foggy Bottom. In conversation…he compared the public diplomacy idea to a benign virus, which he hoped would infect every level of his old workplace." Helms himself was not above using political blackmail to get rid of the USIA, holding a bill on a chemical weapons convention hostage in the Senate until Clinton would agree to his demand to terminate the agency. A bill eventually made its way through Congress and in October 1999 USIA officially entered the world of "former government agencies" and its duties subsumed by the Department of State's Office for Public Diplomacy and

Public Affairs.[38] The impact was immediate, as shown by the fate of the once vibrant art program. As a State report in 2000 put it, "The budget for cultural presentations in FY-2000 is almost exactly what it was in the 1954–1962 period – about $2 million annually – but in dollars NOT adjusted for inflation." America's international art program, which once sent U.S. art circling the globe, was reduced to one State-sponsored tour of an Andy Warhol retrospective.[39]

It was a remarkable, stunning, and, to some, saddening collapse of a program that began with such high ideals and interest in the 1940s and 1950s. With no "evil empire" left to fight, the reasoning seemed to go, why spend time, effort, and money on trying to tell the world the truth – or, for that matter, anything else – about the United States? For most American citizens and political figures, the Cold War had been won through a massive military buildup that simultaneously kept the Soviets in check and also encouraged them to wreak havoc on their already-unsteady economy by trying to match U.S. defense spending. The paintings, operas, symphonies, books, and plays sent abroad now seemed like unimportant footnotes to the colossal political upheavals of the 1980s and 1990s that brought the Soviets to their knees. The need for international understanding and appreciation of American culture was unimportant. All that the world now needed to understand was that America had emerged victorious, the undisputed champion of a fight that lasted over four decades.

Conclusion: The Soul of a Nation

The Department of State is looking for a few good people. Through its Bureau of Education and Cultural Affairs, it is reaching out to find specific individuals and groups to represent the United States abroad. The recruiting standards seem quite minimal: eighteen years of age or older (for some positions, the minimum age is raised to twenty-one); U.S. citizenship; and a willingness to travel abroad for weeks (or months) at a time. Experience working with various groups, particularly young people, is often mentioned; the ability to collaborate or "engage" seems high on the list of priorities. The list of desired specific skills is long, eclectic, and, to people older than twenty-one perhaps a bit baffling: experience in "Beat Making, DJing, B-Boying/B-Girling (or other forms of hip hop dancing), or MCing"; "Innovative musicians either stylistically, lyrically, or technologically within their musical worlds"; expertise in "any characteristically American musical genre...including but not limited to Americana, Blues, Bluegrass, Cajun, Country, Folk, Latin, Native American, Gospel, Hip Hop/Urban, Indie Rock, Jazz, Punk, R&B, and Zydeco"; "Strong record of artistic accomplishments with some international experience"; "Emerging, mid-career or established visual artists"; or have skills in baseball, basketball, martial arts, soccer, swimming, volleyball, or a variety of winter sports. All of these individuals and groups will be part of a concerted effort that "creates long-lasting ties between the United States and other countries by providing Americans with access to international artists, while sharing America's rich culture of performing arts with international audiences." It is 2017 and it seems astounding that cultural diplomacy, apparently down and out for the count in 1999, could stage such an amazing comeback and offer a rich variety of programs in the performing arts of music, theater, and dance; the visual arts, including film; and numerous sports.[1]

It was not a gradual rebirth of interest in cultural diplomacy among U.S. officials. It was, quite literally, an explosion set off by two planes crashing into the World Trade Center, another smashing into the Pentagon, and another falling to earth in Pennsylvania (likely a result of the passengers battling with the hijackers), on September 11, 2001. A group of al-Qaeda terrorists shook America to its core, and new fears arose that just a decade after winning the Cold War the United States was now at war with a new, little understood, and deadly enemy. The reaction by the American government was immediate and far-reaching. Citizens soon became familiar with a reality encompassed in a new vocabulary, including the Department of Homeland Security, the USA PATRIOT Act, a war against terrorism in Afghanistan, another in Iraq, domestic surveillance, radical Islam, waterboarding, and Osama bin Laden. America was quite aware of the military actions taken abroad against this new threat, and long lines at airports to get through tightened security certainly made them cognizant of new and (hopefully) improved anti terrorism acts at home. Given the drama and shock, it is not terribly surprising that another part of the war on terror, involving baseball stars and hip-hop artists, was little noticed by the American public.

The renewed interest in cultural diplomacy on the part of the U.S. government was, in some ways, not terribly surprising. Yes, it had been just two years since the ignominious absorption of the USIA into the Department of State and budget cuts that reduced the cultural programs to a shadow of what they had once been. Even at the time, however, a number of different people made the same point: that during wartime, or threats to national security, all weapons – including culture – would be brought to bear. With the end of the Cold War, the expense, suspect effectiveness, and fears of government intervention in the arts all conspired to portray cultural diplomacy as a force that was no longer needed or desirable. It was a simple, but seemingly accurate, equation: war equals more emphasis on culture as a weapon; peace meant a return to the normal governmental disinterest in anything related to art or culture. Now, America was again at war and policymakers once more grasped at anything that promised to help in achieving victory. And it is entirely appropriate that the former "hot potato" of cultural diplomacy has returned to its original official home: the Department of State, specifically its Bureau of Education and Cultural Affairs (ECA). But, this war was different and, therefore, required a cultural approach that while it had its precedent in Cold War efforts, would reflect the different circumstances and different enemy.

Outwardly, the new cultural diplomacy offensive did not appear substantially different from the preceding offensive during the Cold War. In fact, many observers drew direct connections back to the golden years of cultural diplomacy. One senior diplomat argued that "Like its predecessors during the early Cold War era, the Bush administration must realize that in waging its self-proclaimed war against extremism, winning foreigners' voluntary allegiance to the American project will be the most important prize of all."[2] The U.S. government utilized many of the same "weapons" as it had before: dance, music, theater, museums, sports, film, and literature, for instance. The DanceMotion USA program sent companies (including one of the first dance troupes sent abroad in the 1950s, the Limón Dance Company) to the Middle East, Asia, and Africa. Under the auspices of the Next Level program, "beatmakers," DJs, and dancers travel the world, and the American Music Abroad program sponsors tours by an eclectic array of musicians and groups. In 2006, world champion ice skater Michelle Kwan was named the "first American Public Diplomacy Envoy." She was joined in 2011 by baseball Hall of Fame player Cal Ripken. Under the Sports Envoys program, American athletes travel the world to connect with foreign audiences. In 2010, State jumped back into the world of art by establishing smART Power in conjunction with the Bronx Museum of the Arts, which was designed to "include visual artists like painters and sculptors, who will be asked next year to create public art projects in 15 foreign countries." Other museums cooperate with the Department of State in a program called Museums Connect, which in 2015 established the project "Identities: Understanding Islam in a Cross-Cultural Context" with a museum in Morocco.[3]

The differences, however, are also quite apparent. The most important is that the new cultural diplomacy effort has very distinct target audiences: young people and the Muslim world. The emphasis on Muslim societies is, of course, entirely understandable since for U.S. policymakers it is the Islamic world from which the current threat emanates. Much like during the Cold War, the war on terrorism is seen as much a contest between ideas as it is between armed forces. A 2004 report argued that the "contest of ideas [within Islam] is taking place not just in Arab and other Islamic countries but in the cities and villages of Europe, Asia, Africa, and the Western Hemisphere.... U.S. policies on Israeli-Palestinian issues and Iraq in 2003–2004 have damaged America's credibility and power to persuade." And there is broad agreement in the American government that one factor in that threat is a lack of understanding. As one official put it shortly after the attacks, "There's a worldwide debate about the relationship between Islam and the West, and we don't have a seat at that table."[4]

In fact, even before the USIA died in 1999 the United States was using cultural diplomacy to reach the Middle East. Since 1998, America and Iran have participated in a little-publicized program of cultural exchanges. Wrestlers from America traveled to Iran in 1998; since that time other American athletes, scientists, and artists have visited. In return, Iran sent increasing numbers of its own people to the United States, such as the 2009 trip by Iranian musicians who participated in a bluegrass festival in Kentucky. The State Department's hope was that "these cultural exchanges are helping pave the way for the next step toward easing more than three decades of mutual suspicion and hostility."[5] While some critics argued that the U.S. government should be more heavily publicizing these efforts, rather than conducting them in near-secrecy, after 9/11 the Department of State fully embraced – and advertised – its programs designed to provide outreach to the Muslim world.

The almost laser-like focus on young people, on the other hand, is fairly new. During the Cold War period America's cultural diplomats were certainly aware of the youth audience and they sometimes tailored their programs to reach it, with more modern music, modern art, or film. It was, however, just one of many audiences that State and the USIA sought to contact. The post-9/11 programs, although they might reach somewhat diverse audiences, are clearly designed for the young. Replacing the 1950s emphasis on classical music, the American Music Abroad Program stresses not only traditionally American music such as bluegrass and (as always) jazz but also hip-hop, urban music, indie rock, and punk. The program's website is quite blunt in stating that the artists "represent the new generation of musical ambassadors" who "focus on younger and underserved audiences." The Next Level program seeks to use "multi-disciplinary hip hop collaborations" for its people-to-people diplomacy, "especially among young audiences."[6] Although the reasoning for the extreme emphasis on international youth is never concretely spelled out, it is not hard to imagine. As during the Cold War, American policymakers look at the young people abroad not as today's "kids" but as tomorrow's leaders. In addition, another compelling factor might be the notion that anti-Americanism is so ingrained among the adult populations, particularly in Muslim societies, that efforts to change older minds might prove futile. Perhaps, it is best to focus on the more malleable minds of the young, particularly since those minds seem to crave certain aspects of American popular culture such as sports and contemporary music and dance. They are also the group most actively engaged with social media and other internet sources, which the new cultural diplomacy programs fully exploit.

While some of the cultural forms of outreach might have changed, along with the direction and "target audiences" of the new cultural diplomacy, many of the issues that have always haunted such efforts remain troublingly consistent. As always, the publicity surrounding the program is not being matched by funding. In 2008, America's cultural programs received a mere $10 million. As one former U.S. diplomat complained, "Public diplomacy has an important function in the State Department, but its poor stepchild, ECA, is inadequately staffed and funded to represent the creative sector of the U.S. on the world stage."[7]

Nevertheless, much like a character from one of America's greatest cultural productions, U.S. cultural diplomacy has "always depended on the kindness of strangers." Whether it was relying upon ANTA, MOMA, the AFA, the Smithsonian, and many others, State and the USIA were always more than happy to have the public sector do much of the heavy lifting. The new efforts are no different, as the ECA, with its small budget and staff, depends on the cooperation (and resources) of numerous private artists, groups, and institutions. The relationship, as in the 1950s, remains tempestuous and suspicion-ridden. At the crux of the battles lie two unresolved matters: the "purpose" of America's cultural diplomacy, and the always-controversial matter of government censorship.

In her article about the Museums Connect Program, Natalia Grincheva makes clear the continuing problem of whether cultural programs sent abroad should basically be concerned with human interaction via the arts, or, as the U.S. government often seems to prefer, as another means to power and influence. As she notes, the Department of State "considers several themes in the selection process of the museum projects," such as "empowering women and youth; mitigating religious, cultural, or political tensions, advocating human rights; building civic engagement and volunteerism," and so on. Yet, while State argues that one goal is to foster "such fundamental American values as religious and political freedom and human rights," it also makes clear that its overarching purpose is to "create a more secure, stable, and prosperous global arena in which the United States can advance its national interests." Proponents of Museums Connect respond that "there is no direct interference from the government"; none is needed since "the operational principles of American museums, nurtured within the national economic and political environment, can communicate values of liberal democracy and public engagement without governmental guidance." Others, however, are more skeptical, wondering whether the participating museums "want to be used to promote foreign policy," and claiming that U.S. officials have "suggested museums that they would like to see participate, and topics they would like to see covered, such as outreach to indigenous and minority communities in Muslim-majority societies." Journalist Lee Rosenbaum is more direct: "Cultural ties can assuredly improve relations between countries, but not when they are conceived as an instrument of political propaganda. AAM [American Alliance of Museums] has done a disservice to its members by signing up for this dubious government-curated enterprise." In her analysis of the new dance programs, Clare Croft also sounds a note of caution. While the new cultural diplomacy effort was often hailed by its proponents as "a re-envisioning of American global interactions, privileging listening over speaking, dialogue over 'messaging,'" the first congressional hearings into revitalizing the cultural programs were done under the heading, "The Message is America: Rethinking American Public Diplomacy." To Croft, this suggested "a return to twentieth-century diplomacy strategy focused on exporting American ideals."[8]

Both Grincheva and Croft are supportive of the cultural outreach efforts and argue that without official U.S. support (meager though it might be), private groups and individuals would be unable or unwilling to mount such programs on their own dime. Therefore, a certain amount of tolerance for government involvement is necessary for success. However, there is evidence that State's involvement often amounts to much more than a simple interest in seeing that its investments are put to good use. In her

2010 article announcing State's reentry into the use of art in its cultural diplomacy efforts, Kate Taylor highlighted the tensions between the official and private participants: "the State Department focused on whether local people's perceptions of the United States changed," whereas the Bronx Museum of the Arts was more interested in "whether the artists were able to complete their projects." State would be "reserving final approval over both the artists and their projects." As the Department official in charge of the program put it, "We just want to make sure that there aren't any issues." Pressed by Taylor to explain what was meant by the vaguely ominous term "issues," the answer was less than reassuring: "Oh, who knows? You never know, but you always want to reserve the right to have a final overlook." One artist who was also interviewed argued that the program could have value, "but only if the artists were given sufficient freedom," since the "best projects" might not "take the most obvious form that somebody in the State Department might imagine." A former participant in the Fulbright program, his own perception was that "it was also important to be able to convince people that he spoke and acted for himself, not for the United States." Croft cited one example from the dance program of what could happen when State inserted itself too heavily into the process. State left the choice of choreographers to private professionals, but then "generated the list of countries" to which they would be sent. The selected choreographers named their preferences, "mostly based on availability constraints rather than knowledge of any country or culture." The government's demand for a "quick timetable and selection process" made for problems: "The choreographers who were selected were relatively homogenous: four of the five were white women, and all five were from New York or California's largest cities. There was no attempt to match choreographer to locale, thus treating all of the chosen countries as though they were interchangeable. The choreographers I interviewed cited lack of preparation time as contributing to their significant misperceptions about the countries they would visit."[9]

It is certainly clear from many of the pieces and government reports that have been published in the years since 9/11 that U.S. officials continue to view cultural diplomacy largely in terms of how it promotes U.S. interests, although they are careful to note that those interests and the "desires" of the world's people very often coalesce. Helena Finn, a senior diplomat, wrote in 2003 (in words quite reminiscent of Cold War rhetoric) that cultural diplomacy was important because "dialogue is essential to winning the hearts and minds of moderate elements in societies vulnerable to radicalism." She makes clear, however, that "dialogue" means countering "extremism." The United States should "take inspiration from the successful cultural diplomacy of the Cold War" to "establish meaningful contact with the silent majority in the Muslim world, in ways other than through military force or traditional diplomacy." In her view, "Cultural diplomacy is one of the most potent weapons in the United States' armory," and she concludes with the hope that the U.S. government will realize that "in waging its self-proclaimed war against extremism, winning foreigners' voluntary allegiance to the American project will be the most important prize of all." The 2005 report from the Advisory Committee on Cultural Diplomacy approvingly quoted from the 9/11 Commission, which declared:

> Just as we did in the Cold War, we need to defend our ideals abroad vigorously. America does stand up for its values. The United States defended, and still defends, Muslims against tyrants and criminals in Somalia, Bosnia, Kosovo, Afghanistan, and Iraq. If the United States does not act aggressively to define itself in the Islamic World, the extremists will gladly do the job for us.[10]

Scholar Neal M. Rosendorf takes a more nuanced approach to the "war of ideas" understanding of cultural diplomacy's aims. "This approach," he argues, "is misdirected for several reasons.... It is critical to avoid sounding gratuitously aggressive; lest an approach designed to rehabilitate America's prestige and help create a safer international environment have the perversely opposite effect." Yet, his dislike of the "U.S. versus them" approach is grounded more on the idea that "there is no serious philosophical or ideological competitor to the model of liberal democracy that embraces some variant of capitalism." The "Muslim jihadists and terrorists are not responding to an ideology or philosophy in any secular sense of the term, but to a warped theological interpretation." Thus, he believes that the "monofocusing on the Arab-Muslim world in cultural diplomacy efforts ignores the other five billion people out there whose support or hostility toward the U.S. matters greatly to our ability to lead and maintain both American and international security." Cultural diplomacy's main benefits will be in "rehabilitating America's tattered global prestige and presenting a more accurate picture of American values." If the United States is unwilling or unable to more effectively utilize culture to achieve these goals, "we will not be able to lead effectively." He concludes that "Cultural diplomacy cannot do the job of remaking America's image by itself; but the job of remaking America's image cannot be done without cultural diplomacy."[11]

It might seem a long way from a decaying, stuffed moose being sent to France, to a Brooklyn hip-hop group sent to Syria, but in fact the connections between them – a period of time spanning nearly 250 years – are vivid and meaningful. During that time, the United States – sometimes officially, sometimes unofficially; stopping and starting; battling criticisms from within and outside of the nation – has utilized cultural diplomacy in attempt after attempt in the "remaking of America's image." Or, more accurately, it has tried to *make* a holistic image of America, to try and give meaning, form, and direction to a nation that has, over the last two centuries, stubbornly refused to adhere to a single standard of what is, and what is not, America/American. As one recent report argued, cultural diplomacy is "the linchpin of public diplomacy, for it is in cultural activities that a nation's idea of itself is best represented." In words that harkened back to the passionate defenses of international cultural efforts during the Cold War, the report exclaimed, "The ideals of the Founding Fathers, enshrined in the Declaration of Independence, the Constitution, the Federalist Papers, and the Bill of Rights, take on new life in the vibrant traditions of American art, dance, film, jazz, and literature, which continue to inspire people the world over despite our political differences." "Cultural diplomacy," the committee argued, "reveals the soul of a nation."[12] Perhaps it does. In the controversies and battles, the passion and anger, the conflicted and conflicting messages, the wild and often befuddling array of culture thrown at the world, the fears of being misunderstood, disrespected, or thought less of, the desire to be admired, to be emulated, to be loved, America's cultural diplomacy, from Jefferson to hip-hop, encapsulates all that is intriguing, mystifying, wonderful, appalling, and often aggravating about a nation still seeking an identity.

NOTES

Introduction

1 Michael J. Hogan and Thomas G. Paterson, eds., *Explaining the History of American Foreign Relations* (New York: Cambridge University Press, 1991), contained but one chapter on culture and international affairs by Akira Iriye. By the time the second edition appeared in 2004, a chapter on cultural transfer by Jessica Gienow-Hecht joined Iriye's work to represent culture and diplomacy. If we are to judge from the latest edition (2016, now edited by Frank Costigliola and Michael J. Hogan), there has been a bit of backsliding: both of those chapters are now gone, with Gienow-Hecht's essay on nation branding being the only direct reference to cultural diplomacy.
2 Cynthia P. Schneider, "Cultural Diplomacy: Hard to Define, But You'd Know It If You Saw It," *The Brown Journal of World Affairs* 13:1 (Fall/Winter 2006):191–203.
3 William A. Rugh, "The Case for Soft Power," in Philip Seib, ed., *Toward a New Public Diplomacy: Redirecting U.S. Foreign Policy* (New York: Palgrave MacMillan, 2009), p. 7.
4 Midori Yoshii, Michael L. Krenn, John Day Tully, and Thomas W. Zeiler, "A Roundtable on Thomas W. Zeiler's *Ambassadors in Pinstripes: The Spalding World Baseball Tour and the Birth of the American Empire, Passport: The Newsletter of the SHAFR* 38:2 (August 2007):9.
5 Margaret Cogswell, *Communication through Art*, May 2, 1964, Record Unit 321, Box 109, Communication through Art folder [36 of 36], Smithsonian Institution Archives, Washington, DC.

Chapter 1

1 Lee Alan Dugatkin, *Mr. Jefferson and the Giant Moose: Natural History in Early America* (Chicago: University of Chicago Press, 2009), p. ix.
2 Quote from De Pauw found in ibid., p. 31.
3 Paul Semonin, *American Monster: How the Nation's First Prehistoric Creature Became a Symbol of National Identity* (New York: New York University Press, 2000), p. 6.
4 Dugatkin, *Mr. Jefferson and the Giant Moose,* pp. 59, 60.
5 For a very good study of *Notes,* see David Tucker, *Enlightened Republicanism: A Study of Jefferson's* Notes on the State of Virginia (Lanham, MD: Lexington Books, 2008). Quotes are taken from *Notes on the State of Virginia* contained in Adrienne Koch and William Peden, eds., *The Life and Selected Writings of*

Thomas Jefferson (New York: The Modern Library, 1944), pp. 202, 203, 209. Louis-Jean-Marie Daubenton was a contemporary of and collaborator with Buffon.

6   Koch and Peden, *The Life and Selected Writings,* pp. 213, 215. David Rittenhouse was an American polymath, most noted at the time for his contributions to the study of astronomy.

7   Semonin, *American Monster,* pp. 220, 221.

8   Dugatkin, *Mr. Jefferson and the Giant Moose,* pp. 81, 98, 99; Semonin, *American Monster,* pp. 224, 225.

9   Ussama Makdisi, *Artillery of Heaven: American Missionaries and the Failed Conversion of the Middle East* (Ithaca, NY: Cornell University Press, 2008), p. 58.

10   Makdisi, *Artillery of Heaven,* p. 10; Ian Tyrrell, *Reforming the World: The Creation of America's Moral Empire* (Princeton, NJ: Princeton University Press, 2010), p. 4.

11   In his most famous publication, *Our Country* (1891), Strong fervently declared that "If I read not amiss, this powerful race [the Americans] will move down upon Mexico, down upon Central and South America, out upon the islands of the sea, over upon Africa and beyond. And can anyone doubt that the result of this competition of the races will be the 'survival of the fittest?'" Josiah Strong, *Our Country,* ed. By Jurgen Herbst (Cambridge: Belknap Press of Harvard University Press, 1963), p. 213.

12   Tyrrell, *Reforming the World,* p. 4; Makdisi, *Artillery of Heaven,* p. 84.

13   Melani McAlister, *Epic Encounters: Culture, Media, and U.S. Interests in the Middle East, 1945–2000* (Berkeley: University of California Press, 2001), p. 13.

14   Makdisi, *Artillery of Heaven,* p. 63, 65, 84.

15   Quoted in McAlister, *Epic Encounters,* p. 15.

16   Lawrence S. Little, *Disciples of Liberty: The African Methodist Episcopal Church in the Age of Imperialism, 1884–1916* (Knoxville: The University of Tennessee Press, 2000), pp. xi–xii.

17   Elliott P. Skinner, *African Americans and U.S. Policy toward Africa, 1850–1924* (Washington, DC: Howard University Press, 1992), p. 15.

18   Little, *Disciples of Liberty,* pp. xii, 30, 62, 75, 76, 80.

19   Frederick Douglass, *Life and Times of Frederick Douglass* (New York: Citadel Press, 1983), p. 236.

20   Alan J. Rice and Martin Crawford, eds., *Liberating Sojourn: Frederick Douglass & Transatlantic Reform* (Athens: The University of Georgia Press, 1999), p. 2, 5.

21   "Reception Speech at Finbury Chapel, Moorfields, England, May 12, 1846," in John Blassingame, et al., eds., *The Frederick Douglass Papers; Series Two: Autobiographical Writings; Volume 2: My Bondage and My Freedom* (New Haven: Yale University Press, 2003), p. 24 3.

22   Rice and Crawford, *Liberating Sojourn,* p. 6, 141, 182. As the editors note, Douglass was not so favorably impressed on his return to England in 1859. While some still supported his abolitionist cause, "there were others who had grown weary of such agitation and philanthropy and demanded to know 'what have we to do with American slavery?' Douglass was taken aback by what he called this new doctrine of nonintervention" (p. 188).

23 Aaron W. Marrs, "Chapter 2: The Civil War Origins of the *FRUS* Series, 1861–1868," in William B. McAllister, et al., *Toward "Thorough, Accurate, and Reliable": A History of the* Foreign Relations of the United States *Series* (Washington, DC: U.S. Department of State, 2015), pp. 21–26, 38, 39.

24 Ibid., pp. 26, 27, 39, 41.

25 For the most thorough study of the American participation at the 1867 show, see Carol Troyen, "Innocents Abroad: American Painters at the 1867 Exposition Universelle, Paris," *American Art Journal* 16:1 (Autumn 1984):2–29.

26 Ibid., pp. 4–6, 13.

27 Robert W. Rydell and Rob Kroes, *Buffalo Bill in Bologna: The Americanization of the World, 1869–1922* (Chicago: The University of Chicago Press, 2005), p. 118.

28 Elliott J. Gorn, *The Manly Art: Bare-Knuckle Prize Fighting in America* (Ithaca: Cornell University Press, 1986), p. 19.

29 Ibid., pp. 19–21.

30 Ibid., pp. 148–159.

31 For the best studies of the links between the rising popularity of boxing and American imperial aims, see Gorn and Michael T. Isenberg, *John L. Sullivan and His America* (Chicago: University of Illinois Press, 1988).

32 Ibid., pp. 237–256.

33 Ibid., pp. 293–296.

34 The most in-depth coverage of the links between U.S. foreign policy and Spalding's baseball tour is Thomas W. Zeiler, *Ambassadors in Pinstripes: The Spalding World Baseball Tour and the Birth of the American Empire* (Lanham, MD: Rowman & Littlefield Publishers, Inc., 2006). The tour is put into a larger historical perspective in Robert Elias, *The Empire Strikes Out: How Baseball Sold U.S. Foreign Policy and Promoted the American Way Abroad* (New York: The New Press, 2010).

35 Elias, *The Empire Strikes Out,* pp. 21, 22.

36 Ibid., pp. 21–26; Zeiler, *Ambassadors in Pinstripes.*

37 Zeiler, *Ambassadors in Pinstripes,* pp. ix–xiii, 23. Cleveland's successor, Benjamin Harrison, did not show the same excitement greeting the players upon their return in 1889. Anson remarked after a very brief and uncomfortable meeting with the president that Harrison "was about as warm as an icicle" (Zeiler, *Ambassadors in Pinstripes,* pp. 172, 173).

38 Rydell and Kroes, *Buffalo Bill,* p. 4.

39 Alfred Heller, "Philadelphia 1876," in John E. Findling and Kimberly D. Pelle, eds., *Encyclopedia of World's Fairs and Expositions* (Jefferson, NC: McFarland & Company, Inc., Publishers, 2008), p. 56. Also see, Robert W. Rydell, *All the World's a Fair: Visions of Empire at American International Expositions, 1876–1916* (Chicago: The University of Chicago Press, 1984), Ch. 1.

40 Heller, "Philadelphia 1876," p. 56; Rydell, *All the World's a Fair,* Ch. 2.

41 Rydell, *All the World's a Fair,* pp. 64–68; R. Reid Badger, "Chicago 1893," in *Encyclopedia of World's Fairs,* pp. 119, 120; Robert W. Rydell, John E. Findling, and Kimberly D. Pelle, *Fair America: World's Fairs in the United States* (Washington, DC: Smithsonian Institution Press, 2000), p. 36.

42 Rydell and Kroes, *Buffalo Bill,* pp. 105–111.

43 Ibid., pp. 111–115.

44 Mark Twain, *The Innocents Abroad, or the New Pilgrims' Progress: Being Some Account of the Steamship QUAKER CITY'S Pleasure Excursion to Europe and the Holy Land* (Norwalk, CT: The Easton Press, 1998), pp. 27, 55, 87, 88, 189.
45 Twain, *Innocents Abroad*, pp. 10, 44, 65, 66.
46 Edward Wagenknecht, "Introduction," in Twain, *Innocents Abroad*, pp. ix–x.
47 Twain, *Innocents Abroad*, pp. 493, 494.
48 Dugatkin, *Mr. Jefferson and the Giant Moose*, p. 81.

Chapter 2

1 Theodore Roosevelt, "At the Opening of the Jamestown Exposition, April 26, 1907," http://www.theodore-roosevelt.com/images/research/txtspeeches/247.txt (Accessed March 24, 2017).
2 Lori Lyn Bogle, "TR's Use of PR to Strengthen the Navy," *Naval History Magazine* 21:6 (December 2007):26–31.
3 Candice Millard, *Destiny of the Republic: A tale of Madness, Medicine, and the Murder of a President* (New York: Doubleday, 2013), does a wonderful job of shedding light on the under-appreciated Garfield, whose presidency was tragically cut short by his assassination. Before taking public office, Garfield was the quintessential Renaissance man; a professor of ancient languages, literature, and math; and a published scholar. Unlike Roosevelt, Garfield was a passionate defender of civil rights for African Americans.
4 Richard H. Collin, *Theodore Roosevelt, Culture, Diplomacy, and Expansion: A New View of American Imperialism* (Baton Rouge: Louisiana State University Press, 1985), pp. 1–2, 5, and 7.
5 Information found at http://www.theodorerooseveltcenter.org/Learn-About-TR/TR-Encyclopedia/Culture-and-Society/Louisiana-Purchase-Exposition.aspx (Accessed March 24, 2017).
6 The best study of the St. Louis Exposition is Rydell, *All the World's a Fair*, Ch. 6.
7 Astrid Boger, "St. Louis 1904," in John E. Findling and Kimberly D. Pelle, eds., *Encyclopedia of World's Fairs and Expositions* (Jefferson, NC: McFarland & Company, Inc., Publishers, 2008), p. 173.
8 See Paul A. Kramer, *The Blood of Government: Race, Empire, the United States & the Philippines* (Chapel Hill: The University of North Carolina Press, 2006).
9 Rydell, *All the World's a Fair*, pp. 167, 178.
10 Elihu Root to Secretary Oscar Straus, 2 June 1906, RU 70, Box 79, Commerce and Labor, U.S. Department of Labor, 1906–1908 file (hereafter Commerce and Labor file); Richard Rathbun to Cyrus Adler, August 10, 1906, RU 45, Box 21, Folder 25, SIA; "Fire in Milan Exposition," *New York Times*, August 4, 1906, p. 2. During the late nineteenth and early twentieth centuries, the Smithsonian's role in U.S. participation in international fairs and exhibitions was quite limited. The "Exposition Records of the Smithsonian Institution and the United States National Museum, 1867–1940," reveal that the Institution played a large role in just three exhibits prior to the 1907 exposition in Bordeaux: two fishery exhibits in Berlin and London, and the

Columbian Historical Exposition in Madrid. The finding aid for the records lists just eighteen other foreign expositions before 1907 and suggests that in regard to these shows the Smithsonian took little or no role in the American participation. See the finding aid for RU 70, SIA.

11 "Dictated by the Secretary" (Straus), January 8, 1907; Jules Jusserand to Root, January 8, 1907, RU 70, Box 79, Commerce and Labor file, SIA.

12 Root to Straus, January 12, 1907; Minutes of Meeting, January 17, 1907, RU 70, Box 79, Commerce and Labor file, SIA.

13 Adler to Straus, January 17, 1907; Straus to Root, January 18, 1907, RU 70, Box 79, Commerce and Labor file, SIA.

14 Theodore Roosevelt to Straus, January 18, 1907, RU 70, Box 79, Commerce and Labor file, SIA.

15 For Roosevelt's attitude toward France, see Howard K. Beale, *Theodore Roosevelt and the Rise of America to World Power* (Baltimore, MD: Johns Hopkins University Press, 1956), pp. 355–372; William N. Tilchin, *Theodore Roosevelt and the British Empire: A Study in Presidential Statecraft* (New York: St. Martin's Press, 1997), pp. 92, 93; Raymond A. Esthus, *Theodore Roosevelt and the International Rivalries* (Claremont, CA: Regina Books, 1970), pp. 14–17. A good example of Roosevelt's fondness for Jusserand is found in Roosevelt to Henry Cabot Lodge, June 25, 1903: "What delightful people the Jusserands are! Last night they and Secretary and Mrs. Hay with McVeagh and President Benjamin Ida Wheeler of the University of California dined with me, and it was as pleasant as possible. Jusserand had given me his pamphlet proving that the King's Quhair is rightfully attributed to James I. It is the kind of antiquarian and literary small study in which my soul delights." (*Selections from the Correspondence of Theodore Roosevelt and Henry Cabot Lodge, 1884–1918*, Vol. II [New York: Charles Scribner's Sons, 1925], p. 34.)

16 Collin, *Theodore Roosevelt*, 190.

17 Robert Bacon (Acting Secretary of State) to Secretary Straus, March 7, 1907, RU 70, Box 79, Commerce and Labor file; Bacon to Charles D. Walcott, March 8, 1907, RU 45, Box 21, Folder 25; Walcott to Root, 15, March 1907, RU 70, Box 80, Tittmann, O.H., 1907–1908 file, SIA; "The Smithsonian Institution," *The New York Times* (December 1906). This was not the first time the Smithsonian suffered such insults. See Mark Twain's disparaging remarks about the "mildewed old fossil, the Smithsonian Institute" in Ch. 1.

18 Murphy to Robert Bacon, Feb. 1907, M862, Numerical and Minor Files of the Department of State, 1906–1910 (hereafter M862), Record Group 59, General Records of the Department of State (hereafter RG 59), National Archives and Record Center (hereafter NARA); Root to Murphy, March 7, 1907; Murphy to Root, March 8, 1907; Murphy to Wilson, March 12, 1907, RU 45, Box 21, Expositions: Maritime Exposition International, Bordeaux, France, 1906–1907 Correspondence [folder 25] file, SIA.

19 "Catalogue of U.S. Government Exhibits, International Maritime Exposition, Bordeaux," 1907, RU 70, Box 80, Draft Catalogue of the American Exhibit, 1907 file, SIA.

20 Some wonderful pictures of the American Pavilion are found in RU 45, Box 22, Expositions: Maritime Exposition, International, Bordeaux, France, 1907

Photographs of the United States Exhibit file (folder 2), SIA. The "Catalogue of U.S. Government Exhibits, International Maritime Exposition, Bordeaux," is found in RU 70, Box 80, Draft Catalogue of the American Exhibit, 1907 folder, SIA. Jusserand to Root, March 29, 1907, RU 70, Box 80, State, Department of, 1907 file; William deC. Ravenel to S. A. Daudelin, October 15, 1907 (with "List of Diplomas Retained by Mr. Ravenel"), RU 70, Box 79, D, 1907–1909 file; Ravenel to Daudelin, January 15, 1908, RU 70, Box 79, D, 1907–1909 file, SIA.

21 Woodrow Wilson to Sir William Tyrell, 22 November 1913, in Arthur S. Link, ed., *The Papers of Woodrow Wilson*, Vol. 28 (Princeton, NJ: Princeton University Press, 1979):574, 575.

22 William Starr Myers, *Woodrow Wilson: Some Princeton Memories* (Princeton, NJ: Princeton University Press, 2016), p. 43.

23 Scholars are still debating whether Wilson actually uttered those words. In a recent study of the film, Melvyn Stokes concluded that "He *may* have said this. After all, the film's view of the Civil War and Reconstruction periods was not too different from Wilson's own (his historical writings were several times quoted in the film's intertitles)" (emphasis in original). See, Melvin Stokes, *D.W. Griffith's The Birth of a Nation: A History of "The Most Controversial Motion Picture of All Time"* (New York: Oxford University Press, 2007), 111.

24 Ibid., pp. 111–113; Mary Childs Nerney to George Packard, April 17, 1915, *History Matters*, http://historymatters.gmu.edu/d/4966/. Retrieved March 7, 2016.

25 For histories of the CPI, start with the book by the Committee's director, George Creel: *How We Advertised America* (New York: Arno Press, 1972). Somewhat surprisingly the CPI has been the subject of just a few monographs, including Stephen Vaughn, *Holding Fast the Inner Lines: Democracy, Nationalism, and the Committee on Public Information* (Chapel Hill: The University of North Carolina Press, 1980); James R. Mock and Cedric Larson, *Words That Won the War: The Story of the Committee on Public Information, 1917–1919* (Princeton, NJ: Princeton University Press, 1939). A more recent look at the CPI is found in Christopher E. Howard, "Propaganda against Propaganda: Deconstructing the Dominant Narrative of the Committee on Public Information." MA Thesis, Appalachian State University, 2014. Boone, NC: Appalachian State University Special University Archives Publication.

26 For the controversies associated with the CPI consult the works noted in Note 21. It is interesting to note that although the CPI become universally known as the "Creel Committee" very little scholarship has appeared about this enigmatic personality. Jonathan Auerbach, *Weapons of Democracy: Propaganda, Progressivism, and American Public Opinion* (Baltimore, MD: Johns Hopkins University Press, 2015) is the most recent study to deal with Creel in any depth.

27 Creel, *How We Advertised*, p. 12; Rydell and Kroes, *Buffalo Bill*, p. 137.

28 Mock and Larson, *Words That Won the War*, pp. 237, 244–245, 247; Creel, *How We Advertised*, pp. 3, 4, 9.

29 Mock and Larson, *Words That Won the War*, pp. 9, 237, 238.

30 "Woods to Define Our Aims Abroad," *New York Times*, February 18, 1918, p. 3.
31 Creel, *How We Advertised*, pp. 290–297. Interestingly, Creel dismisses the work of the CPI in England as being "almost a matter of routine" since the situation in that nation "was never very bothersome" (p. 298).
32 Creel, *How We Advertised*, pp. 299–302; Mock and Larson, *Words That Won the War*, pp. 286–292; Charles E. Merriam, "American Publicity in Italy," *The American Political Science Review* 13:4 (November 1919):541–555; "Wilson Greets Italians," *New York Times*, August 13, 1918, p. 7.
33 Creel, *How We Advertised*, pp. 300–302.
34 Gregg Wolper, "Wilsonian Public Diplomacy: The Committee on Public Information in Spain," *Diplomatic History* 17:1 (Winter 1993):17–34. Creel's account of the CPI's work in Spain is limited to one brief chapter, most of which is taken up with a lengthy excerpt from a report by the CPI representative in that nation.
35 James R. Mock, "The Creel Committee in Latin America," *The Hispanic American Historical Review* 22:2 (May 1942):262–279. Both the Creel and Mock and Larson books contain sections on the CPI activities in Mexico, but almost nothing about the Committee's efforts in South America.
36 Kazuyuki Matsuo, "American Propaganda in China: The U.S. Committee on Public Information, 1918–1919," *The Journal of American and Canadian Studies* 14:2 (1996):19–42. The CPI's work in China is barely mentioned in the Mock and Larson study. In Creel's volume, China gets a bit more attention. He also adds a brief mention of the CPI's efforts in Japan (Creel, *How We Advertised*, pp. 358–364).
37 Howard, "Propaganda against Propaganda," pp. 80, 81.
38 Creel, *How We Advertised*, pp. 320, 321; Tibor Glant, "Against All Odds: Vira B. Whitehouse and Rosika Schwimmer in Switzerland, 1918," *American Studies International* 40:1 (February 2002):34–51.
39 Claude E. Fike, "The Influence of the Creel Committee and the American Red Cross on Russian-American Relations, 1917–1919," *The Journal of Modern History* 31:2 (June 1959):93–109; Mock and Larson, *Words That Won the War*, pp. 314–320. The question of whether the Sisson documents were real or fakes continues to be debated. George F. Kennan, in a 1956 article, declared them to be forgeries.
40 "The Committee on Public Misinformation," *New York Times*, July 7, 1917, p. 7; "Attacks Creel Committee," *New York Times*, April 1, 1918, p. 12.
41 "Asks Who Authorizes Creel Propaganda," *New York Times*, February 5, 1918, p. 11. The representative in question was C.B. Miller of Minnesota.
42 Wolper, "Wilsonian Public Diplomacy," p. 31.
43 Rydell and Kroes, *Buffalo Bill*, pp. 137, 140.
44 Howard, "Propaganda Against Propaganda," p. 7; Glant, "Against All Odds," p. 42.
45 Frank A. Ninkovich, *The Diplomacy of Ideas: U.S. foreign policy and cultural relations, 1938–1950* (Cambridge: Cambridge University Press, 1981), p. 13.
46 Mock, "Creel Committee in Latin America," p. 278.
47 Ninkovich, *Diplomacy of Ideas*, p. 13.
48 J. Manuel Espinosa, *Inter-American Beginnings of U.S. Cultural Diplomacy, 1936–1948* (Washington, DC: Department of State, 1976), pp. 48–57.

49 Ninkovich, *Diplomacy of Ideas*, p. 18; Gary E. Kraske, *Missionaries of the Book: The American Library Profession and the Origins of United States Cultural Diplomacy* (Westport, CT: Greenwood Press, 1985).
50 Kraske, *Missionaries*, p. 21.
51 Quote found in Espinosa, *Inter-American Beginnings*, p. 76.
52 Ninkovich, *Diplomacy of Ideas*, pp. 18–20.
53 Ibid., pp. 22, 23.
54 Richard T. Arndt, *The First Resort of Kings: American Cultural Diplomacy in the Twentieth Century* (Washington, DC: Potomac Books, 2005), p. 55; Fredrick B. Pike, *The United States and Latin America: Myths and Stereotypes of Civilization and Nature* (Austin: University of Texas Press, 1992), pp. 288–289; Mark T. Gilderhus, *The Second Century: U.S.-Latin American Relations since 1889* (Wilmington, DE: Scholarly Resources, Inc., 2000), pp. 94–96; Espinosa, *Inter-American Beginnings*, pp. 67–73.
55 Justin Hart, *Empire of Ideas: The Origins of Public Diplomacy and the Transformation of U.S. Foreign Policy* (Oxford: Oxford University Press, 2013), pp. 8, 9.
56 *The Roosevelt Administration and Its Dealings with the Republics of the Western Hemisphere: Address of the Honorable Sumner Welles, Assistant Secretary of State, Read at the Annual Convention of the Association of American Colleges, Atlanta, January 17, 1935* (Washington, DC: United States Government Printing Office, 1935).
57 Espinosa, *Inter-American Beginnings*, p. 1.
58 Hart, *Empire of Ideas*, pp. 18, 20.
59 Ibid., p. 21.
60 Ninkovich, *Diplomacy of Ideas*, p. 31.
61 Darlene J. Sadlier, *Americans All: Good Neighbor Cultural Diplomacy in World War II* (Austin: University of Texas Press, 2012), pp. 10–13.
62 Ibid., pp. 12, 13; Hart, *Empire of Ideas*, 30–32; Ninkovich, *Diplomacy of Ideas*, 35–37. Although the memo Hopkins handed to Roosevelt was unsigned, Hart concludes that the author was, in fact, Rockefeller.
63 For more on the music activities, see Jennifer L. Campbell, "Creating Something Out of Nothing: The Office of Inter-American Affairs Music Committee (1940–1941) and the Inception of a Policy for Musical Diplomacy," *Diplomatic History* 16:1 (January 2012):29–39.
64 Sadlier, *Americans All*, Chs. 2 and 5; Carol A. Hess, *Representing the Good Neighbor: Music, Difference, and the Pan American Dream* (Oxford: Oxford University Press, 2013), pp. 3, 4.
65 Hart, *Empire of Ideas*, pp. 34, 35.
66 Ninkovich, *Diplomacy of Ideas*, pp. 115–118.
67 Ramon Girona and Jordi Xifra, "The Office of Facts and Figures: Archibald MacLeish and the 'strategy of truth'," *Public Relations Review* 35:3 (September 2009):287–290.
68 Dean J. Kotlowski, "Selling America to the World: The Office of War Information's *The Town* (1945) and the *American Scene* Series," *Australasian Journal of American Studies* 35:1 (July 2016):82, 83; Franklin D. Roosevelt, "68—Executive Order 9182 Establishing the Office of War Information, June 13, 1942," http://www.presidency.ucsb.edu/ws/index.php?pid=16273&st=office+of+war+information&st1= (Accessed March 24, 2017). The only

limitation on OWI's overseas activities was that it was prohibited from operating in Latin America, still the bailiwick of the OCIAA.

69 Allan M. Winkler, *The Politics of Propaganda: The Office of War Information, 1942–1945* (New Haven: Yale University Press, 1978), pp. 63–65.
70 Kotlowski, "Selling America," p. 83.
71 Winkler, *Politics of Propaganda*, p. 73; Espinosa, *Inter-American Beginnings*, p. 161.
72 Kraske, *Missionaries*, pp. 139–143; Pamela Spence Richards, "Information for the Allies: Office of War Information Libraries in Australia, New Zealand, and South Africa," *Library Quarterly* 52:4 (October 1982):329, 330.
73 Richards, "Information for the Allies," pp. 325–347.
74 Kotlowski, "Selling America," pp. 83–85.
75 Ibid, pp. 86–94.
76 Ninkovich, *Diplomacy of Ideas*, Ch. 5; Espinosa, *Inter-American Beginnings*, pp. 210–228; Hart, *Empire of Ideas*, Ch. 2.
77 Hart, *Empire of Ideas*, p. 70.

Chapter 3

1 Michael L. Krenn, "Send More Boxing Monkeys: Adventures in U.S. Cold War Propaganda," *The SHAFR Newsletter* 30:1 (March 1999):27, 28.
2 Espinosa, *Inter-American Beginnings*, pp. 228, 229; Hart, *Empire of Ideas*, pp. 110–116; Walter L. Hixson, *Parting the Curtain: Propaganda, Culture, and the Cold War, 1945-1961* (New York: St. Martin's Griffin, 1998), pp. 4, 5. For more on Benton, see Sidney Hyman, *The Lives of William Benton* (Chicago: University of Chicago Press, 1970).
3 James A. Leith, *The Idea of Art as Propaganda in France, 1750–1799: A Study in the History of Ideas* (Toronto: University of Toronto Press, 1965); Todd Porterfield, *The Allure of Empire: Art in the Service of French Imperialism, 1798–1836* (Berkeley: University of California Press, 2000); Anthony Adamthwaite, *Grandeur and Misery: France's Bid for Power in Europe, 1914–1940* (London: Arnold, 1995).
4 Frederick C. Barghoorn, *The Soviet Cultural Offensive: The Role of Cultural Diplomacy in Soviet Foreign Policy* (Princeton, NJ: Princeton University Press, 1960); Toby Miller and George Yudice, *Cultural Policy* (London: Sage Publications, 2002).
5 Jean-Francois Fayet, "VOKS: The Third Dimension of Soviet Foreign Policy," and Rosa Magnusdottir, "Mission Impossible? Selling Soviet Socialism to Americans, 1955–1958," both in Jessica C.E. Gienow-Hecht and Mark C. Donfried, eds., *Searching for a Cultural Diplomacy* (New York: Berghahn Books, 2010), pp. 33–49; 50–72.
6 Kenneth Holland to William T. Stone and William Benton, March 10, 1947, Exhibitions section, Advancing American Art file, USIA Historical Collection, Washington, DC; William Benton to Fred Busbey, April 2, 1947, Record Group 59, Records of the Assistant Secretary of State for Public Affairs, 1945–1950, subject file, box 7, ASNE folder, National Archives, College Park, MD. Department of State Employee Martin Manning put the "USIA Historical

Collection" together. It was moved several times and is today generally referred to as the "Manning Collection."

7 Benton to Howland S. Sargeant, February 20, 1947, RG 59, Records of ASS/PA, 1945–1950, subject file, Box 7, ASNE file, NA. For Benton's interest in radio and Muzak see Cynthia B. Meyers, "From Radio Adman to Radio Reformer: Senator William Benton's Career in Broadcasting, 1930–1960," *Journal of Radio & Audio Media* 16:1 (2009):17–29.

8 Holland to Stone and Benton, March 10, 1947, Exhibitions section, Advancing American Art file, USIA HC.

9 Scholars are still carefully examining the mythology surrounding the It's All True disaster. See Sadlier, *Americans All*, pp. 23–27; Catherine L. Benamou, *It's All True: Orson Welles's Pan-American Odyssey* (Berkeley: University of California Press, 2007); Richard B. Jewell, "Orson Welles, George Schaefer, and IT'S ALL TRUE: A 'Cursed' Production," *Film History* 2 (November 1988):325–335.

10 For the best accounts of *Advancing American Art,* see Margaret Lynne Ausfeld and Virginia M. Mecklenburg, *Advancing American Art: Politics and Aesthetics in the State Department Exhibition, 1946-1948* (Montgomery, AL: Montgomery Museum of Fine Arts, 1984); Taylor D. Littleton and Maltby Sykes, *Advancing American Art: Painting, Politics, and Cultural Confrontation at Mid-Century* (Tuscaloosa: University of Alabama Press, 1989); Michael L. Krenn, *Fall-Out Shelters for the Human Spirit: American Art and the Cold War* (Chapel Hill: University of North Carolina Press, 2005), pp. 26–49. In 2013–2014, a group of American museums reassembled nearly the entire collection and exhibited it across the United States; see Scott Bishop, Robert Ekelund, et al., *Art Interrupted: Advancing American Art and the Politics of Cultural Diplomacy* (Athens: Georgia Museum of Art, 2012).

11 For the story of the disastrous British show, see Krenn, *Fall-Out Shelters*, pp. 24–26.

12 "Questions concerning the Department's Art Program asked by Edward Alden Jewell in the New York Times, June 15, 1947, with answers," July 1947, attached to Lawrence Morris to G. Stewart Brown, July 15, 1947, Advancing American Art (microfilm), Archives of American Art, Washington, D.C. For an interesting study of the rise of American art in the postwar world, see Serge Guilbaut, *How New York Stole the Idea of Modern Art: Abstract Expressionism, Freedom, and the Cold War* (Chicago: Chicago University Press, 1983).

13 Benton to Busbey, April 2, 1947, RG 59, Records of ASS/PA, 1945–1950, subject file, box 7, ASNE folder, NA. For a better understanding of "socialist realism" and Soviet art in general, see Matthew Cullerne Bown, *Socialist Realist Painting* (New Haven, CT: Yale University Press, 1998); C. V. James, *Socialist Realism: Origins and Theory* (New York: St. Martin's Press, 1973); Antoine Baudin, "Why Is Soviet Painting Hidden from Us?': Zhdanov Art and Its International Relations and fallout, 1947–1953," in Thomas Lahusen and Evgeny Dobrenko, eds., *Socialist Realism without Shores* (Durham, NC: Duke University Press, 1997), pp. 227–256; Renee Baigell and Matthew Baigell, eds., *Soviet Dissident Artists: Interviews after Perestroika* (New Brunswick, NJ: Rutgers University Press, 1995).

14 Alfred M. Frankfurter, "American Art Abroad: The State Department Collection," *Art News* (October 1946):21–31, 78.

15   Krenn, *Fall-Out Shelters*, pp. 30–35.
16   Littleton and Sykes, *Advancing American Art*, pp. 26, 27.
17   Ibid., pp. 30, 31; Krenn, *Fall-Out Shelters*, pp. 36, 37.
18   Littleton and Sykes, *Advancing American Art*, pp. 30–37; Krenn, *Fall-Out Shelters*, pp. 37–42.
19   The best analysis of the auctioning of the paintings is found in Littleton and Sykes, *Advancing American Art*, Ch. 2. The chief beneficiaries of the sale were the University of Oklahoma and Auburn University (who would later collaborate in the reassembling of the show for a 2013–2014 exhibit). The O'Keeffe painting went for $50; another by Arthur Dove was sold for $30. Littleton and Sykes estimate that these paintings would bring over $200,000 each at auction today.
20   David F. Krugler, *The Voice of America and the Domestic Propaganda Battles, 1945-1953* (Columbia: University of Missouri Press, 2000), pp. 43–64.
21   Nicholas J. Cull, *The Cold War and the United States Information Agency: American Propaganda and Public Diplomacy, 1945–1989* (Cambridge: Cambridge University Press, 2008), pp. 14, 15; Alan L. Heil, Jr., *Voice of America: A History* (New York: Columbia University Press, 2003), pp. 32–45; Krugler, *The Voice of America*, pp. 30, 31.
22   Krugler, *The Voice of America*, pp. 38, 39, 48, 49.
23   Krugler, *The Voice of America*, pp. 59–70; Heil, *Voice of America*, pp. 47–49; Cull, *The Cold War*, p. 40.
24   Cora Sol Goldstein, "The Control of Visual Representation: American Art Policy in Occupied Germany, 1945–1949," in Giles Scott-Smith and Hans Krabbendam, eds., *The Cultural Cold War in Western Europe, 1945–1960* (London: Frank Cass, 2003), pp. 283, 284; "U.S. Army Sponsors Art Show in Germany," *Art Digest* (June 1, 1946):7, 30. For a more detailed analysis of the use of American art in western Germany in the years immediately after the Second World War, see Cora Sol Goldstein, *Capturing the German Eye: American Visual Propaganda in Occupied Germany* (Chicago: University of Chicago Press, 2009).
25   Cora Sol Goldstein, "Before the CIA: American Actions in the German Fine Arts (1946-1949)," *Diplomatic History* 29:5 (November 2005):747–750; Haynes R. Mahoney, "Windows to the West," in "Educational and Cultural Activities in Germany Today," 1950, Ralph Bunche Library, Department of State, Washington, DC; Reinhold Wagnleitner, "The Irony of American Culture Abroad: Austria and the Cold War," in Lary May, ed., *Recasting America: Culture and Politics in the Age of Cold War* (Chicago: University of Chicago Press, 1989), p. 293; Krenn, *Fall-Out Shelters*, pp. 67, 69–71. The other specific request made by the Germans was for a German-dubbed screening of *Gone with the Wind*.
26   Krenn, *Fall-Out Shelters*, pp. 67–87.
27   For the American libraries, see Arndt, *The First Resort of Kings*, pp. 150–156; for film, see Sarah Nilsen, *Projecting America, 1958: Film and Cultural Diplomacy at the Brussels World's Fair* (Jefferson, NC: McFarland & Company, 2011), pp. 46–50.
28   Sam Lebovic, "From War Junk to Educational Exchange: The World War II Origins of the Fulbright Program and the Foundations of American Cultural Globalism, 1945–1950," *Diplomatic History* 37:2 (2013):280–312. Also

see Randall Bennett Woods, "Fulbright Internationalism," *The Annals of the American Academy of Political and Social Science* 491 (May 1987):22–35.

29   Liping Bu, "Educational Exchange and Cultural Diplomacy in the Cold War," *Journal of American Studies* 33:3, Pt. 1 (December 1999):396–397, 408, 411.

30   Alice Garner and Diane Kirkby, "'Never a Machine for Propaganda'?: The Australian-American Fulbright Program and Australia's Cold War," *Australian Historical Studies* 44 (2013):121–123, 127, 132. As Giles Scott-Smith argues, other "exchange" programs had more definitive political goals. The Foreign Leader Program was a one-way affair that sought to bring foreign opinion makers (political leaders, journalists) to America. The purpose was clear: "to solidify relations with allies." And, unlike many other such programs, the foreign visitors' reaction was "generally ... positive." ("The US State Department's Foreign Leader Program in France During the Early Cold War," *Revue française d'études américaines* 107 (March 2006):47–60.

31   Nancy Snow, "International Exchanges and the U.S. Image," *The Annals of the American Academy of Political and Social Science* 616 (March 2008):200–202; Richard Pells, *Not Like Us: How Europeans Have Loved, Hated, and Transformed American Culture since World War II* (New York: Basic Books, 1997), pp. 172–177.

32   "A Report to the National Security Council—NSC 68," April 12, 1950, Papers of Harry S. Truman, President's Secretary's File, Harry S. Truman Library, Independence, MO; Laura A. Belmonte, *Selling the American Way: U.S. Propaganda and the Cold War* (Philadelphia: University of Pennsylvania Press, 2008), pp. 47, 48.

33   Edward W. Barrett, *Truth Is Our Weapon* (New York: Funk & Wagnalls Company, 1953), p. 69.

34   For more in depth analyses of "The Campaign of Truth" see Barrett, *Truth*, Ch. 6; Hixson, *Parting the Curtain*, pp. 14–17; Arndt, *First Resort*, pp. 254–257; Belmonte, *Selling the American Way*, pp. 39–49.

35   Arndt, *First Resort*, pp. 254–257.

36   Krenn, *Fall-Out Shelters*, pp. 80–87.

37   A good introduction to the civil rights issue in the United States in the wake of World War II is Steven F. Lawson, *Running for Freedom: Civil Rights and Black Politics in America since 1941*, 4th ed. (West Sussex: Wiley-Blackwell, 2014), especially Chs. 1 and 2. For the story of Isaac Woodard, see Rawn James, Jr., *The Double V: How Wars, Protest, and Harry Truman Desegregated America's Military* (New York: Bloomsbury Press, 2013), Ch. 24.

38   Richard Lentz and Karla K. Gower, *The Opinions of Mankind: Racial Issues, Press, and Propaganda in the Cold War* (Columbia: University of Missouri Press, 2010), p. 21; Krenn, *Black Diplomacy: African Americans and the State Department, 1945–1969* (Armonk, NY: M.E. Sharpe, 1999), p. 33.

39   Krenn, *Black Diplomacy*, pp. 31–33; Lentz and Gower, *Opinions*, Chs. 1 and 2.

40   The literature dealing with African Americans and U.S. foreign policy during the Cold War is large and growing. Some of the essential studies are Brenda Gayle Plummer, *Rising Wind: Black Americans and U.S. Foreign Affairs, 1935–1960* (Chapel Hill: University of North Carolina Press, 1996); Brenda Gayle Plummer, *In Search of Power: African Americans in the Era of Decolonization, 1956-1974* (Cambridge: Cambridge University Press, 2013); Brenda Gayle Plummer ed., *Window on Freedom: Race, Civil Rights,*

and Foreign Affairs, 1945–1988 (Chapel Hill: University of North Carolina Press, 2003); Thomas Borstelmann, *Cold War and the Color Line: American Race Relations in the Global Arena* (Cambridge: Cambridge University Press, 2001); Carol Anderson, *Eyes Off the Prize: The United Nations and the African American Struggle for Human Rights, 1944–1955* (Cambridge: Cambridge University Press, 2003); Carol Anderson, *Bourgeois Radicals: The NAACP and the Struggle for Colonial Liberation, 1941–1960* (Cambridge: Cambridge University Press, 2014); Mary Dudziak, *Cold War Civil Rights: Race and the Image of American Democracy* (Princeton: Princeton University Press, 2000); Penny M. von Eschen, *Race against Empire: Black Americans and Anticolonialism, 1937–1957* (Ithaca, NY: Cornell University Press, 1996); Krenn, *Black Diplomacy*; James H. Meriwether, *Proudly We Can Be Africans: Black America and Africa, 1935–1961* (Chapel Hill: University of North Carolina Press, 2002); Gerald Horne, *The End of Empires: African Americans and India* (Philadelphia, PA: Temple University Press, 2008); Jonathan Rosenberg, *How Far the Promised Land? World Affairs and the American Civil Rights Movement from the First World War to Vietnam* (Princeton, NJ: Princeton University Press, 2006); Kevin Gaines, *American Africans in Ghana: Black Expatriates and the Civil Rights Era* (Chapel Hill: University of North Carolina Press, 2006); Linda Heywood, et al., eds., *African Americans in U.S. Foreign Policy: From the Era of Frederick Douglass to the Age of Obama* (Urbana: University of Illinois Press, 2015).

41 George C. Marshall to Charles E. Wilson, June 28, 1947, RG 59, 501.BD-Human Rights/6-547, NA; President's Commission on Civil Rights, *To Secure These Rights* (Washington, DC: Government Printing Office, 1947).

42 Krenn, *Black Diplomacy*, Chs. 1–2; Jake C. Miller, *The Black Presence in American Foreign Affairs* (Washington, DC: University Press of America, 1978), Ch. 1.

43 Krenn, *Black Diplomacy*, pp. 47–50; Krenn, "Edward R. Dudley," in Cathal J. Nolan, ed., *Notable U.S. Ambassadors since 1775: A Biographical Dictionary* (Westport, CT: Greenwood Press, 1997), pp. 88–93. Also see "Interview with Edward R. Dudley, Jr.," found at https://www.loc.gov/item/mfdipbib000313/ (Accessed March 25, 2017).

44 Krenn, *Black Diplomacy*, pp. 54–56; Daniel Brantley, "Black Americans as Participants in the Foreign Service," *Crisis* 93:9 (November 1986):32–33.

45 Krenn, *Black Diplomacy*, pp. 56–58.

46 "Progress Report on the Employment of Colored Persons in the Department of State," enclosed in Clarence Mitchell to Walter White, April 6, 1953, Papers of the National Association for the Advancement of Colored People, Group II, Box A617, State Department, General, 1952–1954 file, Library of Congress.

47 Christian Ravndal to John Peurifoy, May 23, 1949, Truman Papers, White House Central File, Confidential File, State Department Correspondence series, Box 39, 1948–1949 folder, no. 5, Truman Library. For a thorough discussion of Ravndal's report, see Krenn, "'Outstanding Negroes' and 'Appropriate Countries': Some Facts, Figures, and Thoughts on Black U.S. Ambassadors, 1949–1988," *Diplomatic History* 14 (Winter 1990):131–141. It is interesting to note that the appointments after Dudley clearly followed the logic of Ravndal's memo. Although the next three African American ambassadors were named to posts in Africa, the first post–Second World War black diplomat

to head a U.S. mission in Europe was Clifton Wharton, Sr., who was named minister to Romania in 1958. The first two African Americans named as ambassadors to European nations went to Scandinavian nations: Wharton (to Norway in 1961) and Carl Rowan (to Finland, 1963).

48   For more on Bunche, see Brian Urquhart, *Ralph Bunche: An American Life* (New York: W.W. Norton, 1993); Charles P. Henry, *Ralph Bunche: Model Negro or American Other?* (New York: New York University Press, 1999); Jeffrey C. Stewart, "A New Negro Foreign Policy: The Critical Vision of Alain Locke and Ralph Bunche," in Heywood, *African Americans in U.S. Foreign Policy*, pp. 30–57. "Bunche Blasts D.C. Jim Crow," *Pittsburgh Courier*, June 11, 1949, pp. 1, 4, 13.

49   Krenn, *Black Diplomacy*, pp. 37–42.

50   Philip Raine to Mr. Haden, October 20, 1952; John Ordway to Mr. Reid, December 30, 1952, RG 59, 811.411.9-3052, /12-3052, NA.

51   The two best studies of Du Bois and his battles with both the NAACP and the Department of State are Carol Anderson's *Bourgeois Radicals* and *Eyes Off the Prize*. Also see Gerald Horne, *Black and Red: W.E.B. Du Bois and the Afro-American Response to the Cold War, 1944–1963* (Albany: SUNY Press, 1986).

52   For Baker, see Mary L. Dudziak, "Josephine Baker, Racial Protest, and the Cold War," *Journal of American History* 81 (September 1994):543–570; Matthew Pratt Guterl, *Josephine Baker and the Rainbow Tribe* (Cambridge: Belknap Press, 2014). On Robeson, consult Martin B. Duberman, *Paul Robeson* (New York: Knopf, 1989); Gerald Horne, *Paul Robeson: The Artist as Revolutionary* (London: Pluto Press, 2016); and Jordan Goodman, *Paul Robeson: A Watched Man* (London: Verso Books, 2013).

Chapter 4

1   "Art and Entertainment: Latest 'Cold War' Weapon for U.S.," *U.S. News & World Report*, July 1, 1955, pp. 57–59. For a recent and interesting look at the role of maps in the Cold War, see Timothy Barney, *Mapping the Cold War: Cartography and the Framing of America's International Power* (Chapel Hill: University of North Carolina Press, 2015).

2   Kenneth Osgood, *Total Cold War: Eisenhower's Secret Propaganda Battle at Home and Abroad* (Lawrence: University Press of Kansas, 2006), pp. 217, 218.

3   Belmonte, *Selling the American Way*, p. 51.

4   Ibid., pp. 51, 52; Cull, *The Cold War*, pp. 85–90; Arndt, *First Resort*, pp. 256–263.

5   Cull, *The Cold War*, p. 92; Osgood, *Total Cold War*, pp. 295, 296.

6   Barrett, *Truth*, pp. 181–184.

7   Cadra Peterson McDaniel, *American-Soviet Cultural Diplomacy: The Bolshoi Ballet's American Premiere* (Lanham, MD: Lexington Books, 2015), pp. xviii–xix. Also see Barghoorn, *Soviet Cultural Offensive*, Chs. 2–3.

8   Osgood, *Total Cold War*, pp. 88, 89; Cull, *The Cold War*, pp. 92–96.

9   Osgood, *Total Cold War*, p. 89. The OCB was created shortly after USIA came into existence. It replaced the Psychological Strategy Board, established by Truman in 1951 to coordinate America's "psychological" warfare with the Soviets.

10 NSC, "Mission of the United States Information Agency," *Foreign Relations of the United States, 1952–1954, National Security Affairs, Volume II, Part 2* (Washington, DC: Government Printing Office, 1984), pp. 1753–1755.

11 An excellent discussion of ANTA, the USIA, and State is found in Naima Prevots, *Dance for Export: Cultural Diplomacy and the Cold War* (Hanover, NH: University Press of New England, 1998), pp. 37–52.

12 Lisa E. Davenport, *Jazz Diplomacy: Promoting America in the Cold War Era* (Jackson: University Press of Mississippi, 2009), p. 39.

13 Danielle Fosler-Lussier, *Music in America's Cold War Diplomacy* (Berkeley: University of California Press, 2015), pp. 23–24. Also see Jessica C.E. Gienow-Hecht, "*The World Is Ready to Listen*: Symphony Orchestras and the Global Performance of America," *Diplomatic History* 36:1 (January 2012):17–28.

14 There are a number of good studies of the role of classical music in America's cultural diplomacy during the Cold War, including the previously cited work by Fosler-Lussier and James E. Wierzbicki, *Music in the Age of Anxiety: American Music in the Fifties* (Urbana: University of Illinois Press, 2016); Jessica Gienow-Hecht, ed., *Music and International History in the Twentieth Century* (New York: Berghahn Books, 2015), particularly the excellent essay by Jonathan Rosenberg, "'To Reach…into the Hearts and Minds of Our Friends': The United States' Symphonic Tours and the Cold War"; Emily Abrams Ansari, "'A Serious and Delicate Mission': American Orchestras, American Composers, and Cold War Diplomacy in Europe," in Felix Meyer, et al., eds, *Crosscurrents: American and European Music in Interaction, 1900–2000* (Woodbridge: Boydell & Brewer, 2008), pp. 287–298.

15 The London review is quoted in Prevots, *Dance for Export*, p. 22. The chapter entitled "The Avant-Garde Conundrum" pp. 53–68 provides an insightful analysis of the discussions and debates concerning sending more modern dance companies abroad. It is interesting to note that ballet did appear at the 1952 Berlin Cultural Festival, with performances by the New York City Ballet (pp. 20–22), but as noted previously in discussing the U.S. participation in the 1951 festival in Berlin because these shows were largely "hidden" from the American public and press there was little in the way of a concerted follow-up.

16 Prevots, *Dance for Export*, pp. 23–26; Victoria Phillips Geduld, "Dancing Diplomacy: Martha Graham and the Strange Commodity of Cold-War Cultural Exchange in Asia, 1955 and 1974," *Dance Chronicle* 33:1 (2010):45, 58–59. Other significant works on the role of dance in America's cultural diplomacy during the Cold War are Clare Croft, *Dancers as Diplomats: American Choreography in Cultural Exchange* (New York: Oxford University Press, 2015); Catherine Gunther Kodat, *Don't Act, Just Dance: The Metapolitics of Cold War Culture* (New Brunswick: Rutgers University Press, 2014); McDaniel, *American-Soviet Cultural Diplomacy*.

17 Osgood, *Total Cold War*, pp. 225–226. Also see Davenport, *Jazz Diplomacy*, pp. 44–46.

18 Davenport, *Jazz Diplomacy*, p. 33.

19 Richard Pells, *Modernist America: Art, Music, Movies, and the Globalization of American Culture* (New Haven, CT: Yale University Press, 2011), p. 154.

20 There have been a number of works on the Till murder; the most recent is Devery S. Anderson, *Emmitt Till: The Murder That Shocked the World*

and Propelled the Civil Rights Movement (Jackson: University Press of Mississippi, 2015).

21   Marshall W. Stearns, "Is Jazz Good Propaganda? The Dizzy Gillespie Tour," *The Saturday Review*, July 14, 1956, pp. 28–31. For Conover's influence see Pells, *Modernist America*, pp. 154, 155; Cull, *The Cold War*, pp. 107, 108; Mindy L. Clegg, "When Jazz Was King: Selling Records with the Cold War," *Journal of American Culture* 38:3 (September 2015):243–254.

22   For more on jazz diplomacy, see the previously mentioned works by Pells, Clegg, and Davenport as well as Penny M. Von Eschen, *Satchmo Blows Up the World: Jazz Ambassadors Play the Cold War* (Cambridge: Harvard University Press, 2004); Scott Gac, "Jazz Strategy: Dizzy, Foreign Policy, and Government in 1956," *Americana: The Journal of American Popular Culture (1900 to Present)* 4:1 (Spring 2005): http://www.americanpopularculture.com /journal/articles/spring_2005/gac.htm (Accessed March 25, 2017); David M. Carletta, "'Those White Guys Are Working for Me': Dizzy Gillespie, Jazz, and the Cultural Politics of the Cold War during the Eisenhower Administration," *International Social Science Review* 82:3 & 4 (2007):115–134.

23   Martin J. Medhurst, "Eisenhower's 'Atoms for Peace' Speech: A Case Study in the Strategic Use of Language," *Communication Monographs* 54 (June 1987):204, 209–210, 214.

24   Cull, *The Cold War*, p. 106.

25   Ran Zwigenberg, "'The Coming of a Second Sun': The 1956 Atoms for Peace Exhibit in Hiroshima and Japan's Embrace of Nuclear Power," *The Asia-Pacific Journal* 10:6, No. 1 (February 2012):1–15.

26   See Robert H. Haddow, *Pavilions of Plenty: Exhibiting American Culture Abroad in the 1950s* (Washington, DC: Smithsonian Institution Press, 1997), pp. 47–59; Cull, *The Cold War*, pp. 117, 118; Belmonte, *Selling the American Way*, pp. 131–133.

27   Krenn, *Black Diplomacy*, pp. 90, 91; also see Cull, *The Cold War*, Ch. 2; Belmonte, *Selling the American Way*, pp. 164–177; Osgood, *Total Cold War*, pp. 226–229, 275–287.

28   Krenn, *Black Diplomacy*, Ch. 5.

29   Krenn, "Carl Rowan and the Dilemma of Civil Rights, Propaganda, and the Cold War," in Linda Heywood, et al., eds., *African Americans in U.S. Foreign Policy: From the Era of Frederick Douglass to the Age of Obama* (Urbana: University of Illinois Press, 2015), pp. 61–63.

30   Davenport, *Jazz Diplomacy*, pp. 66–69.

31   Ellen Noonan, *The Strange Career of Porgy & Bess: Race, Culture, and America's Most Famous Opera* (Chapel Hill: University of North Carolina Press, 2012), p. 188–189, 195–196. A briefer, but still very good, introduction to the long history of the show is James Standifer, "The Tumultuous Life of *Porgy and Bess*," *Humanities* 18:6 (November/December 1997), http:// www.neh.gov/humanities/1997/novemberdecember/feature/the-tumultuous -life-porgy-and-bess. The Truman administration actually sponsored the first overseas show, to the 1952 Berlin Cultural Festival, but little came of this until two years later under Eisenhower.

32   Krenn, *Black Diplomacy*, p. 91.

33   For the Globetrotters and America's cultural diplomacy in the Cold War, see Damion L. Thomas, *Globetrotting: African American Athletes and Cold War*

Politics (Urbana: University of Illinois Press, 2012); Russ Crawford, *The Use of Sports to Promote the American Way of Life during the Cold War: Cultural Propaganda, 1945–1963* (Lewiston, NY: Edwin Mellen Press, 2008).

34　Barbara J. Keys, *Globalizing Sport: National Rivalry and International Community in the 1930s* (Cambridge: Harvard University Press, 2006), particularly Chs. 4, 5, and 7.

35　Toby C. Rider, *Cold War Games: Propaganda, the Olympics, and U.S. Foreign Policy* (Urbana: University of Illinois Press, 2016), p. 88. The Soviets actually bested the Americans at the 1956 Winter Olympics in Italy, winning sixteen medals to just seven for the United States. However, the Winter Games were traditionally more sparsely attended and usually dominated by European nations more engaged in many winter sports. The Summer Games, at least during the 1950s, were seen as the real arena for battle with the Soviets.

36　Rider, *Cold War Games*, pp. 94–99.

37　Rademacher's victory illustrated boxing's continuing importance in the field of cultural relations between nations, first highlighted by John L. Sullivan's overseas tours of the late 1800s. During the Cold War, as the United States and the Soviet Union fought on the world stage, American and communist boxers (first the Soviets, then the Cubans) slugged it out for national pride every four years at the Summer Games.

38　Rider, *Cold War Games*, Ch. 6.

39　Krenn, *Fall-Out Shelters*, Ch. 3.

40　Ibid., pp. 105–108.

41　Fosler-Lussier, *Music*, p. 1. Sebastian was the father of John B. Sebastian, who became famous in the 1960s as a founding member of the popular band The Lovin' Spoonful.

42　Krenn, *Fall-Out Shelters*, pp. 98, 99.

43　Prevots, *Dance for Export*, pp. 26–30. For a more detailed analysis of the constant budget battles to support the USIA, see Cull, *The Cold War*.

44　Donald C. Meyer, "The NBC Symphony Orchestra," PhD dissertation (University of California, Davis, 1994), Ch. 7. Also see Prevots, *Dance for Export*, pp. 33–35.

45　Krenn, *Fall-Out Shelters*, pp. 105–110.

46　Ibid., pp. 107–108, 201–202. For a detailed look at the development of the 1953 list of "prohibited" books and authors, see Louise S. Robbins, "The Overseas Libraries Controversy and the Freedom to Read: U.S. Librarians and Publishers Confront Joseph McCarthy," *Libraries & Culture* 36:1 (Winter 2001):27–39. And for one of the first stories to break the news about the blacklist, see the story "Secret Blacklist: Untold Story of the U.S.I.A.," *Nation* (October 30, 1954):376–378.

47　Krenn, *Fall-Out Shelters*, pp. 109, 110.

48　Davenport, *Jazz Diplomacy*, pp. 63, 64.

49　Lentz and Gower, *Opinions of Mankind*, pp. 97–104. For more on the significance of the Little Rock incident for American foreign relations, see Mary L. Dudziak, "The Little Rock Crisis and Foreign Affairs: Race, Resistance, and the Image of American Democracy," *South California Law Review* (September 1997):1641–1716; Cary Fraser, "Crossing the Color Line in Little Rock: The Eisenhower Administration and the Dilemma of Race for U.S. Foreign Policy," *Diplomatic History* 24:2 (Spring 2000):233–264.

50 Krenn, *Black Diplomacy*, pp. 104, 105.
51 Literature on the U.S. participation at the 1958 World's Fair is plentiful: Hixson, *Parting the Curtain*, pp. 141–150; Haddow, *Pavilions of Plenty*, Chs. 3–7; Rydell, *World of Fairs*, Ch. 7; Nilsen, *Projecting America*, Chs. 2–6.
52 For a full treatment of the American art exhibit at the 1958 fair, see Krenn, *Fall-Out Shelters*, Ch. 4.
53 Michael L. Krenn, "'Unfinished Business': Segregation and U.S. Diplomacy at the 1958 World's Fair," *Diplomatic History* 20:4 (Fall 1996):591–612.
54 Krenn, *Fall-Out Shelters*, pp. 134–137. The only official response to the criticisms was to send a collection of fifteen other paintings from the Whitney Museum in New York that were hung in the offices of the U.S. commissioner general for the fair. While these new paintings also contained some works of abstract expressionism, there were a number of other different genres represented.
55 Krenn, "Unfinished Business."
56 Hixson, *Parting the Curtain*, p. 167. Chapters 6 and 7 of the book constitute a wonderful examination of the establishment, impact, and importance of the exhibition. Also see Andrew James Wulf, *U.S. International Exhibitions during the Cold War: Winning Hearts and Minds through Cultural Diplomacy* (Lanham, MD: Rowman & Littlefield, 2015), Ch. 3.
57 Hixson, *Parting the Curtain*, pp. 179, 180.
58 Ibid., pp. 208, 209.
59 Krenn, *Fall-Out Shelters*, pp. 159–168.
60 Ibid., pp. 169–170.

Chapter 5

1 The standard work on Murrow remains A. M. Sperber, *Murrow: His Life and Times* (New York: Fordham University Press, 1999).
2 Krenn, *Fall-Out Shelters*, pp. 180–188.
3 Ibid., pp. 189–192.
4 The best general study of the Biennale is Lawrence Alloway, *The Venice Biennale, 1895–1968: From Salon to Goldfish Bowl* (Greenwich, CT: New York Graphic Society, 1968). For the U.S. participation during the 1950s and early 1960s, see Krenn, *Fall-Out Shelters*, pp. 79–81, 85, 86; Nancy Jachec, *Politics and Painting at the Venice Biennale, 1948–1964: Italy and the Idea of Europe* (Manchester: Manchester University Press, 2007); Frances K. Pohl, "An American in Venice: Ben Shahn and United States Foreign Policy at the 1954 Venice Biennale or Portrait of the Artist as an American Liberal," *Art History* 4:1 (March 1981):80–113. There is also a "Brief History of U.S. Participation in the Venice Biennale," c. 1968, in Record Unit 321, Box 150, Venice Biennale XXXIV [42 of 73] folder, Smithsonian Institution Archives, Washington, DC.
5 Krenn, *Fall-Out Shelters*, pp. 197–200.
6 Krenn, *Black Diplomacy*, pp. 124, 125.
7 Krenn, "Carl Rowan," pp. 66, 67; Cull, *The Cold War*, pp. 233–236.

8   The best examination of the use of film by the USIA during the Cold War is Nicholas J. Cull, "Film as Public Diplomacy: The USIA's Cold War at Twenty-Four Frames per Second," in Kenneth A. Osgood and Brian C. Etheridge, *The United States and Public Diplomacy: New Directions in Cultural and International History* (Leiden: Martinus Nijhoff Publishers, 2010), pp. 257–284.

9   Krenn, *Black Diplomacy*, pp. 141–143.

10 Davenport, *Jazz Diplomacy*, Chs. 5–6.

11 Prevots, *Dance for Export*, pp. 77, 81–84.

12 "ANTA May Be Out in Cultural Shakeup," *Billboard*, January 5, 1963, p. 8.

13 Davenport, *Jazz Diplomacy*, pp. 133, 134; Assistant Secretary Lucius D. Battle, Interviewed by Dayton Mak, July 10, 1991, p. 58, The Association for Diplomatic Studies and Training, Foreign Affairs Oral History Project, Arlington, VA, www.adst.org.

14 Prevots, *Dance for Export*, p. 134

15 Davenport, *Jazz Diplomacy*, pp. 98–100.

16 Krenn, *Fall-Out Shelters*, pp. 200–206.

17 Ibid., pp. 209–221.

18 Ibid., pp. 222–226; Claire Bower, "Paintbrush Politics: The Collapse of American Arts Diplomacy, 1968–1972," Hallvard Notaker, et al., *Reasserting America in the 1970s: U.S. Public Diplomacy and the Rebuilding of America's Image Abroad* (Manchester: Manchester University Press, 2016), pp. 111–125.

19 Krenn, *Fall-Out Shelters*, pp. 226–232; Bower, "Paintbrush Politics," pp. 118–121.

20 Noonan, *Strange Career of Porgy & Bess*, pp. 266, 275, 281.

21 Thomas, *Globetrotting*, pp. 156–162.

22 Krenn, "'The Low Key Mulatto Coverage:' Race, Civil Rights, and American Public Diplomacy, 1965–1976," in Notaker, et al., eds, *Reasserting America*, pp. 98–101; Krenn, *Black Diplomacy*, pp. 142–144.

23 Cull, *Cold War*, pp. 317–319; Krenn, "Mulatto Coverage," pp. 101–104.

24 Krenn, "Mulatto Coverage," pp. 103–106; Dean Kotlowski, "Black Power—Nixon Style: The Nixon Administration and Minority Business Enterprise," *The Business History Review* 72:3 (Autumn 1998):413, 417.

25 The article, "The C.I.A.: Maker of Policy, or Tool?," by Tom Wicker, John W. Finney, Max Frankel, H.W. Kenworthy, and other staff, appeared in the *New York Times* on April 26, 1966, on p. 1. Four more articles in the series appeared before the end of April. Sol Stern, "A Short Account of International Student Politics & the Cold War with Particular Reference to the NSA, CIA, Etc.," *Ramparts Magazine* (March 1967):29–39. This was followed by another report, entitled "Three Tales of the CIA," in the April 1967 edition, pp. 15–28, that continued the story of CIA infiltration of student groups and unions.

26 Hugh Wilford, "Calling the Tune? The CIA, The British Left and the Cold War, 1945–1960," in Giles Scott-Smith and Hans Krabbendam, eds., *The Cultural Cold War in Western Europe, 1945–1960* (London: Frank Cass Publishers, 2003), pp. 44, 45; Cassandra Pybus, "CIA as Culture Vultures," *Jacket2* 12 (October 2000): jacketmagazine.com/12/pybus-quad.html; Paul McGarr, "'Quiet Americans in India:' The CIA and the Politics of Intelligence in Cold War South Asia," *Diplomatic History* 38:5 (2014):1046, 1047.

27 John A. Davis, "Black Americans and United States Policy toward Africa," *Journal of International Affairs* 23:2 (1969):238.

28 Nicholas J. Cull, "How We Got Here," in Philip Seib, ed., *Toward a New Public Diplomacy: Redirecting U.S. Foreign Policy* (New York: Palgrave Macmillan, 2009), p. 32.

29 Cull, *Cold War*, pp. 302–304; Nicholas Griffin, *Ping-Pong Diplomacy: The Secret History Behind the Game That Changed the World* (New York: Scribner, 2014); Nicholas J. Cull, "The Devil at the Crossroads: USIA and American Public Diplomacy in the 1970s," in Notaker, et al., eds., *Reasserting America*, p. 28.

30 Wulf, *U.S. International Exhibitions*, pp. 180–191.

31 Ibid., pp. 191–202. An interesting study of "space diplomacy" is Teasel Muir-Harmony, "Selling Space Capsules, Moon Rocks, and America: Spaceflight in U.S. Public Diplomacy, 1961–1979," in Notaker, et al., eds., *Reasserting America*, pp. 127–142.

32 Cull, "How We Got Here," pp. 32–38; Cull, *The Decline and Fall of the United States Information Agency: American Public Diplomacy, 1989–2001* (New York: Palgrave Macmillan, 2012), pp. 60, 183; Juliet Antunes Sablosky, "Reinvention, Reorganization, Retreat: American Cultural Diplomacy at Century's End, 1978–1998," *Journal of Arts Management, Law & Society* 29:1 (Spring 1999):30–46.

33 Allen Guttmann, "The Cold War and the Olympics," *International Journal* 43:4 (Autumn 1988):554.

34 For a thorough analysis of the U.S.-Soviet rivalry at the Olympics, see Rider, *Cold War Games.*

35 Kevin B. Witherspoon, "'Fuzz Kids' and 'Musclemen:' The US-Soviet Basketball Rivalry, 1958–1975," in Heather C. Dichter and Andrew L. Johns, eds., *Diplomatic Games: Sport, Statecraft, and International Relations since 1945* (Lexington: University Press of Kentucky, 2014), pp. 304–307.

36 Guttmann, "The Cold War and the Olympics," pp. 559–567; Thomas, *Globetrotting*, pp. 168, 169; Philip A. D'Agati, *The Cold War and the 1984 Olympic Games: Soviet-American Surrogate War* (New York: Palgrave Macmillan, 2013). For the hockey rivalry, see John Soares, "The Cold War on Ice," *The Brown Journal of World Affairs* 14:2 (Spring/Summer 2008):77–87.

37 Sablosky, "Reinvention," pp. 8, 11.

38 Cull, *Decline and Fall*, pp. 105, 163, 164.

39 Krenn, *Fall-Out Shelters*, p. 237.

Conclusion

1 All of the information about these programs can be found at https://eca.state .gov/programs-initiatives/cultural-diplomacy; https://eca.state.gov/programs -initiatives/sports-diplomacy (Accessed March 25, 2017).

2 Helena K. Finn, "The Case for Cultural Diplomacy: Engaging Foreign Audiences," *Foreign Affairs* 82:6 (November/December 2003):20.

3 See the websites listed above for descriptions of the programs and participants. Numerous articles have appeared in newspapers, journals, and magazines in recent years highlighting various aspects of the cultural diplomacy program: Natalia Grincheva, "Democracy for Export: Museums Connect Program as a

Vehicle of American Cultural Diplomacy," *Curator: The Museum Journal* 58:2 (April 2015):137–149; Kate Taylor, "U.S. to Send Visual Artists as Cultural Ambassadors," *New York Times*, October 25, 2010, C1; Hishaam Aidi, "Leveraging Hip hop in US Foreign Policy," *Aljazeera*, November 7, 2011, http://www.aljazeera.com/indepth/opinion/2011/10/2011103091018299924. html; Clare Croft, "Dance Returns to American Cultural Diplomacy: The U.S. State Department's 2003 Dance Residency Program and Its After Effects," *Dance Research Journal* 45:1 (April 2013):23–39.

4   Advisory Committee on Cultural Diplomacy, U.S. Department of State, "Cultural Diplomacy: The Linchpin of Public Diplomacy" (Washington, DC: U.S. Department of State, September 2005), p. 3.

5   Jonathan Broder, "Banjo Diplomacy: Can Art, Sports and Science Create a Thaw between the U.S. and Iran? Ping-Pong Anyone?," *Newsweek,* July 24, 2015, pp. 16–19.

6   See the websites listed in Note 1.

7   Cynthia P. Schneider, "The Unrealized Potential of Cultural Diplomacy: 'Best Practices' and What Could Be, If Only …," *The Journal of Arts Management, Law, and Society* 39:4 (Winter 2009):266, 276.

8   Grincheva, "Democracy for Export," pp. 141, 146; Croft, "Dance Returns," pp. 27–28.

9   Taylor, "Visual Artists"; Croft, "Dance Returns," pp. 25, 26.

10 Finn, "The Case for Cultural Diplomacy," pp. 15, 16, 20; Advisory Committee, "Cultural Diplomacy," p. 20.

11 Neal M. Rosendorf, "A Cultural Public Diplomacy Strategy," in Seib, *Toward a New Public Diplomacy*, pp. 173–194.

12 Advisory Committee, "Cultural Diplomacy," p. 2.

BIBLIOGRAPHY

Adamthwaite, Anthony. *Grandeur and Misery: France's Bid for Power in Europe, 1914-1940*. London: Arnold, 1995.

Aidi, Hishaam. "Leveraging Hip Hop in US Foreign Policy." *Aljazeera*, http://www.aljazeera.com/indepth/opinion/2011/10/2011103091018299924.html (Accessed November 7, 2011).

Alloway, Lawrence. *The Venice Biennale, 1895–1968: From Salon to Goldfish Bowl*. Greenwich, CT: New York Graphic Society, 1968.

Anderson, Carol. *Bourgeois Radicals: The NAACP and the Struggle for Colonial Liberation, 1941–1960*. Cambridge: Cambridge University Press, 2014.

Anderson, Carol. *Eyes Off the Prize: The United Nations and the African American Struggle for Human Rights, 1944–1955*. Cambridge: Cambridge University Press, 2003.

Anderson, Devery S. *Emmitt Till: The Murder That Shocked the World and Propelled the Civil Rights Movement*. Jackson: University Press of Mississippi, 2015.

Ansari, Emily Abrams. "'A Serious and Delicate Mission:' American Orchestras, American Composers, and Cold War Diplomacy in Europe." In *Crosscurrents: American and European Music in Interaction, 1900–2000*, eds. Felix Meyer, Carol J. Oja, Wolfgang Rathert and Anne C. Shreffler. Woodbridge: Boydell & Brewer, 2008, pp. 287–298.

Arndt, Richard T. *The First Resort of Kings: American Cultural Diplomacy in the Twentieth Century*. Washington, DC: Potomac Books, 2005.

Auerbach, Jonathan. *Weapons of Democracy: Propaganda, Progressivism, and American Public Opinion*. Baltimore, MD: Johns Hopkins University Press, 2015.

Ausfeld, Margaret Lynne and Virginia M. Mecklenburg. *Advancing American Art: Politics and Aesthetics in the State Department Exhibition, 1946–1948*. Montgomery, AL: Montgomery Museum of Fine Arts, 1984.

Baigell, Renee and Matthew Baigell, eds., *Soviet Dissident Artists: Interviews after Perestroika*. New Brunswick, NJ: Rutgers University Press, 1995.

Barghoorn, Frederick C. *The Soviet Cultural Offensive: The Role of Cultural Diplomacy in Soviet Foreign Policy*. Princeton, NJ: Princeton University Press, 1960.

Barney, Timothy. *Mapping the Cold War: Cartography and the Framing of America's International Power*. Chapel Hill: University of North Carolina Press, 2015.

Barrett, William W. *Truth Is Our Weapon*. New York: Funk & Wagnalls Company, 1953.

Baudin, Antoine. "Why Is Soviet Painting Hidden from Us?: Zhadanov Art and Its International Relations and Fallout, 1947–1953." In *Socialist Realism without Shores*, eds. Thomas Lahusen and Evgeny Dobrenko. Durham, NC: Duke University Press, 1997, pp. 227–256.

Beale, Howard K. *Theodore Roosevelt and the Rise of America to World Power.* Baltimore, MD: Johns Hopkins University Press, 1956.

Belmonte, Laura A. *Selling the American Way: U.S. Propaganda and the Cold War.* Philadelphia: University of Pennsylvania Press, 2008.

Benamou, Catherine L. *It's All true: Orson Welles's Pan-American Odyssey.* Berkeley: University of California Press, 2007.

Bishop, Scott, Robert Ekelund, Danielle Mohr Funderburk, Dennis Harper, J. Andrew Henley, Jessica Hughes, Marilyn Laufer, Paul Manoguerra, Daniel Scott Neil, Heather Read, Sunny Stalter-Pace and Mark White. *Art Interrupted: Advancing American Art and the Politics of Cultural Diplomacy.* Athens, GA: Georgia Museum of Art, 2012.

Blassingame, John, Peter P. Hinks and John R. McKivigan, eds., *The Frederick Douglass Papers: Series Two: Autobiographical Writings: Volume 2: My Bondage and My Freedom.* New Haven, CT: Yale University Press, 2003.

Boger, Astrid. "St. Louis 1904." In *Encyclopedia of World's Fairs and Expositions,* eds. John E. Findling and Kimberly D. Pelle. Jefferson, NC: McFarland & Company, Inc., Publishers, 2008.

Bogle, Lori Lyn. "TR's Use of PR to Strengthen the Navy." *Naval History Magazine* 21:6 (December 2007):26–31.

Borstelmann, Thomas. *Cold War and the Color Line: American Race Relations in the Global Arena.* Cambridge: Cambridge University Press, 2001.

Bower, Claire, "Paintbrush Politics: The Collapse of American Arts Diplomacy, 1968–1972." In *Reasserting America in the 1970s: U.S. Public Diplomacy and the Rebuilding of America's Image Abroad,* eds. Hallvard Notaker, Giles Scott-Smith and David J. Snyder. Manchester: Manchester University Press, 2016, pp. 111–125.

Bown, Matthew Cullerne. *Socialist Realist Painting.* New Haven, CT: Yale University Press, 1998.

Brantley, Daniel. "Black Americans as Participants in the Foreign Service." *Crisis* 3:9 (November 1986):32–33.

Broder, Jonathan. "Banjo Diplomacy: Can Art, Sports and Science Create a Thaw between the U.S. and Iran? Ping-Pong Anyone?" *Newsweek* 24 (July 2015):16–19.

Bu, Liping. "Educational Exchange and Cultural Diplomacy in the Cold War." *Journal of American Studies* 33:3, Pt. 1 (December 1999):393–415.

Campbell, Jennifer L. "Creating Something Out of Nothing: The Office of Inter American Affairs Music Committee (1940–1941) and the Inception of a Policy for Musical Diplomacy." *Diplomatic History* 16:1 (January 2012):29–39.

Carletta, David M. "'Those White Guys Are Working for Me:' Dizzy Gillespie, Jazz, and the Cultural Politics of the Cold War during the Eisenhower Administration." *International Social Science Review* 82:3 & 4 (2007):115–134.

Clegg, Mindy L. "When Jazz Was King: Selling Records with the Cold War." *Journal of American Culture* 38:3 (September 2015):243–254.

Collin, Richard H. *Theodore Roosevelt, Culture, Diplomacy, and Expansion: A New View of American Imperialism.* Baton Rouge: Louisiana State University Press, 1985.

Crawford, Russ. *The Use of Sports to Promote the American Way of Life during the Cold War: Cultural Propaganda, 1945–1963.* Lewiston, NY: Edwin Mellen Press, 2008.

Creel, George. *How We Advertised America*. New York: Arno Press, 1972.

Croft, Clare. *Dancers as Diplomats: American Choreography in Cultural Exchange*. New York: Oxford University Press, 2015.

Croft, Clare. "Dance Returns to American Cultural Diplomacy: The U.S. State Department's 2003 Dance Residency Program and Its After Effects." *Dance Research Journal* 45:1 (April 2013):23–39.

Cull, Nicholas J. *The Cold War and the United States Information Agency: American Propaganda and Public Diplomacy, 1945–1989*. Cambridge: Cambridge University Press, 2008.

Cull, Nicholas J. "The Devil at the Crossroads: USIA and American Public Diplomacy in the 1970s." In *Reasserting America in the 1970s: U.S. Public Diplomacy and the Rebuilding of America's Image Abroad*, eds. Hallvard Notaker, Giles Scott-Smith and David J. Snyder. Manchester: Manchester University Press, 2016, pp. 25–41.

Cull, Nicholas J. "Film as Public Diplomacy: The USIA's Cold War at Twenty-Four Frames per Second." In *The United States and Public Diplomacy: New Directions in Cultural and International History*, eds. Kenneth A. Osgood and Brian C. Etheridge. Leiden: Martinus Nijhoff Publishers, 2010, pp. 257–284.

Cull, Nicholas J. "How We Got Here." In *Toward a New Public Diplomacy: Redirecting U.S. Foreign Policy*, ed. Philip Seib. New York: Palgrave Macmillan, 2009, pp. 23–47.

D'Agati, Philip A. *The Cold War and the 1984 Olympic Games: Soviet-American Surrogate War*. New York: Palgrave Macmillan, 2013.

Davenport, Lisa E. *Jazz Diplomacy: Promoting America in the Cold War Era*. Jackson: University Press of Mississippi, 2009.

Davis, John A. "Black Americans and United States Policy toward Africa." *Journal of International Affairs* 23:2 (1969):236–249.

Douglass, Frederick. *Life and Times of Frederick Douglass*. New York: Citadel Press, 1983.

Duberman, Martin B. *Paul Robeson*. New York: Knopf, 1989.

Dudziak, Mary L. *Cold War Civil Rights: Race and the Image of American Democracy*. Princeton, NJ: Princeton University Press, 2000.

Dudziak, Mary L. "Josephine Baker, Racial Protest, and the Cold War." *Journal of American History* 81 (September 1994):543–570.

Dudziak, Mary L. "The Little Rock Crisis and Foreign Affairs: Race, Resistance, and the Image of American Democracy." *South California Law Review* (September 1997):1641–1716.

Dugatkin, Lee Alan. *Mr. Jefferson and the Giant Moose: Natural History in Early America*. Chicago: University of Chicago Press, 2009.

Elias, Robert. *The Empire Strikes Out: How Baseball Sold U.S. Foreign Policy and Promoted the American Way Abroad*. New York: The New Press, 2010.

Espinosa, J. Manuel. *Inter-American Beginnings of U.S. Cultural Diplomacy, 1936–1948*. Washington, DC: Department of State, 1976.

Esthus, Raymond A. *Theodore Roosevelt and the International Rivalries*. Claremont, CA: Regina Books, 1970.

Fayet, Jean-Francois. "VOKS: The Third Dimension of Soviet Foreign Policy." In *Searching for a Cultural Diplomacy*, eds. Jessica C. E. Gienow-Hecht and Mark C. Donfried. New York: Berghahn Books, 2010, pp. 33–49.

Fike, Claude E. "The Influence of the Creel Committee and the American Red Cross on Russian-American Relations, 1917–1919." *The Journal of Modern History* 31:2 (June 1959):93–109.

Finn, Helena K. "The Case for Cultural Diplomacy: Engaging Foreign Audiences." *Foreign Affairs* 82:6 (November/December 2003):15–20.

Fosler-Lussier, Danielle. *Music in America's Cold War Diplomacy*. Berkeley: University of California Press, 2015.

Fraser, Cary. "Crossing the Color Line in Little Rock: The Eisenhower Administration and the Dilemma of Race for U.S. Foreign Policy." *Diplomatic History* 24:2 (Spring 2000):233–264.

Gac, Scott. "Jazz Strategy: Dizzy, Foreign Policy, and Government in 1956." *Americana: The Journal of American Popular Culture (1900 to Present)* 4:1 (Spring 2005), http://www.americanpopularculture.com/journal/articles/spring_2005/gac.htm.

Gaines, Kevin. *American Africans in Ghana: Black Expatriates and the Civil Rights Era*. Chapel Hill: University of North Carolina Press, 2006.

Garner, Alice and Diane Kirkby. "'Never a Machine for Propaganda'?: The Australian-American Fulbright Program and Australia's Cold War," *Australian Historical Studies* 44 (2013):117–133.

Geduld, Victoria Phillips. "Dancing Diplomacy: Martha Graham and the Strange Commodity of Cold-War Cultural Exchange in Asia, 1955 and 1974." *Dance Chronicle* 33:1 (2010):44–81.

Gienow-Hecht, Jessica C. E., ed. *Music and International History in the Twentieth Century*. New York: Berghahn Books, 2015.

Gienow-Hecht, Jessica C. E. "*The World Is Ready to Listen*: Symphony Orchestras and the Global Performance of America." *Diplomatic History* 36:1 (January 2012):17–28.

Gilderhus, Mark T. *The Second Century: U.S.-Latin American Relations since 1889*. Wilmington, DE: Scholarly Resources, Inc., 2000.

Girona, Ramon and Jordi Xifra. "The Office of Facts and Figures: Archibald MacLeish and the 'Strategy of Truth.'" *Public Relations Review* 35:3 (September 2009):287–290.

Glant, Tibor. "Against All Odds: Vira B. Whitehouse and Rosika Schwimmer in Switzerland, 1918." *American Studies International* 40:1 (February 2002):34–51.

Goldstein, Cora Sol. "Before the CIA: American Actions in the German Fine Arts (1946–1949)." *Diplomatic History* 29:5 (November 2005):747–778.

Goldstein, Cora Sol. *Capturing the German Eye: American Visual Propaganda in Occupied Germany*. Chicago: University of Chicago Press, 2009.

Goldstein, Cora Sol. "The Control of Visual Representation: American Art Policy in Occupied Germany, 1945–1949." In *The Cultural Cold War in Western Europe, 1945–1960*, eds. Giles Scott-Smith and Hans Krabbendam. London: Frank Cass Publishers, 2003, pp. 283–299.

Goodman, Jordan. *Paul Robeson: A Watched Man*. London: Verso Books, 2013.

Gorn, Elliott J. *The Manly Art: Bare-Knuckle Prize Fighting in America*. Ithaca, NY: Cornell University Press, 1986.

Griffin, Nicholas. *Ping-Pong Diplomacy: The Secret History behind the Game That Changed the World*. New York: Scribner, 2014.

Grincheva, Natalia. "Democracy for Export: Museums Connect Program as a Vehicle of American Cultural Diplomacy." *Curator: The Museum Journal* 58:2 (April 2015):137–149.

Guilbaut, Serge. *How New York Stole the Idea of Modern Art: Abstract Expressionism, Freedom, and the Cold War*. Chicago: Chicago University Press, 1983.

Guterl, Matthew Pratt. *Josephine Baker and the Rainbow Tribe*. Cambridge: Belknap Press, 2014.

Guttmann, Allen. "The Cold War and the Olympics." *International Journal* 43:4 (Autumn 1988):554–568.

Haddow, Robert H. *Pavilions of Plenty: Exhibiting American Culture Abroad in the 1950s*. Washington, DC: Smithsonian Institution Press, 1997.

Hart, Justin. *Empire of Ideas: The Origins of Public Diplomacy and the Transformation of U.S. Foreign Policy*. Oxford: Oxford University Press, 2013.

Heil, Alan L., Jr. *Voice of America: A History*. New York: Columbia University Press, 2003.

Henry, Charles P. *Ralph Bunche: Model Negro or American Other?*. New York: New York University Press, 1999.

Hess, Carol A. *Representing the Good Neighbor: Music, Difference, and the Pan-American Dream*. Oxford: Oxford University Press, 2013.

Heywood, Linda, Allison Blakely, Charles Stith and Joshua C. Yesnowitz, eds., *African Americans in U.S. Foreign Policy: From the Era of Frederick Douglass to the Age of Obama*. Urbana: University of Illinois Press, 2015.

Hixson, Walter L. *Parting the Curtain: Propaganda, Culture, and the Cold War, 1945–1961*. New York: St. Martin's Griffin, 1998.

Horne, Gerald. *Black and Red: W.E.B. Du Bois and the Afro-American Response to the Cold War, 1944–1963*. Albany, NY: SUNY Press, 1986.

Horne, Gerald. *The End of Empires: African Americans and India*. Philadelphia, PA: Temple University Press, 2008.

Horne, Gerald. *Paul Robeson: The Artist as Revolutionary*. London: Pluto Press, 2016.

Howard, Christopher E. "Propaganda against Propaganda: Deconstructing the Dominant Narrative of the Committee on Public Information." MA Thesis, Appalachian State University, 2014.

Hyman, Sidney. *The Lives of William Benton*. Chicago: University of Chicago Press, 1970.

Isenberg, Michael T. *John L. Sullivan and His America*. Urbana: University of Illinois Press, 1988.

Jachec, Nancy. *Politics and Painting at the Venice Biennale, 1948–1968: Italy and the Idea of Europe*. Manchester: Manchester University Press, 2007.

James, C. V. *Socialist Realism: Origins and Theory*. New York: St. Martin's Press, 1973.

James, Rawn, Jr. *The Double V: How Wars, Protest, and Harry Truman Desegregated America's Military*. New York: Bloomsbury Press, 2013.

Jewell, Richard B. "Orson Welles, George Schaefer and IT'S ALL TRUE: A 'Cursed' Production." *Film History* 2 (November 1988):325–335.

Keys, Barbara J. *Globalizing Sport: National Rivalry and International Community in the 1930s*. Cambridge: Harvard University Press, 2006.

Koch, Adrienne and William Peden, eds. *The Life and Selected Writings of Thomas Jefferson*. New York: The Modern Library, 1944.

Kodat, Catherine Gunther. *Don't Act, Just Dance: The Metapolitics of Cold War Culture*. New Brunswick, NJ: Rutgers University Press, 2014.

Kotlowski, Dean. "Black Power—Nixon Style: The Nixon Administration and Minority Business Enterprise." *The Business History Review* 72:3 (Autumn 1998):409–455.

Kotlowski, Dean. "Selling America to the World: The Office of War Information's *The Town* (1945) and the *American Scene* Series." *Australasian Journal of American Studies* 35:1 (July 2016):79–101.

Kramer, Paul A. *The Blood of Government: Race, Empire, the United States & the Philippines*. Chapel Hill: The University of North Carolina Press, 2006.

Kraske, Gary E. *Missionaries of the Book: The American Library Profession and the Origins of United States Cultural Diplomacy*. Westport, CT: Greenwood Press, 1985.

Krenn, Michael L. *Black Diplomacy: African Americans and the State Department, 1945–1969*. Armonk, NY: M.E. Sharpe, 1999.

Krenn, Michael L. "Carl Rowan and the Dilemma of Civil Rights, Propaganda, and the Cold War." In *African Americans in U.S. Foreign Policy: From the Era of Frederick Douglass to the Age of Obama*, eds. Linda Heywood, Allison Blakely, Charles Stith and Joshua C. Yesnowitz. Urbana: University of Illinois Press, 2015, pp. 58–80.

Krenn, Michael L. *Fall-Out Shelters for the Human Spirit: American Art and the Cold War*. Chapel Hill: University of North Carolina Press, 2005.

Krenn, Michael L. "'The Low Key Mulatto Coverage:' Race, Civil Rights, and American Public Diplomacy, 1965–1976." In *Reasserting America in the 1970s: U.S Public Diplomacy and the Rebuilding of America's Image Abroad*, eds. Hallvard Notaker, Giles Scott-Smith and David J. Snyder. Manchester: Manchester University Press, 2016, pp. 95–110.

Krenn, Michael L. "'Outstanding Negroes' and 'Appropriate Countries': Some Facts, Figures, and Thoughts on Black U.S. Ambassadors, 1949–1988." *Diplomatic History* 14 (Winter 1990):131–141.

Krenn, Michael L. "Send More Boxing Monkeys: Adventures in U.S. Cold War Propaganda." *The SHAFR Newsletter* 30:1 (March 1999):27–28.

Krenn, Michael L. "'Unfinished Business:' Segregation and U.S. Diplomacy at the 1958 World's Fair." *Diplomatic History* 20:4 (Fall 1996):591–612.

Krugler, David F. *The Voice of America and the Domestic Propaganda Battles, 1945–1953*. Columbia: University of Missouri Press, 2000.

Lawson, Steven F. *Running for Freedom: Civil Rights and Black Politics in America since 1941*. 4th ed. West Sussex: Wiley-Blackwell, 2014.

Lebovic, Sam. "From War Junk to Educational Exchange: The World War II Origins of the Fulbright Program and the Foundations of American Cultural Globalism, 1945–1950." *Diplomatic History* 37:2 (2013):280–312.

Leith, James A. *The Idea of Art as Propaganda in France, 1750–1799: A Study in the History of Ideas*. Toronto: University of Toronto Press, 1965.

Lentz, Richard and Karla K. Gower. *The Opinions of Mankind: Racial Issues, Press, and Propaganda in the Cold War*. Columbia: University of Missouri Press, 2010.

Link, Arthur, ed. *The Papers of Woodrow Wilson.* Vol. 28. Princeton, NJ: Princeton University Press, 1979.

Little, Lawrence S. *Disciples of Liberty: The African Methodist Episcopal Church in the Age of Imperialism, 1884–1916.* Knoxville: The University of Tennessee Press, 2000.

Littleton, Taylor D. and Maltby Sykes. *Advancing America Art: Painting, Politics, and Cultural Confrontation at Mid-Century.* Tuscaloosa: University of Alabama Press, 1989.

Magnusdottir, Rosa. "Mission Impossible? Selling Soviet Socialism to Americans, 1955–1958." In *Searching for a Cultural Diplomacy,* eds. Jessica C. E. Gienow-Hecht and Mark C. Donfried. New York: Berghahn Books, 2010, pp. 50–72.

Makdisi, Ussama. *Artillery of Heaven: American Missionaries and the Failed Conversion of the Middle East.* Ithaca, NY: Cornell University Press, 2008.

Matsuo, Kazuyuki. "American Propaganda in China: The U.S. Committee on Public Information, 1918–1919." *The Journal of American and Canadian Studies* 14:2 (1996):19–42.

McAlister, Melani. *Epic Encounters: Culture, Media, and U.S. Interests in the Middle East, 1945–2000.* Berkeley: University of California Press, 2001.

McAllister, William B., Joshua Botts, Peter Cozzens and Aaron W. Marrs. *Toward "Thorough, Accurate, and Reliable": A History of the* Foreign Relations of the United States *Series.* Washington, DC: U.S. Department of State, 2015.

McDaniel, Cadra Peterson. *American-Soviet Cultural Diplomacy: The Bolshoi Ballet's American Premiere.* Lanham, MD: Lexington Books, 2015.

McGarr, Paul. "'Quiet Americans in India:' The CIA and the Politics of Intelligence in Cold War South Asia." *Diplomatic History* 38:5 (2014):1046–1082.

Medhurst, Martin J. "Eisenhower's 'Atoms for Peace' Speech: A Case Study in the Strategic Use of Language." *Communication Monographs* 54 (June 1987):204–220.

Meriwether, James H. *Proudly We Can Be Africans: Black America and Africa, 1935–1961.* Chapel Hill: University of North Carolina Press, 2002.

Merriam, Charles E. "American Publicity in Italy." *The American Political Science Review* 13:4 (November 1919):541–555.

Meyer, Donald C. "The NBC Symphony Orchestra." PhD dissertation, University of California, Davis, 1994.

Meyers, Cynthia B. "From Radio Adman to Radio Reformer: Senator William Benton's Career in Broadcasting, 1930–1960." *Journal of Radio & Audio Media* 16:1 (2009):17–29.

Millard, Candice. *Destiny of the Republic: A Tale of Madness, Medicine, and the Murder of a President.* New York: Doubleday, 2013.

Miller, Jake C. *The Black Presence in American Foreign Affairs.* Washington, DC: University Press of America, 1978.

Miller, Toby and George Yudice. *Cultural Policy.* London: Sage Publications, 2002.

Mock, James R. "The Creel Committee in Latin America." *The Hispanic American Historical Review* 22:2 (May 1942):262–279.

Mock, James R. and Cedric Lawson. *Words That Won the War: The Story of the Committee on Public Information, 1917–1919.* Princeton, NJ: Princeton University Press, 1939.

Muir-Harmony, Teasel. "Selling Space Capsules, Moon Rocks, and America: Spaceflight in U.S. Public Diplomacy, 1961–1979." In *Reasserting America in the 1970s: U.S. Public Diplomacy and the Rebuilding of America's Image*

Abroad, eds. Hallvard Notaker, Giles Scott-Smith and David J. Snyder. Manchester: Manchester University Press, 2016, pp. 127–142.

Myers, William Starr. *Woodrow Wilson: Some Princeton Memories*. Princeton, NJ: Princeton University Press, 2016.

Nilsen, Sarah. *Projecting America, 1958: Film and Cultural Diplomacy at the Brussels World's Fair*. Jefferson, NC: McFarland & Company, 2011.

Ninkovich, Frank A. *The Diplomacy of Ideas: U.S. Foreign Policy and Cultural Relations, 1938–1950*. Cambridge: Cambridge University Press, 1981.

Noonan, Ellen. *The Strange Career of Porgy & Bess: Race, Culture, and America's Most Famous Opera*. Chapel Hill: University of North Carolina Press, 2012.

Osgood, Kenneth. *Total Cold War: Eisenhower's Secret Propaganda Battle at Home and Abroad*. Lawrence: University Press of Kansas, 2006.

Pells, Richard. *Modernist America: Art, Music, Movies and the Globalization of American Culture*. New Haven, CT: Yale University Press, 2011.

Pells, Richard. *Not Like Us: How Europeans Have Loved, Hated, and Transformed American Culture since World War II*. New York: Basic Books, 1997.

Pike, Frederick B. *The United States and Latin America: Myths and Stereotypes of Civilization and Nature*. Austin: University of Texas Press, 1992.

Plummer, Brenda Gayle. *In Search of Power: African Americans in the Era of Decolonization, 1956–1974*. Cambridge: Cambridge University Press, 2013.

Plummer, Brenda Gayle. *Rising Wind: Black Americans and U.S. Foreign Affairs, 1935 1960*. Chapel Hill: University of North Carolina Press, 1996.

Plummer, Brenda Gayle, ed. *Window on Freedom: Race, Civil Rights, and Foreign Affairs, 1945–1988*. Chapel Hill: University of North Carolina Press, 2003.

Pohl, Frances K. "An American in Venice: Ben Shahn and United States Foreign Policy at the 1954 Venice Biennale or Portrait of the Artist as an American Liberal." *Art History* 4:1 (March 1981):80–113.

Porterfield, Todd. *The Allure of Empire: Art in the Service of French Imperialism, 1798–1836*. Berkeley: University of California Press, 2000.

Prevots, Naima. *Dance for Export: Cultural Diplomacy and the Cold War*. Hanover, NH: University Press of New England, 1998.

Pybus, Cassandra. "CIA as Culture Vultures." *Jacket2* 12 (October 2000), jacketmagazine.come/12/pybus-quad.html.

Rice, Alan J. and Martin Crawford, eds., *Liberating Sojourn: Frederick Douglass & Transatlantic Reform*. Athens: The University of Georgia Press, 1999.

Richard, Pamela Spence. "Information for the Allies: Office of War Information Libraries in Australia, New Zealand, and South Africa." *Library Quarterly* 52:4 (October 1982):325–347.

Rider, Toby C. *Cold War Games: Propaganda, the Olympics, and U.S. Foreign Policy*. Urbana: University of Illinois Press, 2016.

Robbins, Louise S. "The Overseas Libraries Controversy and the Freedom to Read: U.S. Librarians and Publishers Confront Joseph McCarthy." *Libraries & Culture* 36:1 (Winter 2001):27–39.

Rosenberg, Jonathan. *How Far the Promised Land? World Affairs and the American Civil Rights Movement from the First World War to Vietnam*. Princeton, NJ: Princeton University Press, 2006.

Rosendorf, Neal M. "A Cultural Public Diplomacy Strategy." In *Toward a New Public Diplomacy: Redirecting U.S. Foreign Policy*, ed. Philip Seib. New York: Palgrave Macmillan, 2009, pp. 173–194.

Rydell, Robert W. *All the World's a Fair: Visions of Empire at American International Expositions, 1876–1916.* Chicago: The University of Chicago Press, 1984.

Rydell, Robert W. *World of Fairs: The Century-of-Progress Expositions.* Chicago: The University of Chicago Press, 1993.

Rydell, Robert W. and Rob Kroes. *Buffalo Bill in Bologna: The Americanization of the World, 1869–1922.* Chicago: The University of Chicago Press, 2005.

Rydell, Robert W., John E. Findling and Kimberly D. Pelle. *Fair America: World's Fairs in the United States.* Washington, DC: Smithsonian Institution Press, 2000.

Sablosky, Juliet Antunes. "Reinvention, Reorganization, Retreat: American Cultural Diplomacy at Century's End, 1978–1998." *Journal of Arts Management, Law & Society* 29:1 (Spring 1999):30–46.

Sadlier, Darlene J. *Americans All: Good Neighbor Cultural Diplomacy in World War II.* Austin: University of Texas Press, 2012.

Schneider, Cynthia P. "Cultural Diplomacy: Hard to Define, but You'd Know It If You Saw It." *The Brown Journal of World Affairs* 13:1 (Fall/Winter 2006):191–203.

Schneider, Cynthia P. "The Unrealized Potential of Cultural Diplomacy: 'Best Practices' and What Could Be, If Only …," *The Journal of Arts Management, Law, and Society* 39:4 (Winter 2009):260–279.

Scott-Smith, Giles. "The US State Department's Foreign Leader Program in France During the Early Cold War," *Revue française d'études américaines* 107 (March 2006):47–60.

Semonin, Paul. *American Monster: How the Nation's First Prehistoric Creature Became a Symbol of National Identity.* New York: New York University Press, 2000.

Skinner, Elliott P. *African Americans and U.S. Policy toward Africa, 1850–1924.* Washington, DC: Howard University Press, 1992.

Snow, Nancy. "International Exchanges and the U.S. Image." *The Annals of the American Academy of Political and Social Science* 616 (March 2008):198–222.

Soares, John. "The Cold War on Ice." *The Brown Journal of World Affairs* 14:2 (Spring/Summer 2008):77–87

Sperber, A. M. *Murrow: His Life and Times.* New York: Fordham University Press, 1999.

Standifer, James. "The Tumultuous Life of *Porgy and Bess.*" *Humanities* 18:6 (November/December 1997), http://www.neh.gov/humanities/1997/novemberdecember/feature/the-tumultuous-life-porgy-and-bess.

Stewart, Jeffrey C. "A New Negro Foreign Policy: The Critical Vision of Alain Locke and Ralph Bunche." In *African Americans in U.S. Foreign Policy: From the Era of Frederick Douglass to the Age of Obama*, eds. Linda Heywood et al. Urbana: University of Illinois Press, 2015, pp. 30–57.

Stokes, Melvin. *D.W. Griffith's* The Birth of a Nation: *A History of "The Most Controversial Motion Picture of All Time."* New York: Oxford University Press, 2007.

Thomas, Damion L. *Globetrotting: African American Athletes and Cold War Politics.* Urbana: University of Illinois Press, 2012.

Tilchin, William N. *Theodore Roosevelt and the British Empire: A Study in Presidential Statecraft.* New York: St. Martin's Press, 1997.

Troyen, Carol. "Innocents Abroad: American Painters at the 1867 Exposition Universelle, Paris." *American Art Journal* 16:1 (Autumn 1984):2–29.

Tucker, David. *Enlightened Republicanism: A Study of Jefferson's Notes on the State of Virginia.* Lanham, MD: Lexington Books, 2008.

Twain, Mark. *The Innocents Abroad, or the New Pilgrims' Progress: Being Some Account of the Steamship QUAKER CITY'S Pleasure Excursion to Europe and the Holy Land.* Norwalk, CT: The Easton Press, 1998.

Tyrrell, Ian. *Reforming the World: The Creation of America's Moral Empire.* Princeton, NJ: Princeton University Press, 2010.

Urquhart, Brian. *Ralph Bunche: An American Life.* New York: W.W. Norton, 1993.

Vaughn, Stephen. *Holding Fast the Inner Lines: Democracy, Nationalism, and the Committee on Public Information.* Chapel Hill: The University of North Carolina Press, 1980.

Von Eschen, Penny M. *Race against Empire: Black Americans and Anticolonialism, 1937–1957.* Ithaca, NY: Cornell University Press, 1996.

Von Eschen, Penny M. *Satchmo Blows Up the World: Jazz Ambassadors Play the Cold War.* Cambridge: Harvard University Press, 2004.

Wagnleitner, Reinhold. "The Irony of American Culture Abroad: Austria and the Cold War." In *Recasting America: Culture and Politics in the Age of the Cold War,* ed. Lary May. Chicago: University of Chicago Press, 1989, pp. 285–302.

Wierzbicki, James E. *Music in the Age of Anxiety: American Music in the Fifties.* Urbana: University of Illinois Press, 2016.

Wilford, Hugh. "Calling the Tune? The CIA, The British Left and the Cold War, 1945–1960." In *The Cultural Cold War in Western Europe, 1945–1960,* eds. Giles Scott-Smith and Hans Krabbendam. London: Frank Cass Publishers, 2003, pp. 41–50.

Winkler, Allan M. *The Politics of Propaganda: The Office of War Information, 1942–1945.* New Haven, CT: Yale University Press, 1978.

Witherspoon, Kevin B. "'Fuzz Kids' and 'Musclemen:' The US-Soviet Basketball Rivalry, 1958–1975." In *Diplomatic Games: Sport, Statecraft, and International Relations since 1945,* eds. Heather C. Dichter and Andrew L. Johns. Lexington: University Press of Kentucky, 2014.

Wolper, Gregg. "Wilsonian Public Diplomacy: The Committee on Public Information in Spain." *Diplomatic History* 17:1 (Winter 1993):17–34.

Woods, Randall Bennett. "Fulbright Internationalism." *The Annals of the American Academy of Political and Social Science* 491 (May 1987):22–35.

Wulf, Andrew James. *U.S. International Exhibitions during the Cold War: Winning Hearts and Minds through Cultural Diplomacy.* Lanham, MD: Rowman & Littlefield, 2015.

Yoshii, Midori, Michael L. Krenn, John Day Tully and Thomas W. Zeiler. "A Roundtable on Thomas W. Zeiler's *Ambassadors in Pinstripes: The Spalding World Baseball Tour and the Birth of the American Empire.*" *Passport: The Newsletter of the SHAFR* 38:2 (August 2007):4–15.

Zeiler, Thomas W. *Ambassadors in Pinstripes: The Spalding World Baseball Tour and the Birth of the American Empire.* Lanham, MD: Rowman & Littlefield Publishers, Inc., 2006.

Zwigenberg, Ran. "'The Coming of a Second Sun:' The 1956 Atoms for Peace Exhibit in Hiroshima and Japan's Embrace of Nuclear Power." *The Asia-Pacific Journal* 10:6, No. 1 (Feb. 2012):1–15.

INDEX